electronic portfolios

Emerging Practices in

Student, Faculty, and Institutional

Learning

Barbara L. Cambridge, *volume editor*

Susan Kahn, Daniel P. Tompkins, and Kathleen Blake Yancey, *section editors*

Lacey Hawthorne, *editorial assistant*, and Emily Springfield, *technology assistant*

AMERICAN ASSOCIATION
FOR HIGHER EDUCATION

The editorial team worked collaboratively on this project addressing the scholarship of teaching and learning. We learned about portfolios and electronic portfolios in new areas and for new purposes, and we expanded our thinking about our own areas of responsibility. Preparing this book was knowledge-building for us all. *Left to right:* Susan Kahn, Daniel Tompkins, Lacey Hawthorne, Barbara Cambridge, Kathleen Blake Yancey, and Emily Springfield.

Recommended bibliographic listing:
Cambridge, B.L., Kahn, S., Tompkins, D.P., and Yancey, K.B. (Eds.). (2001). *Electronic portfolios: Emerging practices in student, faculty, and institutional learning*. Washington, DC: American Association for Higher Education.

Contents

Institutional Portfolios

I am pleased to write the foreword for this edited volume, *Electronic Portfolios: Emerging Practices in Student, Faculty, and Institutional Learning*. This compilation represents the merging of two currents of AAHE work in an exciting and innovative way. The first current is AAHE's long-time focus on assessing student learning and disseminating best practices across the higher education community. Recent research and practice have been devoted to documenting and assessing student learning, documenting and assessing faculty roles in student learning, and assessing overall institutional effectiveness in terms of student success.

We here at AAHE, like others in higher education, are trying to determine the multiple ways that technology enhances the learning process. The second piece of this exciting volume is the focus on electronic portfolios as the vehicle to discuss student, faculty, and institutional learning. The authors in this volume demonstrate in concrete, creative, and innovative ways how technology has the power to enhance the processes of learning in the classroom, for both students and faculty members, as well as to assist organizing for learning on a larger institutional scale.

Technology can extend the existing work of students, faculty, and institutions. In the hands of innovators, technology can transform the portfolio from a paper record to a more accessible and effective tool. Teaming learning practices with technological opportunities creates a new sum total, greater than the two separate parts.

Barbara Cambridge, vice president for program integration at AAHE, and her colleagues present us with a unique and ground-breaking book. This volume provides a window into emerging practices from institutions around the country that are revolutionizing the way portfolios are used to build knowledge, create knowledge communities, and transform the concept of the learning process.

As you read these chapters, begin to consider how you will act on what best suits your individual and institutional needs. I hope you find this resource to be beneficial to your present and future goals.

Yolanda T. Moses
President, American Association for Higher Education

Sometimes a book can reshape our thinking. My recent reading and rereading of John Seely Brown and Paul Duguid's *The Social Life of Information* (Harvard Business School Press, 2000) prompted me to rethink what I am up to when I consider the value of portfolios, a topic that has intrigued me for many years. In 1988, I chaired a group of faculty members at Indiana University, self-selected colleagues who, like me, wondered how we could as a university with seven campuses help students on all those sites analyze their own learning and help faculty members also understand and learn from student learning. Although we hadn't yet envisioned institutional portfolios, we did write a document addressed to the faculty and administration suggesting that all students graduating from Indiana University have an undergraduate portfolio that represented what they had learned during their undergraduate careers. The document stated that portfolios offer a broader view than was undertaken at that time to understand and integrate learning across a curriculum. Although undergraduate portfolios were not adopted across the university, individual programs and departments began to experiment with various forms of portfolios.

Continuing to practice with varieties of portfolios in the classroom and across a writing program, 10 years later I wrote with a colleague *Portfolio Learning* (Prentice Hall, 1998), a textbook based on five assumptions: Students are in control of the topics and sources for their writing; students need to discover ideas and synthesize them with the ideas of others, collaborating with teachers and classmates; making mistakes can be productive; a body of work represents learning better than a single piece of writing does; and writing in a single course is simply a part of a lifetime of writing. That textbook demonstrated that our practice had theoretical underpinnings based on an explicit epistemology and on the perspective of learning over time. I had, in fact, used those underlying theories in the teaching portfolio that I had submitted when I was promoted to full professor.

In that interval between 1988 and 1998, technology had, of course, expanded at a rate faster than I could have ever imagined. I now taught in a computer classroom, knew that composing on-line changed the actual composing process, heard *distance education* lauded and lamented at every conference I attended, and read about virtual universities that some feared would dominate higher education. Having moved to AAHE to lead its Assessment Forum and then its Teaching Initiatives, I was intrigued by the possibilities for electronic versions of portfolios, especially a new genre called *institutional portfolios*. And I was most intrigued by the possibilities that technology offered, for the first time, to link that new genre with student and faculty portfolios that were being used more and more prevalently. This intrigue led to the Urban Universities Portfolio Project, which figures prominently in the third section of this volume.

Why did Brown and Duguid's *The Social Life of Information* then spur new thinking about portfolios?

One reason is that these two scientists who are experts in technology applications believe that we must include both information and individuals in multiple social networks. They make the case that knowledge is more important than information and that knowledge is created socially. Applied to portfolios, then, technology can help us turn information into knowledge and support the social networks that are the fabric of human society. A tall order for portfolios? Yes, but a realistic order if we decide that filling the order is worth it.

The contributors to *Electronic Portfolios* want to explore the possibilities for filling that order through electronic portfolios created by students, faculty members, and institutions. They are aware that the digital medium is new enough that many unanswered questions need investigation, but they are excited enough about what we've learned so far to pursue the answers. We editors even envision the day that electronic portfolios of students, faculty members, and institutions will be interactive in a dynamic and generative way.

Please examine, analyze, and dream with us through this volume. It does not presume to cover all the possibilities for future practice — or all current portfolio practices for that matter. But it does invite you to read about the practices of individuals and institutions, pose questions, offer examples, and imagine along the way what might be as we move at ever more accelerating rates into new possibilities.

You can comment on anything in this volume, think through some new ideas, or suggest other possibilities by logging on to http://www.aahe.org/electronicportfolios. At this site, you will find some message threads begun, but you can suggest additional topics of interest to you. Let's use the Web to augment this print medium as we continue the conversation about electronic portfolios.

Barbara L. Cambridge
May 2001

Electronic Portfolios as Knowledge Builders

by Barbara L. Cambridge

> *Growth is the only evidence of life.*
> — John Henry Newman

Portfolios offer rich possibilities for learning and assessment. With increased pressure for better understanding of college and university students' learning and external pressure for better representation of it, portfolios enable learning for the creator and the user and demonstrate learning for multiple audiences. This book, with its focus on electronic portfolios, adds the extra value of technology to prompt learning and assessment.

Each section of this book contains a rationale for electronic portfolios for the creator (student, faculty member, or institution), possible features of an electronic portfolio, examples of current practice, cautions, and recommendations. Our examples are not exhaustive but offer instances of real people engaged in actual practice with the emerging medium of the electronic portfolio. This baseline book will undoubtedly be followed by others that scan the horizon for best practices, provide detailed analyses of a particular type of portfolio, or move toward integration of electronic portfolios by students, faculty members, and institutions. As editors of this volume, we hope that this foundational book paves the way for further inquiry into and practice with electronic portfolios for many audiences.

Features of Portfolios

Portfolios have features that can make them powerful tools of learning and assessment. Four characteristics adapted from Liz Hamp-Lyons and William Condon's *Assessing the*

Barbara L. Cambridge is vice president of the American Association for Higher Education and director of the Carnegie Academy Campus Program. She developed with colleagues a portfolio program for writing students at Indiana University Purdue University Indianapolis, has done workshops nationally on teaching and course portfolios, and serves on the leadership team of the Urban Universities Portfolio Project. She is coauthor of the textbook *Portfolio Learning* (Prentice Hall, 1998).

Portfolio: Principles for Practice, Theory and Research (1998) set the stage for features of electronic portfolios:

- *Portfolios can feature multiple examples of work.* Through multiple examples, portfolios authentically represent a range of work. For example, students can better demonstrate their progress toward increased critical reasoning during their undergraduate career if they include samples of early and late work, of reasoning in different disciplines, or of varied ways of showing critical thinking. Faculty members show their skill as teachers if they include students' work from the range of courses they teach, a comparative analysis of syllabi from the first and most recent time they have taught a course, or several peer observations of their classes in different semesters. Institutions include comparative data about retention across a number of years, examples of students' writing from across the curriculum, and studies of the impact of community involvement by the institution. In these ways, portfolios draw on basic premises about assessment and learning: A more accurate read is possible when varied measures are used, and through learning we change over time.

- *Portfolios can be context rich.* It is difficult to understand the grade on a student's essay if the reader has not seen the assignment, is not aware of the instruction before the assignment, and does not know the rubrics for grading. Fortunately, a portfolio can surround a student's essay with this context to make the learning and assessment more understandable. Faculty members who receive high student evaluations can surround those ratings with descriptions of pedagogies, classroom assessment techniques, and out-of-classroom interactions that help to explain those evaluations. High satisfaction on alumni surveys can be contextualized in a portfolio with employer survey results, information on an institution's career counseling, and statements from faculty mentors. In other words, the portfolio can provide the kind of thick description that helps a user understand an outcome and the reasons for the outcome.

- *Portfolios can offer opportunities for selection and self-assessment.* Because the reader of the portfolio sees evidence of the portfolio creator's ability to make choices based on criteria, the portfolio demonstrates decisions about quality. Although I will argue later that including only best work may foster a negative emphasis on success only, the selection process does demonstrate rhetorical savvy. Determining what products and processes will be warranted by which audiences is part of the selection process.

- *Portfolios can offer a look at development over time.* Because creators can add to and reflect on previous entries in a portfolio, they can demonstrate their learning over a period of time. For example, students who keep undergraduate portfolios will show progress at differing degrees in different areas of learning. After a shaky beginning with unsuccessful collaborative learning strategies, faculty members may have done professional development to learn and apply more fruitful practices. Based on input from students and new technologies, institutions may have added on-line mentoring to aid commuting students. This look across a sequence of activities enables readers to understand or assess decisions and achievement over a span of time.

The word *can* appears before each verb in the previous italicized statements because portfolios offer potential. In particular, portfolios can help turn information into knowledge, assessing into an integral part of learning, and failure into occasion for learning. Electronic portfolios can facilitate each of these outcomes if we consider technology as one of multiple essential features of decision making.

Turning Information Into Knowledge

Predictable responses to the advent of print portfolios were "How can we read them all?" and "Where will we store them?" Faculty members already overwhelmed by reading individual papers or exams shuddered at the thought of more information to digest and process. Discouraged with a single letter grade on tests or papers, students were, nonetheless, aghast at the thought of revising papers or reflecting on tests, especially in quantity and during a semester. Faculty and students both were apprehensive about having just too much information.

The difference between information and knowledge becomes crucial here. John Seely Brown and Paul Duguid (2000) note three "generally accepted distinctions between knowledge and information. . . . First, knowledge usually entails a knower." We may ask about the location of information ("Where can we find that information?"), but we expect an agent of knowledge ("Who knows that?"). Second, "knowledge appears harder to detach than information." Verbs used with information but not easily with knowledge are "pick up, possess, pass around, put in a database, lose, find, [and] accumulate." Third, "knowledge seems to require more by way of assimilation. It entails the knower's understanding and some degree of commitment" (pp. 119-120). Information theory, in fact, holds information to be independent of meaning.

Two important practices supported by the use of electronic portfolios offer ways of making meaning of information: reflection and social construction.

Reflection is central to learning. For example, service-learning has been particularly helpful in emphasizing the difference between doing and learning. Students may volunteer in the community, doing good but learning little. Service-learning insists that students reflect on their activity, putting it in the context of what they are learning in their class and in the context of the service. It is by stepping back from the experience and contemplating and analyzing it that students become knowledgeable about it.

Throughout this book, reflection is identified as crucial to the practice of creating portfolios. A scrapbook of materials is only an accumulation of information. What turns the data into evidence is reflection about the meaning of selected materials. Moreover, continued reflection can evoke new meaning from those materials so that the electronic medium supports continued learning. Students and faculty members can use recent experience as fodder for new reflection, which can make new meaning. Learners can report new insights easily over time as they demonstrate the value of learning across a lifetime.

Social construction of knowledge is also an important tenet of portfolios. According to Chris Dede in "Rethinking How to Invest in Technology" (2000), much research documents that

> helping students make sense of something they have assimilated but do not yet understand is crucial to inducing learning that is retained and generalized. Learners must engage in reflective discussion of shared experiences from multiple perspectives if they are to convert information into knowledge and master the collaborative creation of meaning and purposes. (p. 187)

Throughout this book, reflection is identified as crucial to the practice of creating portfolios.

Dede goes on to say that "distributed learning involves orchestrating educational activities among classrooms, workplaces, homes, and community settings. This pedagogical strategy models for students that learning is a part of all aspects of life" (p. 187) and, I would add, all levels of activity in the university and beyond.

In addition to Brown and Duguid, Scardamalia and Bereiter (2000) have imagined

> a network of networks — people from schools, universities, cultural institutions, service organizations, businesses — simultaneously building knowledge within their primary groups while advancing the knowledge of others. We might call such a community network a knowledge-building society. Electronically networked environments expand the possibilities for what such productive, mutually supportive communities can produce. (p. 312)

In fact, Scardamalia and Bereiter were part of a team of cognitive research and computer scientists who developed CSILE (computer-supported intentional learning environment) for use at all educational levels from first grade through the university. Analysis of CSILE shows that students who use the network system "are better able to comprehend difficult informative texts" than are their counterparts not using the system. They also demonstrate higher quality of portfolio commentaries, general depth of explanation, and facility with graphics. "They even demonstrate more mature beliefs about learning." The diverse group of participants in the system includes "elementary and high school students and their parents, postsecondary teacher education and medical school students, museum staff, engineering firm staff, and staff from a science center and an art gallery" (p. 314).

Another project that demonstrates the possibilities of extended communities of learners is a partnership of Stetson University and Disney that uses a fiber-optic network linking houses, apartments, and businesses in a community with the local school. Students have personalized learning plans, manage their own electronic portfolios, and achieve graduation through an exhibition. Students choose a pivotal topic early in their senior year, approved by their graduation committee and assessed at various decision points throughout the year. Potential graduates demonstrate their knowledge and skills to that graduation committee and invited guests through multimedia that encompass the students' portfolios, including dance, song, oratory, video, and print. Criteria include evidence of communication, personal development, critical thinking, and social responsibility (Triedemann, 1996, p. 18).

These examples are offered not to promote any one model for a knowledge-building society but to suggest that electronic portfolios can be part of a larger endeavor to link learners across our society. Instead of drowning in information, a network of people can turn that information into knowledge to benefit multiple constituencies. Although this book focuses on students, faculty members, and institutions of higher education, technology offers the potential for ever widening circles of linked learners.

Establishing how the network of linked learners works successfully, however, involves assessment. Although in the past some students and some faculty have seen assessment as a necessary evil imposed on them by some external force, it is clear that assessment can be a way of knowing how we are turning information into knowledge, moving beyond surface learning to deep learning.

Incorporating Assessment as an Integral Part of Learning

Students often dread quizzes, tests, and papers. The threat of a poor grade looms large, an incentive to study for the occasion but not a motivator for deep learning. Hansen and Stephens (2000) note that "many college students today (unrealistically) judge their own academic competence to be high, and tend to blame low performance on poor instruction" (p. 42). "Schools tend to condition students to focus on products and ignore the process that leads to those products" (p. 45).

Assessment systems for teachers also focus on product, not process. The most widely used tools for assessing teaching are ubiquitous end-of-semester student ratings. Their use for improvement almost obviated by placement at the end of the class, the rankings offer information at the conclusion of a unit of work — the class — rather than during the class when changes can be made. In addition, during high-stakes evaluations, teachers are often asked to supply only products such as unanalyzed syllabi and assignment sheets and not analyses of the process such as responses to students' work with subsequent revisions by students or evidence of positive pedagogical changes based on faculty development.

Institutions have their own mordant products. Accreditation self-studies collect more dust than any other document generated in a college or university. When a regional accreditation visit looms, institutions gear up to collect information, write it up, present it to visitors, and, with a sigh of relief if the visit goes well, place it on the shelf until it is referred to just before the next visit. This heavy product has little influence on vital processes of change in the institution.

Electronic portfolios, however, incorporate assessment into the process and recording of learning for students, faculty, and institutions. The premise that assessment can be designed to improve learning during the process of learning is demonstrated in examples in this book. For example, Alverno College, long known for designing its curriculum to work toward competencies affirmed by assessments that signal students' levels of achievement and need for improvement, recently implemented the next stage of that commitment to assessment as a part of learning: the diagnostic digital portfolio. As students identify "key learning experiences," they include the events, criteria for assessment, and self-, internal, and external assessments. Students can thus both plan and plot their growth. Planning and plotting as process is a main point.

Faculty electronic portfolios that focus on process as well as product are being developed by a range of faculty members in multiple disciplines. For example, a group of members of the Mathematics Association of America determined that creating electronic course portfolios is important, but knowing how to read and interpret the portfolios is equally challenging. Two faculty members are generating portfolios, and other group members are responding, in the process raising a multitude of questions about the purposes of teaching mathematics to different groups of students, the most effective pedagogies, and appropriate ways of assessing students' work. All faculty involved are reassessing and altering their own practices as they engage in the social construction of knowledge about learning mathematics.

Changes made by the Western Association of Schools and Colleges in its accrediting process are described in this book in the institutional portfolios section. Particularly illuminating is the sense that accreditation can become consultative as well as evaluative, partly through the electronic institutional portfolio that enables institutions to communicate internally and externally on a continuous basis. The need for hurried assembly of information, collected by a few people and used by fewer, is overcome through institutional choices about focus and continuous generation of assessment information turned into knowledge through application, revision, and reapplication.

The feedback loop has been a fundamental premise of assessment. Information gathered through assessment must be fed back into practice to alter that practice; a subsequent round of assessment determines whether the altered practice gets the practitioner closer to achieving goals. Visuals of the feedback loop feature arrows pointing to next steps, emphasizing the connections among assessing, applying, and learning. Electronic portfolios enable movement around the loop through hyperlinks, among other methods, so that a person can move through the loop or back into the loop to understand the process. The electronic portfolio embodies the principle that assessment is part of the learning process.

Sheingold and Frederiksa (2000) point to the importance of transparency in assessment:

> The positive systemic effects of performance assessments depend critically on the openness or transparency of the values and criteria used in those assessments. . . . The goal of transparency is important precisely because it requires reflective practice. . . . For students, understanding and participating in the performance assessment process should encourage reflection on their own work — the personal styles, strengths, and weaknesses it may reveal and the ways it can be improved. For teachers, understanding the performance assessment process should encourage reflection on their own and others' classroom practices and on ways to support students' development in a manner consistent with what is valued in the assessment system. . . . This activity of social construction should be an ongoing one, allowing for the constant renewal of the assessment system through the invention of new activities, the improvement of scoring frameworks, and the incorporation of new ideas about the goals of teaching and learning. . . . Ideally, the resulting socially distributed assessment system will be a self-improving process for enriching the view of competence incorporated within the educational system. (pp. 326, 327, 332)

Syverson's model of an integrated portfolio system

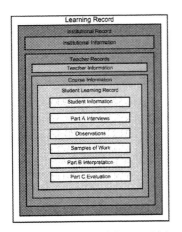

www.cwrl.utexas.edu/~syverson/olr/

An exciting thought for the future is the integration of student, faculty, and electronic portfolios as a "socially distributed assessment system" that becomes "a self-improving process for enriching" educational systems. Margaret Syverson, at the University of Texas at Austin, has designed an integrated system that offers this interactivity among portfolios (see figure opposite). Although not yet in use, this model promises connectivity that supports the kind of social fabric central to the vision of Brown and Duguid and of Scardamalia and Bereiter.

But that social fabric will be rent if we continue to regard disappointing assessment results as fatal. In education, and elsewhere, we must learn how to turn failure into occasion for learning. As Salvatori (2000) demonstrates in theory and practice, "moments of difficulty" are prime opportunities for growth, which, as John Henry Newman tells us, is the only sign of life.

Turning Failure Into Occasion for Learning

We all fail sometimes. Even with carefully established goals and conscientiously executed work, we do not meet the goals because of any number of circumstances. Yet we set up systems that condemn students, faculty members, and institutions for not meeting goals. Portfolios can be part of such systems if we choose to include in them only those pieces of evidence that bear good news: the exemplary essay in a student portfolio, the well balanced syllabus in a faculty portfolio, or selected statistics about minority participation in the institutional portfolio.

Some systems punish for not meeting goals, no matter the reason. Students receive a failing grade when they do not meet expectations — no matter the cause of the failure; faculty who risk trying new pedagogies that take time to learn and implement well lose points toward merit raises because of initial low student ratings; and institutions that include in accreditation self-studies unfavorable retention rates risk requirements for extra reports or visits. Although we know that learning can and often does occur at times of dissonance or moments of difficulty, we look there not for the learning but for the problems.

Two practices are particularly problematic. First, our reporting mechanisms disallow explanations. Tests rarely encourage explanation of reasons for answers. Student course ratings provide few or no contextual explanations. Accrediting self-studies telescope so much material that explanations appear defensive. Second, we use snapshots for important evaluations. A single test speaks to a moment in time. A single student rating occurs at only one point in a semester of work. And a self-study every 10 years freezes at only one point what is fluid and changing in the many years before and after the study.

Portfolios can be structured to include lack of success as the inevitable and potentially educational experience that it can be. Because portfolios are albums rather than single snapshots, they can illustrate process. For example, a student who writes a paper whose sections reveal no organization can, with feedback from peers and the instructor, revise the piece. In her portfolio she can explain the reasoning behind her changes and situate the piece among other examples of well organized work or a series of increasingly well organized pieces. A faculty member whose classroom assessment techniques reveal students' discomfort with initial applications of problem-based learning can trace how he modifies instructions and practices for better results. When an institution finds that its new summer orientation does not supply all the information students need to begin the fall semester, it can describe changes in length, activities, and follow-up that lead to more satisfaction and a pattern of self-assessment portending more changes.

Electronic portfolios especially can provide contextual responses to failure so that readers can see continuously how individuals or institutions use lack of success as impetus to change. A student who stumbles in an oral presentation can include videos of both the original unsuccessful and subsequent more successful speeches, with analysis of changes made in preparation and execution of the speeches. A faculty member's analysis of efficacy of assignments given and revised in subsequent semesters can be buttressed with students' work and students' responses. When institutions gradually reallocate funds to improve library services described as insufficient, the emergent pattern of support speaks to realization of and response to need.

Any information can be misinterpreted or misused. The section on student portfolios cautions about the need to consider carefully who has access to student portfolios on the Web. The section on faculty portfolios includes worries about the possible repercussions of going public with lack of success, i.e., what will happen to faculty who admit to failure? The section on institutional portfolios also deals with the risks of misuse of information to denounce the quality of an institution.

Electronic portfolios open possibilities for putting failure in context.

In an important meeting of a project described in the section on institutional portfolios, members of multiple publics — media, state governments, accrediting bodies, and public policy centers — said loudly and clearly to project leaders that institutional portfolios will be useless if they present only a rosy picture. Everyone knows that institutions, however successful in multiple aspects, have areas that need improvement. Not representing those areas only makes the portfolio suspect. When change is warranted, however, an institution should feature its strategies for change, with results posted as soon as possible. Repeated failure is cause for alarm; failure that is addressed with concrete steps is more readily understood.

This book does not claim that electronic portfolios will solve the problems related to misuse of failure. It does claim, however, that electronic portfolios open possibilities for putting failure in context, demonstrating how it can spur learning and acknowledging that everyone has areas in which they can improve. Before we move to electronic portfolios, however, we must confront issues about usability and availability of technology that changes rapidly.

Choosing Electronic Portfolios

In *Dancing With the Devil: Information Technology and the New Competition in Higher Education,* Katz and his colleagues contend that higher education can be successful in dealing with the challenges of technologies that change quickly. For example, Lehigh University president Gregory Farrington writes that "a good assumption is that within ten years inexpensive technology will allow each of us to send and receive video, audio, graphics, and text, synchronously or asynchronously, wherever we are in the world" (1999, p. 76). Katz, vice president of EDUCAUSE, identifies two of the central assumptions of the next decade: "Ubiquitous, high-speed, economically accessible network capacity will exist nationally, and, to a great extent, globally [and] affordable, multimedia-capable computers will be commonplace, and most leading universities will assume student ownership of such devices" (p. 28).

Yet other people worry about the inequality of access to computers and the resulting "digital divide." Seven percent of lower income households have a computer, compared with 32 percent in the $30,000-50,000 income bracket, 53 percent in households making more than $50,000 annually, and more than 70 percent in those with incomes higher than $75,000 annually (Tapscott, 2000, p. 131). The "leading universities" mentioned by Katz may indeed expect students to own a computer, but how about the majority of students attending community colleges and comprehensive universities? Even if computers are supplied by institutions, what is needed to prepare students and faculty for their use on behalf of learning? Will there be technical support, appropriate training, and maintenance of equipment and systems over time? An essay in the section on student portfolios worries about these issues as campuses consider requiring or even making optional the use of electronic portfolios.

The researchers identified five key factors to address in making a digital portfolio system work: vision, assessment, technology, logistics, and culture.

The Annenberg Institute for School Reform and the Coalition of Essential Schools Exhibition Project had some of the same questions as they considered the use of electronic portfolios in grades K-12. "When it became clear that ordinary mortals, not just computer techie types, could put together multimedia collections of student work, we began to study how such technology could supplement a school's reform process" (Niguidula, 1999, p. 26). Over 1993-1996 they studied six Coalition schools — rural, suburban, and urban; traditional and alternative; technology rich and technology strapped — assuming that ordinary people are capable of creating such portfolios, that portfolios are part of a process of change, and that portfolios can be used in multiple contexts.

The researchers identified five key factors to address in making a digital portfolio system work: vision, assessment, technology, logistics, and culture. The central question under vision is "What should a student know and be able to do?" Vision thus becomes the main menu of the portfolio. Four questions apply to assessment: "How can students demonstrate the school vision? Why do we collect student work? What audiences are most important to us? How do we know what's good?" Questions about technology underlie these factors: "What hardware, software, and networking will we need? Who are the primary users of the equipment? Who will support the system?" With regard to logistics: "Where will information be digitalized? Who will do it? Who will select the work? Who will reflect on the work?" The fifth feature, culture, is the most crucial: "Is the school used to discussing student work? Is the school open to sharing standards? With whom?" The researchers conclude that "school culture is perhaps the most critical component in making digital portfolios a tool for reform rather than a technological version of a set of file folders" (p. 28). Key elements are relationships with the school, regular discussions of students' work, and openness to examining the school's vision with others outside the school.

Technology is only one component of decision making about the use of electronic portfolios and, in this analysis, not the most crucial one. The availability of resources to provide the necessary technology must be part of the consideration, but as is established elsewhere in this book, the range of possibilities for electronic portfolios includes low-cost and high-cost varieties. A careful decision-making process will examine more than technological constraints and possibilities. The major challenges for institutions in the Urban Universities Portfolio Project described in the institutional portfolios section of this book and those of the Coalition schools centered on the culture of the institution. As more technology becomes more and more universally available, institutions that have developed a culture of practice around student learning and a culture of assessment around improvement will be ready for the rich possibilities of electronic portfolios.

References

Brown, J.S., & Duguid, P. (2000). *The Social Life of Information.* Boston: Harvard Business School Press.

Dede, C. (2000). Rethinking how to invest in technology. In *The Jossey-Bass Reader on Technology and Learning* (pp. 184-191). San Francisco: Jossey-Bass.

Hamp-Lyons, L., & Condon, W. (1998). *Assessing the Portfolio: Principles for Practice, Theory and Research.* Cresskill, NJ: Hampton Press.

Hansen, E.J., & Stephens, J.A. (2000, September/October). The ethics of learner-centered education: Dynamics that impede the process. *Change 32* (5), 40-47.

Katz, R.N., & Associates. (1998). *Dancing With the Devil: Information Technology and the New Competition in Higher Education.* San Francisco: Jossey-Bass.

Niguidula, D. (1997, November). Picturing performance with digital portfolios. *Educational Leadership,* 26-29.

Salvatori, M.R. (2000). Difficulty: The great educational divide. In P. Hutchings (Ed.), *Opening Lines: Approaches to the Scholarship of Teaching and Learning* (pp. 81-93). Palo Alto, CA: Carnegie Foundation for the Advancement of Teaching.

Scardamalia, M., & Bereiter, C. (2000). Engaging students in a knowledge society. In *The Jossey-Bass Reader on Technology and Learning* (pp. 312-319). San Francisco: Jossey-Bass.

Sheingold, K., & Frederiksa, J. (2000). Using technology to support innovative assessment. In *The Jossey-Bass Reader on Technology and Learning* (pp. 320-337). San Francisco: Jossey-Bass.

Tapscott, D. (2000). The digital divide. In *The Jossey-Bass Reader on Technology and Learning* (pp. 127-154). San Francisco: Jossey-Bass.

Triedemann, D. (1996, October). New Florida school celebrates education and technology. *Techtrends,* 14-18.

Student Portfolios

Digitized Student Portfolios

by Kathleen Blake Yancey

A sophomore majoring in packaging science has come to my office. A good student who likes his major, Steve is excited about applying for a co-op experience required by that major. Not quite sure how to make his qualifications and interests known to potential employers, he thinks an electronic portfolio might work. He created a print portfolio in our composition class last year, so he understands something about how to create one to showcase his progress as a student and his potential as a co-op employee. This year for a general education computer class, for which he received an A, he created an electronic portfolio. Steve wonders whether he needs an electronic portfolio to secure a co-op position. Should he delete some material in his current electronic portfolio, including cartoon clips and humorous stories? Should he explain more about the samples of schoolwork he has included so that potential employers will understand about the value of that work? "Good questions," I respond. "Why don't we take a look at the portfolio?" He gives me his URL, I open his Web page on my computer screen, and together we look at it on-line.

Welcome to the world of digitized student portfolios.

An Introduction to Print and Electronic Student Portfolios

About 15 years ago, all across the country and at institutions of every kind, faculty began asking students to compile something new: a record of their work called *portfolios*. To create portfolios, students engaged in three primary processes. First, students *collected* all their work. Second, they *selected* from this archive samples of work to share with others. Third, and perhaps most important, students *reflected* on that work — to think about what they had learned, to assess which of their exhibits was the strongest and why, or to use their review of the entire portfolio to plan future activities. Portfolios also began serving different purposes. Sometimes they were like Steve's in my writing class: a vehicle

---

Kathleen Blake Yancey, editor of this section on student portfolios, is R. Roy Pearce Professor of Professional Communication at Clemson University, where she also directs the Roy and Marnie Pearce Center for Professional Communication. Yancey is editor of *Portfolios in the Writing Classroom: An Introduction* (NCTE, 1992) and coeditor of *Situating Portfolios: Four Perspectives* (Utah State University Press, 1997).

for classroom learning and assessment. Other times, they crossed classroom boundaries, such as for securing a co-op position. And still other times, portfolios were used for program assessment.

Portfolios, then, are unified as a construct. Created by the three principal activities of collection, selection, and reflection, student portfolios can be succinctly defined as collections of work selected from a larger archive of work, upon which the student has reflected. Portfolios can be created in many different contexts, serve various purposes, and speak to multiple audiences.

Within the last five years, student portfolios have begun to go electronic. To talk about this shift in portfolios, we need to consider many questions. What do we mean by the expression *electronic portfolio*? Is it simply a digitized version of the more familiar print portfolio? Or is it something completely different? Why are students, faculty, and institutions interested in electronic portfolios? To answer these questions, a quick explanation of print portfolios — their contents, processes, and types — provides a useful context for understanding how print and electronic portfolios compare and what electronic portfolios offer. After a review of six critical issues surrounding electronic portfolios, we hear from six faculty and administrators who have used electronic student portfolios for diverse purposes and with varying degrees of success. Moving then beyond individual models, we consider when electronic portfolios are the appropriate choice and how they can best be designed.

Classroom Portfolios

The first student portfolios appeared in print; they served diverse purposes and took a variety of forms. In general, they can be categorized as classroom portfolios and program portfolios.

Classroom portfolios vary as much as classrooms themselves do. In a first-year composition class, for example, each of the students might compile and reflect on several writings to serve several purposes:
- to show how they have improved as writers during a term;
- to demonstrate their competence in a variety of genres (such as lab reports, essays, resumes, and research-based arguments); and
- to show their ability to revise texts for different purposes and audiences.

In an honors class on economic systems, each of the students might include a midterm test, a project summary, three journal entries, and printouts of a PowerPoint presentation. The portfolios then culminate in final reflective essays in which the students refer to these exhibits as they assess and comment on:

- their understanding of the key concepts in the course;
- their ability to apply those concepts in both global and local contexts; and
- their development over the course of the term, including the ability to use reflection and self-assessment to improve their work.

In yet another class, an undergraduate class on research methods in psychology, students open their portfolio with a reflective synthesis of enclosed materials as well as a statement of the materials' relevance to their development of an independent research project. Other exhibits include a statement of progress on the independent project, a write-up of one experiment, a peer review of that write-up, and other materials (homework assignments and summaries of class readings, for example) chosen by the student.

As these examples suggest, classroom portfolios can vary considerably, especially when we think about them along four parameters or dimensions: (1) type and level of class (in general education or in the major, for example); (2) purpose of the portfolio; (3) audience for the portfolio; and (4) criteria for assessment. Regardless of the diversity of portfolio models, however, they all make the same request: that students assume responsibility for documenting and interpreting their own learning. This responsibility extends through collection, selection, and reflection. Students archive all their work — homework, class projects, journals, lab reports, spreadsheets, notes for presentations, drafts of assignments, peer review notes, and so on. At a designated time — sometimes at midterm, often at the end of a term — students select from this archive exhibits that demonstrate stipulated criteria: development, best work, understanding of concepts, critical thinking, or connection to other classes. Often, they are asked to revisit or revise their work. For example, students may rewrite incorrect answers from a midterm exam, indicating not only how the new answers are correct but also how the student would not create the same incorrect answer again. Revisiting past work, students often improve the earlier work but also comment in a way that demonstrates their thinking around that work. In such a reflective text, *students make their thinking visible.*

Reflection: The Key Portfolio Piece

Most portfolio advocates choose portfolios because of their understanding that reflection enhances learning. Basically, reflection is the process by which we think about how we learn.

Collectively, Dewey, Vygotsky, and Polyani define reflection as a process by which we think: *reviewing,* as we think about the products we create and the ends we produce, but also about the means we use to get to those ends; and *projecting,* as we plan for the learning we want to control and accordingly, manage, contextualize, understand. We learn to reflect as we learn to talk: in the company of others. To reflect, as to learn (since reflection is a kind of learning), we set a problem for ourselves, we try to conceptualize

---

Before this semester I had never done any exploratory writing. "Writing History: What Are the Central Issues?" taught me how to think on paper. It was the first time I was actually forced to organize my thoughts in such a way. Writing history can be looked at from several different perspectives. I had to take these ideas that were floating around and put them in some semblance of order on the page. I did this by breaking it into sections.

Greg Mathews, student

that problem from diverse perspectives — the scientific and the spontaneous — for it is in seeing something from divergent perspectives that we see it fully. Along the way, we check and confirm, as we seek to reach goals that we have set for ourselves. Reflection becomes a habit, one that transforms. (Yancey, 1998, pp. 11-12)

A reflection can take a variety of forms:
- a *letter* synthesizing purpose and introducing the collected texts to a reader;
- *annotations on individual pieces* commenting quite specifically on each text;
- an *essay* whose purpose is to conclude the collected text in some evaluative way;
- an *independent document* covering one of several topics or one of multiple genres seeking to summarize, interpret, and evaluate the work/learning/understanding of a term; or
- all these genres, seeking to embody all these purposes.

A reflection can also serve a variety of purposes. Sometimes students principally assess their own work. How do they evaluate the contents of their own portfolio? How do they evaluate their own learning? How do they evaluate their own learning relative to their own goals? In other situations, students are asked to synthesize material in the portfolios and comment on the significance of it, and/or to connect the learning from the portfolio course to the learning in another course or to learning taking place outside of school. And in some instances students are asked to project into their own future, in part by looking back at what they have accomplished to date.

How we ask for reflection, what genre we prefer, and how we respond to reflection are key issues surrounding portfolios.

Program Portfolios

A second type of student portfolio is the program portfolio, which is a model that draws from several classes, from extracurricular activities, and/or from internships, service-learning, and other experiential learning. Two similar examples of program portfolios include the writing-across-the-curriculum program portfolio model at Eckerd College, which students must "pass" to graduate, and the rising junior writing portfolio at Washington State University (http://www.wsu.edu:8080/~bcondon/portpage.html), which students must "pass" before matriculating in a required writing-in-the-disciplines course in their major. Both these program portfolios, created at very different kinds of institutions — one a small, private liberal arts institution, the other a large research institution — draw on work completed in the classroom. At the same time, the purpose for these portfolios transcends the classroom; it is more cumulative in nature. Students create these portfolios to satisfy outside readers (typically faculty from the campus) that they are competent writers, defined in the first case as the writing performance of a college graduate and in the second as preparation to take on the more sophisticated writing tasks associated with writing in the major.

Another program portfolio that provides a variation on this theme is the Missouri Western State College capstone portfolio. Like the Eckerd model, this portfolio functions as an exit portfolio, but it is located within a discipline and its purpose is twofold. First, students are asked to provide evidence of their disciplinary competence by providing documents attesting to it; the portfolio is reviewed by faculty who pass or fail the portfolio. Second, students use the portfolio to acquire a job. Its opening document, a resume, is thus a work-related text that acts as a bridge between the college curriculum and the world beyond college.

Finally, a more generalized program portfolio is one targeted toward advising students as they progress through their academic career. The Department of Consumer and Family Science at the University of Wyoming, for example, asks students to keep a portfolio as they complete their first two years of school. Advisers meet with students to ensure that they are acquiring the skills and competencies they will need to succeed in school and beyond. Like its counterparts elsewhere — at Kalamazoo College, for instance, and at Olivet College — this portfolio invites each student to reflect on past learning as he or she plans courses, internships, and other academic experiences. This portfolio, then, is oriented toward the future as much as toward the past. And more generally, portfolios bring with them three key characteristics:

- They function as a means of both review and planning.
- They are social in nature.
- They are grounded in reflection.

The Role of Portfolios in Fostering and Enhancing Learning

A final aspect of student portfolios is their emphasis on two dimensions of the learning environments where they are produced. First, precisely because they make learning visible, portfolios allow both faculty and students to focus on learning in a new way. Portfolios bring together visibility, process, and reflection as students chart and interpret their own learning. Students are responsible for telling their own stories of learning: for explaining what they did and did not learn, for assessing their own strengths and weaknesses as learners, for evaluating their products and performances, for showing how that learning connects with other kinds of learning (in the classroom and without), and for using the review of the past to think about paths for future learning.

Likewise, because of the portfolio's design — its inclusion of many entries of different kinds — the portfolio reader, whether student or faculty member, has access to multiple kinds of materials. Reviewing those materials can help readers see patterns within and across them. A key question, then, is what those patterns are and how they might be interpreted. And not least, in the reflection, the student can speak to the individual entries, to the patterns of several entries, and to other learning experiences in ways the review of no other single vehicle — homework assignment, journal, lab report, or research paper — permits. In terms of assessment, portfolios provide rich material for formative assessment, which is in part why they are often associated with learner-centered education and with increased student responsibility for learning.

Second, again in part because portfolios can include such a rich mix of students' work, they are often used in summative assessment, some institutional and some life-based, as when portfolios are used in a job search. Sometimes, the institutional assessment takes place within the classroom, particularly when portfolios are graded. Again, practice here varies: Sometimes the portfolio carries the major grade in a course, and other times it counts as an exam grade. (And often the grading is facilitated by use of a scoring guide.) Portfolio advocates have often argued that grading a set of work at the end of the term permits a more accurate reading of a student's performance. They point out that because the portfolio includes so many samples of a student's performance, because it is finally sampled at the conclusion of a course, and because it includes the student's interpretation of the experience, a portfolio is an especially rich means of assessment. Portfolios permit other kinds of summative assessment as well, however, as we see in the student who compiles one for a rising junior portfolio or for a job interview.

The Electronic Portfolio

What happens to portfolios when we introduce the electronic into the portfolio mix? In some ways, nothing changes; yet changes in key features — especially the addition of linking — seem to make the electronic portfolio a different kind of portfolio altogether, a difference almost of kind rather than degree. Key to this difference is the role that inter-activity plays in students' digital portfolios, the interactivity both of the digital medium and of social action.

Like their paper counterparts, electronic portfolios are governed by purpose and audience. They allow students, for instance, to showcase their best work for an employer (as shown in the Dartmouth model). Alternatively, they allow students to document learning for their teachers that takes place in a course (as the portfolio design from California State University Monterey Bay suggests). Electronic portfolios are created through the same basic processes used for print portfolios: collection, selection, and reflection.

At the same time, electronic portfolios are quite different from print portfolios. Consider, for example, how we learn about each. In general, if we want to learn about print portfolios, we go to physical representations in print, such as journals and books. If we want to

Precisely because they make learning visible, portfolios allow both faculty and students to focus on learning in a new way.

Dartmouth College's student portfolio program site

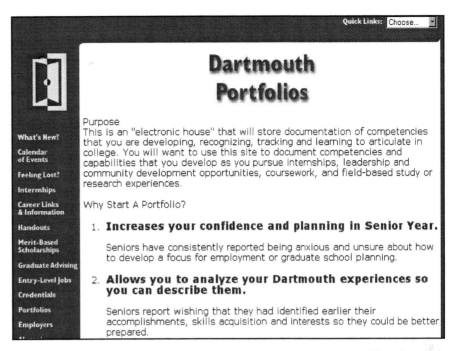

Dartmouth Portfolios

Purpose
This is an "electronic house" that will store documentation of competencies that you are developing, recognizing, tracking and learning to articulate in college. You will want to use this site to document competencies and capabilities that you develop as you pursue internships, leadership and community development opportunities, coursework, and field-based study or research experiences.

Why Start A Portfolio?

1. **Increases your confidence and planning in Senior Year.**

   Seniors have consistently reported being anxious and unsure about how to develop a focus for employment or graduate school planning.

2. **Allows you to analyze your Dartmouth experiences so you can describe them.**

   Seniors report wishing that they had identified earlier their accomplishments, skills acquisition and interests so they could be better prepared.

Quick Links: Choose...

What's New?
Calendar of Events
Feeling Lost?
Internships
Career Links & Information
Handouts
Merit-Based Scholarships
Graduate Advising
Entry-Level Jobs
Credentials
Portfolios
Employers

www.dartmouth.edu/~csrc/students/portfolios/welcome.shtml

A student portfolio for a California State University Monterey Bay social and behavioral sciences course

Portfolio Contents

You will turn in all of your work for SBSD 212 in the form of a Portfolio. You will need a loose-leaf binder for hardcopies. It should have a title page with your name, the number of the course and the semester. This should be followed by a table of contents indicating the order in which you have placed material in the portfolio. Your formal written assignments may be submitted in the form of a set of linked web pages. In this case you need to submit these assignments on a disk placed in the front pocket of your portfolio and provide me with the address on the web where I can find it online. Your binder will then only contain the in-class work.

I. Title Page

II. Roots Essay/Family History

III. Report on Political Project with Historical Context and Personal Reflection

IV. Appendices

A. Description of, and personal response to, origin myths
B. Description of and personal response to, philosophies that underlie the United States Constitution

C. Brief essay defining what politics means to you

D. Written evaluation of the philosophies that underlie the California Constitutions of 1850 and 1879.

E. Personal reflections on, and evaluations of, readings, videos & class discussions through March 3.

F. One-page description of your political project (March 15)

G. Personal response to Rosa and Rockefeller

http://www.monterey.edu/academic/centers/sbsc/sbsc212/portfolio.html

learn about electronic portfolios, however, we can use an electronic medium such as the Web or the electronic database assembled by AAHE (www.aahe.org). And a quick trip on the Web, delivered in print, will show us electronic models that look quite different from their print predecessors.

Migrating From Print or Starting Anew

Some digital portfolio programs have migrated from print to digital. Alverno College, for instance, has long been recognized for its work with student self-assessment. Now, by means of a digitized portfolio, that work is taking an electronic turn. The Alverno portfolio, used as an advising tool, includes three kinds of exhibits or contents: (1) descriptions of "key performances," or learning experiences, that take place within and outside courses; (2) self-assessments of the key performances; and (3) feedback on them.

Alverno College's "Diagnostic Digital Portfolio Program" site

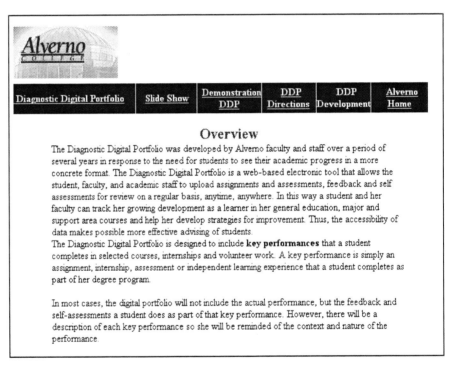

http://www.ddp.alverno.edu/

Interestingly, representations of the key performances themselves are not included: Rather, what is valued here is what is learned from them.

A similar model, tied specifically to general education reform, is being developed at Babson College. As Carolyn Meghan explains, the new curriculum is conceptualized in terms of competencies:

Babson has just completed the first cycle of its new curriculum. The goal of the curriculum is to create student-centered learning built around a set of competencies. The competencies cover a broad range from Numeracy and Rhetoric to Leadership and Multi-Cultural Awareness. As part of the curriculum, students have three gateposts, or moments of reflection, during the first three years. As the close of the first year, students write a self-reflective statement and then meet with a faculty adviser to discuss and reflect on the first year experience. During the sophomore year, students meet with an administrator to create a Learning Plan — a document that narrates the expected course of study for the final two years at Babson. During the junior year, the student meets with a faculty adviser to finalize the Learning Plan. These, as well as other supportive structures, encourage the student to take responsibility for what he/she is learning and to partake in meaningful dialogue about the nature of learning. (personal communication, August 2000)

Although the project is still in development, the value of the electronic portfolio, according to Meghan, lies in the portfolio's ability to prompt dialogue:

> It raises the dialogue and discussion around learning — students are clearer about the competencies and in turn ask professors how assignments relate to the competencies. It addresses a need for more creativity on campus and yet is embedded in a [technological] venue that our students feel comfortable in using. (personal communication, August 2000)

Petition to Major Portfolio

Table of Contents
1. Statement of Intent
2. Career Aspirations and Personal History Statement (Assignment I)
3. Professional Resume / CV
4. Annotated List of SBS Classes taken
5. Transcripts
6. Writing Sample (Sample of Best Works)
7. Individual Learning Plan (ILP)
Description of the ILP and ILP Worksheet (required in portfolio)
8. Supporting Documentation

A model at a different kind of school — Rose-Hulman, a four-year engineering school — also relies on a construction of curriculum oriented to what students know and can do, what Rose-Hulman calls "objectives": ethics, contemporary issues, global issues, teams, communication, engineering practices, interpreting data, experiments, design, and career services. Like their counterparts at Babson and Alverno, students chart their own progress and accomplishments so that the portfolio becomes a prompt for discussions with advisers about their academic experiences.

Yet another portfolio model, this one at California State University Monterey Bay, takes the approach one additional step. There, students intending to major in social and behavioral science are asked to submit a portfolio (see left) as part of their application process for permission to major in the field.

Like the advising models, this electronic portfolio asks students to look forward — to plan — as much to look backward. We see the intent to plan in documents such as the resume and the statement of intent.

Not every model of electronic portfolio, however, is oriented toward students' immediate use. For instance, Stanford University is developing a student portfolio so that the institution can track how students learn. Specifically, through students' collection of data and reflection on them, Stanford hopes to answer the following questions (excerpted from http://sll.stanford.edu/projects/hlc.exploration.htm):

1. How do exploratory changes like those introduced in The Word and the World [a general education course] relate to other experiences in the humanities and in general education as a whole?
2. How do these changes influence an individual undergraduate's subsequent academic experience and contribute to his/her intellectual and professional development?
3. How are various kinds of formal and informal learning woven together to produce "an individual undergraduate experience"?

Digital portfolios, like their print counterparts, can do very different kinds of intellectual work.

Patterns in Digital Portfolios

In general, even very different electronic portfolios point to consistent patterns.

1. Learning tends to be constructed inside *and* outside the "classroom box." Whether conceptualized as key performances or competencies or outcomes, the curriculum includes the classroom but is not constrained by it. Accordingly, space is provided for many kinds of learning experiences, among them internships and extracurricular activities. Likewise, nonschool exhibits — such as resumes — are included as well.
2. Students are asked to look backward at past experiences of all kinds and to think about them in terms of what they contributed to learning and what story they tell about the ways the students learn.
3. Students are expected to use this review of their own learning to plan for the future, whether classes for next year or a career.
4. Electronic portfolios are social. They are used as a vehicle for dialogue among students and faculty, between students and advisers.
5. Electronic portfolios are live texts. They inform the students' choices, and they continue over time.

Six Critical Issues

Making the portfolio electronic requires planning, regardless of whether the model under consideration is a new invention such as Babson's or a migrated model such as Alverno's. Specifically, digital portfolio developers speak in terms of a planning process that attends to six critical issues:

- identifying the "place" where the portfolio will be accessed: on a disk, on the Web;

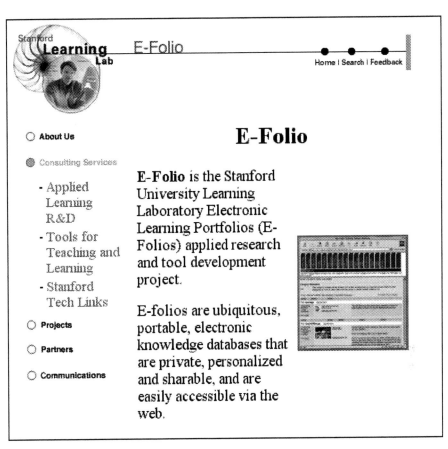

http://sll.stanford.edu/consulting/tools/efolio/

- exploiting appropriately the potential of the electronic environment, including hyperlinks, design of pathways for different purposes and audiences, and use of multiple kinds of information, such as graphics, sound, and video;
- deciding how much technological skill will be required of students and faculty and what, if any, pedagogical changes will be entailed;
- considering the role, if any, that design will play, including the design of interactivity;
- deciding when faculty will read and review the portfolios — and why;
- defining options as to the "life cycle" of the electronic portfolio.

Storing the portfolio

In some ways, the question about location may seem trivial, but it can be the most important one. And it is a question with several variables.

One variable is purpose. Suppose, for instance, that the purpose of the portfolio is to help a student in applying for a job. Is it better to have the portfolio on a CD and take it to the interview, where the student can walk the potential employer through it? Or is it wiser to include the Web-based portfolio's URL in a letter of application?

A second variable is access to information. If the portfolio is housed on a CD or Zip disk, then its creator can exercise a fair measure of control over who sees it. Web-based access can be controlled, but the student's access to the Web may cease if he or she drops out of school or graduates. For institutions with highly transient populations, format can be a significant factor: What commitment can the institution make to students as they move in and out of school? Related to access to information is security. Is it desirable to have students post identifying information on the Web?

A third factor is the allocation of resources. Especially for institutions with minimal resources, it might be best to begin a project with students supplying the CDs and disks, with the understanding that the risk of losing data is higher.

Exploiting the potential of the electronic environment

The electronic environment, whether a disk or a Web page, offers multiple opportunities for representing learning. Students can include performances through sound and video; they can show multiple ways of understanding through graphical, numerical, and verbal representations of data; they can link these representations one to the next or all at once; and they can provide multiple points of entry for different audiences into the various exhibits. As Emily Springfield points out later in this section, however, the fact that a student *can* link two exhibits does not ensure that a substantial connection has been made. In other words, it is true that the digital environment offers new ways of working for both students and faculty. But what it actually *means* — in terms of connecting and synthesizing information, for instance — is still an open question. Accordingly, building a portfolio model that permits collaborative exploration of this question will benefit students and faculty.

Defining technological skills and pedagogical changes required

Some models of the e-portfolio seem fairly high tech, and in disciplines where electronic technology is already part of the skill set, the technological leap may be fairly easily made. (Whether or not the associated leap in active learning and reflective discourse can be made as easily is another question.) Other models of digital portfolios, such as the model discussed by Rich Rice later in this section, are lower tech. By definition, however, an electronic portfolio requires technological skill of both faculty members and students. Identifying how much and what kinds of skills are needed for both stakeholders is a key consideration. Likewise, electronic portfolios are connected to changes in pedagogy. Sometimes, as in the case of the Hartwick nursing portfolios (as described by Peggy Jenkins), they come after the e-portfolio is introduced; sometimes, as in the case of the

Hartwick management portfolios (as described by Katrina Zalatan), they come before the introduction.

Defining the role of design in students' electronic portfolios

Some situations seem to call for templated design. At the beginning of a course or program portfolio, for example, a template might make expectations clear. The design itself, however, is key to the electronic portfolio. For instance, design includes audience issues and thus navigational issues. Likewise, hyperlinking is itself a design issue. Is the linking straightforward and analytical or is it associative? Even when templates are provided, students might well be asked to provide two kinds of links: internal, to exhibits created by the student and within the portfolio itself; and external, to items outside the immediate portfolio of student work. Building into the design both kinds of links works to ensure that at least two contexts are included: internal and external.

Deciding when faculty will read and review the portfolios

In some situations, faculty clearly will review electronic portfolios: during the class in the case of classroom portfolios, for example. But will portfolios be reviewed before they are submitted? Will others review them? Or will they be reviewed only once? In team-teaching or during program assessment, how will the review be structured, especially if multiple pathways are possible? Are faculty in fact reading and reviewing the same portfolio? And once they are read, how will the portfolios be used? Faculty are likely to generate these kinds of questions, questions that need at least tentative answers before a plan is implemented.

Determining the "life cycle" of an electronic portfolio

Eventually, mythology suggests, print items are discarded — or sent to rare book rooms. Not so for digital portfolios: In theory, given enough Web space and time, they can last into the next decade — or millennium. As important, because of hyperlinking and their tendency to move beyond one setting, electronic portfolios have a special potential for durability. That, of course, is part of their appeal. Ironically, the number of dead links increases with time, as well. It is therefore useful to think in terms of the "life cycle" of an electronic portfolio: when it is introduced, how it is developed, and when it comes to completion.

Specific Models of Digital Portfolios

Another way to think about electronic portfolios is to consider specific portfolio models and the lessons learned from them. The work at many institutions — from two-year schools to liberal arts colleges to research institutions — can help us think about how electronic portfolios can change both learning and teaching. This volume's selected samples of experience represent a wide range of institutional type, geographical location, student body, and purpose. The general intent in this representation is, first, to include a diverse set of electronic portfolios. This set shows both common principles and, concurrently, variations in practice. Second, even within those variations, we can discern patterns among practices. In other words, through reviewing these individual models of classroom and program portfolios, we will be able to talk more generally and synthetically about the kinds of models being developed, their key features, their benefits, and their risks.

The seven contributions in this section fall into two general categories. The first category is portfolios for students in the classroom, the second for beyond the classroom. Thus, for classroom electronic portfolios, we move from a focus on the teacher, in Donna Reiss's account, to a focus on the student, in Rich Rice's, to a focus on curriculum, in Katrina Zalatan's. For program electronic portfolios, we move from Emily Springfield's cautionary tale of a portfolio used for advising, to Chris Hult's explanation of an electronic portfolio used for program assessment, to Peggy Jenkins's discussion about digital career portfolio development motivating major curricular reforms. And not least, Emily Springfield's culminating contribution examines a key question: Given a perceived need for portfolios, why print and why electronic?

The Portfolio Models in Brief

A brief introduction to each of the seven contributions can help us see different aspects of electronic portfolios. In the first contribution, "Reflective Webfolios in a Humanities Course," Donna Reiss provides an account of why and how she took a humanities class at a two-year college on-line to electronic portfolios. Motivated to find a vehicle to showcase students' work that is congruent with a learner-centered pedagogy, Reiss suggests that basic Web technology is sufficient. And she makes a claim that we will see repeated: that the electronic medium is particularly suited to two needs of portfolio users. First, it provides a place to house students' work. And second, through hyperlinking, it invites students to make connections between and among classes, experiences, and observations.

To illustrate what a student electronic portfolio looks like, Rich Rice focuses on the portfolio of a specific student in "Composing the Intranet-Based Electronic Portfolio Using 'Common' Tools." We see in student Sharon's words and Rice's analysis thinking both creative and critical. As important, through this focus and Rice's discussion, we see how the electronic dimension of the portfolio "works" — through Sharon's explanation of her navigation system, for example, which provides both pathways for portfolio readers and a central concept unifying Sharon's experiences. Similarly, the links that Sharon identifies animate her central concept. Not least, Rice also shows us how an electronic portfolio can be created from commonplace software.

In "Electronic Portfolios in a Management Major Curriculum," Katrina Zalatan outlines how electronic portfolios have functioned in the reform of a management curriculum at Hartwick College, especially as it begins to emphasize an "active learning culture." As a vehicle, portfolios seem appropriate, given their emphasis on making critical connections and their opportunity for students to assess their own learning and reflect on it. As in several other models of program portfolios, this Hartwick model emphasizes both course and curricular competencies. Also germane is the choice of medium: Students chose not to share their portfolios on the Web, so that they could keep their reflections confidential. Portfolios thus were submitted on a CD or disk (the latter of which was preferred).

In the fourth contribution, "A Major Redesign of the Kalamazoo Portfolio," Emily Springfield provides a cautionary tale about the use of a program portfolio, in this case an electronic portfolio to be used in advising, and what can go wrong. Intended as a "reflective document," the Kalamazoo e-portfolio required that students work in Netscape Composer — a common theme among contributors here — and Springfield shares a workshop format used to acclimate students to this software. She also reports that most users of the e-portfolio (students and advising faculty and staff) appreciated the portability that comes with an electronic portfolio. And, she notes, as the program continued, the quality of the portfolios improved. Still, the fact that it is electronic does not mean that the portfolio is reflective — or, as Springfield puts it, links themselves do not equal reflection. In fact, apart from some resistance to the technology and additional resistance to using advising as a genuinely reflective occasion, reflection itself — what it is, how we ask for it, and how we respond — seems to be a major challenge.

Christine Hult reports on a capstone portfolio program in "Using On-Line Portfolios to Assess English Majors at Utah State University." Motivated by issues related to accreditation, an entire department decides to review programs by asking students to collect and reflect on what they have accomplished in a culminating Web-based electronic portfolio. Like many other programs, this portfolio model required that faculty think in terms new for them — of outcomes and competencies that spanned the classroom experience. As important, a new piece of the curriculum was added — the capstone experience — so that students could create the portfolio. Annually, the faculty review the portfolios, discuss them in terms of how well they meet appropriate expectations, and revise curriculum based on their observations.

In "Development of Electronic Portfolios for Nursing Students," Peggy Jenkins explains that the creation of portfolios in her department was motivated by an interest in helping students move beyond the classroom to find jobs. The first model engaged students in creating CD-based portfolios that students took with them to job interviews, and administrators found that this model of portfolio provided a window into students' competencies that potential employers appreciated. At the same time, they found that asking students to create this portfolio at the end of their academic careers was too little, too late. Consequently, the administrators designed another portfolio that would begin in the students' junior year. This portfolio, like the Kalamazoo portfolio, is primarily a vehicle for reflection, and because it builds on students' experiences in hospital practica where no computer support is available, it takes the form of print. One interesting observation, then, is that in this situation, the electronic portfolio used to get a job has motivated a redesigned focus on reflection in the curriculum that all agree makes for a better student and a better professional, even if it does necessarily take the form of print. In this situation, the result is neither electronic nor print, and it is not optional: It is both electronic and print.

How and whether to migrate the Hartwick print portfolio model to a digital model is a key question, one we have seen before — in the Kalamazoo reflective portfolio and the Alverno digitized portfolio, for example — and portfolio designers will want to think about the question carefully. Emily Springfield's "Comparing Electronic and Paper Portfolios," which includes observations and recommendations from the designers of several programs, addresses three key features that can help guide others: (1) the audience; (2) hardware and software availability and infrastructure; and (3) technological skills of both faculty and students.

Reference

Yancey, K.B. (1998). *Reflection in the Writing Classroom.* Logan, UT: Utah State University Press.

Reflective Webfolios in a Humanities Course

by Donna Reiss

Unlike my colleagues who have migrated their existing portfolio practices to the Web, I had never used portfolios in my face-to-face classes when I developed what I call "Webfolios." In adopting digital portfolios, I was not looking for a new means of assessment either. Rather, I was exploring ways to take advantage of the Internet and to provide alternative ways of learning for both my face-to-face classes and my Web-based classes. Because I had been introduced to Web development during the time I was revising my teaching methods — to incorporate more active, collaborative, writing-to-learn approaches from writing/communication across the curriculum and to reduce or eliminate the predominantly lecture-test techniques modeled by my own teachers — I was focusing on ways to connect students through language and images in on-line environments. The Webfolio project, http://onlinelearning.tc.cc.va.us/faculty/tcreisd/resource/webfolio/intro.htm, became one of those ways.

A Portfolio for Humanities 105

Although my composition and literature students also construct electronic portfolios, my focus here is an on-line elective course, Humanities 105, Technology and the Liberal Arts, in which students read, write, draw, observe, and interview as they explore the relationship between technology and the arts "from the inside." These students composed creatively and published their work on-line with enthusiasm and expertise. Students' informal contributions to electronic mail list discussions and their more carefully composed interactions on threaded Web discussion forums were the primary class learning spaces. To expand beyond the small on-line audience of their classmates to the broader audience of the World Wide Web as a way to display and reflect on their learning, however, seemed an appropriate and appealing next step for me and them.

What a waste it would be, I thought as I developed the Webfolio concept, if the only audience for students' creative efforts were the teacher or a small group of classmates. What a shame if the only record of their work were a typed manuscript or a photocopied booklet. And for my Web-based classes, where students might never meet face to face, what isolation might be fostered by their not sharing their work, and what connections

Donna Reiss is an associate professor at Tidewater Community College (Virginia), where her Web-enhanced and Web-based classes in writing, literature, and humanities include electronic portfolios. She is a writer, an editor, and a consultant on incorporating electronic communication throughout the curriculum: http://www.wordsworth2.net/.

could be generated by their doing so? Sending word-processed files to each other would have made their works visible to their classmates, and posting documents to a Web site would have provided a showcase for their work. But my goals were becoming multiple, no longer just disseminating their work for its own sake or for display but also for several other objectives:

- cooperative and collaborative on-line projects for interacting with each other and course content, including electronic discussion groups;
- publication of student texts for recording and sharing their own learning and that of their class community on, for example, individual and group Web sites;
- identification of college and career interests in an editable form that might be of value as part of an electronic resume, for example, a college record Web page;
- ongoing active reflection that reconsiders individual and group compositions in relation to the class objectives and the students' own thinking, presented as a culminating reflective composition with hyperlinks to their own and others' on-line work;
- demonstration of student learning through processes as well as products, primarily through links to and citations of electronic discussions as well as to finished compositions.

Students' reflective writing is to consider and synthesize the semester's work, citing and hyperlinking to examples from the student's own writing and to dialogues with classmates and appropriate external resources.

The evaluative function is last on this list, as I already had graded most of the individual elements of the collected works that appeared in the Webfolio. Some components were given credit rather than grades, notably the students' college pages of academic and career interests, which were based on a standardized template, and their creative compositions (writing and visual images). Their final reflective essay received a grade in conjunction with the entire Webfolio: If all elements were included as required, students received an A. If the Webfolio project was incomplete, that grade was reduced. As their combined culminating activity and final exam, this project counted 20-25% of their grade for the course.

The Portfolio Model

In a series of on-line templates that students can copy and edit in any Web editor without learning hypertext markup language (HTML), each technology and liberal arts Webfolio includes the following elements:

- A standardized page, identifiable as a college Webfolio by its prescribed format and content requirements — curricular plans, career goals, college activities, and courses (hyperlinked to classes that had Web sites). Figure 1 is an abbreviated version of the college page template (accessible at http://onlinelearning.tc.cc. va.us/faculty/tcreisd/resource/webfolio/).
- A Humanities 105 class Web page, with considerable flexibility for format and design but minimum content requirements. The class page template (accessible at

Figure 1. Tidewater Community College's student Webfolio template page

Pat S Student Webfolio [modified template]
Tidewater Community College

Curriculum
[Here include a 150-250-word description of your educational plans and goals. Related links are welcome.]

Career
[Here include a 150-250-word description of your career plans and goals. You can include a link to an online resume if you wish.]

Personal
[Optional information--but keep in mind that your Web pages are published to the world. You can include information on and links to special interests, hobbies, and a photograph. If you have a personal page elsewhere, you can include a link to it here. Delete this entire personal section if you wish.]

Classes
[Here you can add links to your Web page for every class you take at TCC if you would like to build an electronic portfolio. Add a link to ***your own Web page*** for the class if you have one rather than to the main class page. If your class does not have a Web site, you might want to link to the appropriate Course Description on the TCC Web.]

http://onlinelearning.tc.cc.va.us/faculty/tcreisd/resource/webfolio/minitemp.htm

http://onlinelearning.tc.cc.va.us/faculty/tcreisd/resource/webfolio/hum105.htm) does include a requirement for reflective writing and hyperlinks to the student's major term projects.

Reflective writing

Students' reflective writing is to consider and synthesize the semester's work, citing and hyperlinking to examples from the student's own writing and to dialogues with classmates and appropriate external resources. The exact assignment reads: "Write a 500-word focused reflection on technology and art based on your thinking about the topic throughout the semester as well as other experiences that have influenced your thinking." For instance, in his reflective piece, student Jay R. cited one of his own previous works as well as Mary Shelley's *Frankenstein* and Nathaniel Hawthorne's "The Birthmark" to exemplify one of his points:

> In Hawthorne's short story "The Birthmark," we see that Aylmer's overconfidence in technology and science brought about, like Frankenstein, the death of his wife and thus the destruction of the emotional component of his life. . . . In these examples, we see people placing too much trust in the power of technology while ignoring the "humanity" in themselves:

their consciences, their hearts and the unique abilities that each homo-sapien possesses. (http://onlinelearning.tc.cc.va.us/faculty/tcreisd/resource/webfolio/samples/tcwebjgr/hum105.htm)

In her reflective writing, student Karen S. mentioned the ways that interaction on-line contributed to the course experience: "We wrote notes to classmates, or about someone's homework assignment. We received feedback from each other as well as from our professor, creating our own little cyber-community." She included a link to the threaded discussion forum where she and her classmates worked in small on-line groups for exploratory and problem-solving activities. (http://onlinelearning.tc.cc.va.us/faculty/tcreisd/techarts/1999FALL/webfolio/tcwebkjs/reflect.htm)

Hyperlinks
Hyperlinks to the students' major term projects included both critical and creative works related to the class:

- The text of their original poem about technology and its impact on their lives or on "modern life," illustrated with scanned or computer-generated original work or with found art to complement their small-group discussions of these three poems "about technology": "All Watched Over by Machines of Loving Grace," by Richard Brautigan; "I like to see it lap the miles," by Emily Dickinson; and "The Secretary Chant," by Marge Piercy.
- Texts of their letters to classmates about artwork; films; readings about technology in business, education, and society; and site visits to technology-based businesses, including links to the electronic discussion forum where they interacted with classmates.
- A scanned original or computer-generated image based on a work of art from an exhibit or gallery in the community and accompanied by a reflective writing about the gallery art and the student's version plus information about the creative process for the student artist (as shown in Figure 2).

Although some students initially resisted or even resented this unfamiliar Webfolio project, even the most reluctant were proud of their accomplishment in developing Web sites and publishing their compositions. At the same time they achieved the academic objectives of the course, students enjoyed such creative elements as incorporation of graphics, colors, various fonts, fiction and poetry, and hyperlinks to external resources. They valued the opportunity to reflect on and synthesize the semester's work with a hypertext Webfolio more than they would have a cumulative essay exam. Novices were pleased to increase their skills using computers and new media. Everybody liked the option of sharing their achievements with friends, family, the world — and classmates.

Field Trip to the Chrysler Museum of Art

Dear Classmates,

I recently visited a fascinating exhibit at the Chrysler Museum of Art in Norfolk, Virginia. When I visited the exhibit, Sacred Sites Then & Now, The American Civil War, on June 28th, 1998, I was fascinated by what I observed. The exhibit is a collection of works by various artists. It focuses on the way places have changed since the Civil War. What they have done is to research old photographs, battlefield sketches, and maps, then show the sites as they appear today, using many different media. The way the exhibit is presented, it really illustrates the differences in the way things and places were then versus the way they are today. The sites today differ greatly from the way they appeared then, and believe me, the impact is very strong. Not only are the appearances different, the changes in technology are also very apparent. There were many different types of art in the exhibit, including photographs, murals, collages, and paintings.

The work of art I chose to describe was done in the traditional medium of oil on panel. It is entitled *Clark's Mountain Confederate Signal Station, 1991,* and is by James McElhiney, a contemporary American artist. At about 9 inches by 12 inches, it is relatively small when compared to many of the other works in the exhibit, some of which covered entire walls or large areas of the floor. Like most paintings, it is one-dimensional. The techniques used to create it, physically, probably have not changed in many years. The artist's "vision" is what makes this work so special. When I saw it, I knew immediately that I had found the subject of my letter. There was a message in the painting so powerful that it seemed to shout to me. The painting itself if of average quality, a traditional (at first glance) painting of a Shenandoah Mountain area valley. What affected me was the microwave tower, standing atop the mountain in the foreground. I attempted to recreate the painting, although I will admit it is a very crude representation. That, in itself isn't much to get excited about, until you read the title the artist has given his work, *Clark's Mountain Confederate Signal Station, 1991.*

The painting captures the essence of the way technology has changed our world and our lives. Looking at the picture, I could easily make the microwave tower disappear.

http://onlinelearning.tc.cc.va.us/faculty/tcreisd/resource/webfolio/samples/tcwebkcm/trip2kcm.htm

Recommendations

For teachers who want to develop similar reflect-and-display Webfolios for their classes, I recommend the following strategies:

1. *Provide clear instructions and expectations for students* about required and optional textual and graphic elements, hyperlinks, and method of evaluation. A template of some kind is especially helpful for students new to Web page development. Templates for my classes in composition, introductory literature, and the humanities at Tidewater Community College, used for both classroom and Web-based classes, are on-line at http://onlinelearning.tc.cc.va.us/faculty/tcreisd/resource/ webfolio/intro.htm.

2. *Begin the term with an overview* of this culminating project so that students can be thinking about both the technical aspects (designing and developing Web pages, scanning or downloading graphics, converting word-processed files to Web pages) and the ways they might want to display and connect their texts. In my introductory literature classes, students worked in teams of three to six to develop Web sites about a play they had read, and every student in the group linked from his or her individual portfolio to this collaborative site. I hope to include such Web collaborations in future offerings of Technology and the Liberal Arts.

3. *Offer training with a focus on a specific class Web page* rather than a session that focuses on the technology itself. For my on-line students, I held two optional workshops to teach and practice tools and principles, using Webfolio templates

that I had created. Rather than offer a separate lesson in Web development, develop a workshop activity where students construct the "official college page" and one other page, link the two together, incorporate a hyperlink to an external site, and integrate a graphical element. We use the free Composer Web developer-editor in Netscape because it is easy to learn and use, students can download it at home, and they can advance to more sophisticated tools later if they choose. In future classes, I plan to include incorporation of audio and video components.

4. *Encourage students to link* to relevant external Web sites and to their classmates' Web sites, incorporating these links into their own compositions in meaningful ways. If they include lists of recommended external sites — for example, e-journal articles and other scholarship related to a research project — they should adequately annotate those links.

5. *Permit and encourage as much creativity as you are comfortable with.* Some fundamentals of readability and design will help students make judgments. Some basics of copyright and fair use will help them avoid accidental misuse of others' text and images.

Composing the Intranet-Based Electronic Portfolio Using "Common" Tools

by Rich Rice

Listen to Sharon, as she thinks about how her electronic portfolio will work:

"This teacher's pretty cool," Sharon thinks to herself. "He lets us catch-up on email and check out web-pages during class. And I like how he said we should try to make this portfolio project thing 'personally meaningful.' It's like, in other English classes, most teachers make us write only academic papers, and it's hard to see that stuff in real life. You know? What are we supposed to do with these kinds of writing, anyway, after we get our final grades? Oh, what'd he say? Now he's talking about something called an 'intranet.' Hmm ... how's that different than the Internet? Yeah, that makes sense — a system we share, through computers, and can pop into at any time. Kind of like email. But with our own resources. Talking with other students, my friends, teachers, pretty much anytime I think of something good to say. Sharing and making what we write together. Public vs. private? What's that all about. Oh I get it, makes sense. Work on stuff for the portfolio — stuff that is going on outside school and then relate it to stuff going on in school. Yeah, an IN-tranet. Hmm, yeah. Cool. Tying stuff I already know to new things I'm learning. And doing this by using programs I know, like Word and PowerPoint and email. Cool!"

Electronic portfolios enable learners like Sharon to make reflective connections between the known and the new, the public and the private, and the academic and the personal. They also can suggest development, document diversity, communicate personal interests, and serve as highly authentic assessment tools (Yancey, 1996, p. 130). And as Hawisher and Selfe point out, students can build portfolios from the "common" programs they are already using (1997, p. 306). In sum, as we shall see, composing and interacting with electronic portfolios through the means of intranet spaces — using both virtual space and the "space" between the personal and the private — foster a new kind of learning for students.

Intranet-Based Pedagogy and Composing Communities

An intranet is an electronic network that is local to a specific institution or company; it is like a listserv, only it belongs to the class in question, or to any specific set of partici-

Rich Rice teaches in the Department of English at Ball State University. He also serves on various faculty development initiatives and curriculum design committees for portfolio assessment.

pants. Students can use the intranet as a space where they can share both ideas and writing. And from a teacher's perspective, an intranet makes sense as well: It is a dynamic and flexible space lending itself to a variety of activities, it can be consistent over a number of courses and across disciplines, and it stands the test of time well even with other technological innovations. It is a common tool in many classes, and as Sharon will explain, it works well with a digital portfolio.

Three other tools common to the teachers, students, and administrators in my institution are Microsoft Word, Microsoft PowerPoint, and Centrinity's FirstClass Collaborative Classroom. The first is considered a word-processing tool, the second is traditionally understood as a presentation tool, and the third is a transactional intranet system that includes synchronous and asynchronous features as well as shared folders where users can exchange files. (Your school may use different programs that serve as word-processing, presentation, and information-sharing tools.) We have ready access to them in the classroom, in offices, in 24-hour computer labs, in dorms, and at home. Additionally, at our institution, students use these programs for classes other than mine. And while we are far from creating an ideal intranet campus community ethos, many teachers are using FirstClass in conjunction with Internet Web pages in pedagogically sound ways that encourage students to see this shared space as one in which they can take considerable residence.

Sharon is one of the students who learned very quickly how to adapt these tools to create an electronic portfolio. Most of our students do, because they are relatively familiar with the software. Her portfolio demonstrates how students can integrate intranet contexts and portfolio content. Sharon created an off-line PowerPoint shell with hyperlinks to Word files as well as other nodes in her PowerPoint file. At the beginning of the semester, Sharon did not know how to make hyperlinks in any program. But because she was familiar with composing in Word, learning how to select a word, phrase, or object and then choosing Insert-Hyperlink took only a few minutes. She saved her files on disk and through the intranet so that she could work on pieces of her electronic portfolio on different machines whenever she wanted. Instead of learning different technologies that she would not likely use in any form after college, she spent her time developing a navigational scheme that represented her work in the course and her developing growth as a writer. In these ways, her portfolio is *scalable* (able to be enlarged congruent with the purpose), *reliable* (able to be accessed), and *sustainable* (able to be maintained).

Sharon's navigational theme is very well developed, and the jumping-off points took different forms and contextual themes as her portfolio content changed. As Sharon thought about her audience and what was personally meaningful, she considered "metaphorical ways of moving from piece to piece because there [were] no paper pages to turn" (Fischer, 1996, p. 177). She ended up with the section headings *writer* ("a curious girl

Electronic portfolios enable learners like Sharon to make reflective connections between the known and the new, the public and the private, and the academic and the personal.

The opening page of Sharon's portfolio, and some samples of her work from it

will write"), *good girl* ("a good girl will write in the lines"), *bad girl* ("a bad girl will write in the margins"), and *eccentric girl* ("an eccentric girl will write in anything").

Sharon begins her reflection letter and electronic portfolio by letting her development as a writer and artist begin in narrative. She shares the story of coming to find her identity through literacy. For Sharon and many of today's learners, the electronic portfolio is a valuable presentation device because literacy today is more visually oriented, and the digital portfolio offers the flexible option of using multimedia. Learners often come to words or ideas through pictures. And if a single essay is a *textual representation* of a student's writing skill level for a particular academic standard at one specific moment, a selected collection of one's work is a *contextual picture* of a student's learning process. Sharon reflects:

Words are funny things. They textualize both the real and the abstract, capturing them in neat categories like nouns, adjectives, and verbs. They are strange and elusive sounds to shape and articulate thought. They are the tools of writing and define people and ideas.

I learned to write my name at age five. Sitting awkwardly cross-legged in my room surrounded by a rainbow mess of crayons, I copied the neat print of my teacher who had inscribed my name for me on the interior cover of a book about Prince Charles. I struggled over the perfection of those lines and contours and finally, after painstaking deliberation, managed a fairly legible line of text in the thin layer of wax from a fat, purple crayon. Prince Charles grinned up at me from the front page and I grinned back. I had made my mark.

Eighteen years later I'm still practicing the difficult craft of writing (though only occasionally in crayon). I have always thought that first attempt — how I tried to copy text as I would a picture — was responsible for my development as both a visual and a literary person. The fine arts are as important to me as the literary arts (I am a double major in both graphic design and creative writing), and I believe that effective communication in either medium is powerful and essential.

In five years of university study, my goal in writing has primarily been the same: to create clear, persuasive, and honest prose. I have a deep respect for the reader's attention and for the art of writing, and I thus continue to strive toward truth in a unique and personal style. I suppose these are the goals of many writers, but I have increasingly learned in these five years of study of the importance of keeping my mind open to all experiences that may influence me. Whether I'm reading *Newsweek* or *Angela's Ashes,* cooking dinner or painting a canvas, riding my bike or traveling across Europe, I stay aware and watchful, ready to reflect, react, and refract the world around me from within my own microcosm of words.

George Orwell, one of my favorite writers, once said that all literature is political. I also believe it is mostly autobiographical. And in that sense, my writing defines me.

Elsewhere in her reflection letter, she continues to examine audience in the context of how writing redefines both reader and writer.

Sharon also reflects on how her writing developed from "authoritarian" five-paragraph theme templates to more personally meaningful forms of writing. Because she is able to use those earlier pieces, still saved as Word files, and hyperlink to specific sections that reinforce her points, she is able to reflect more holistically about her thinking and writing and authentically highlight her growth along the lines of logic, personal adaptation, and her own writing style:

These first essays for university classes in this style forced me into a generic, authoritarian tone with little room to explore. My Honors 203 final, "Nature, Love, and Suffering: Relations Within the Human Experience," however, provided me the opportunity to relate several disciplines — literature, philosophy, visual and performing arts — to a central idea, an opportunity for more creativity. The basic theme of this piece is strong and some of my connections are perceptive. Unfortunately, logic is stretched a few times as some of my *examples* feel far-fetched and contrived, particularly the comparisons made among a comedic play, an Italian film, and the philosophy of mythologist Joseph Campbell.

My English 230 essay discussing the Ambrose Bierce short story "An Occurrence at Owl Creek Bridge" began to more deftly weave in such examples to support my premises. In a number of passages I use quotations from several sources — the opinions of writers and other critics — in addition to examples from the text, to *illustrate a point*. I also began to find my own allusions to add dimension to the introduction and added body to my conclusion with more consideration of the story's *significance to the reader.*

By the time I wrote the essay on poet Marianne Moore entitled "From Toads to Schoolbooks. . .," I felt greater confidence in my writing abilities and shifted farther away from overly dogmatic structure. While my introduction still begins with broad statements about literature and artistry, the whole of the essay flows more organically and is less dependent on any point-by-point illustration of the *thesis,* which is still strong, but not so forced and predictable. While the analysis of the poem is detailed and specific, several passages are very *thick with the opinions of others,* and I'm afraid they began to overshadow my own voice in the essay. My writing style is still developing as I'm trying to balance the elements that are strong (organization, clarity) with a more flexible and organic style. Taking creative writing classes has helped me tremendously in this respect, especially after the dozens of drafts and rewrites I prepared for my Honors Thesis project, "The Cipher Box."

Her "cipher box" and contextual, Campbellian movement from the known to the new and from an "overly dogmatic structure" to more confident, personally meaningful forms are the source for her navigational structure and portfolio content. She discovers that her growth in "trying to balance the elements" is a process similar to that of creating her encapsulating boxes. Her portfolio becomes a cipher box, a metaphor that helps her discover more about herself as she hypertextually circles around her personal and academic work. She moves a little further in each node from her crayon picture-writing days, but with each step she strengthens her understanding of those foundations. About a creative writing piece, Sharon points out that "what attracted me so much to 'Box' was how it helped me articulate my own ideas about art. . . . I wanted to push the character, Alexis, even further — to give more details on his past, his feelings and his world because I was learning to see through them to find truths about myself." These are the types of findings Sharon discovered in her section called "a curious girl will write."

Closely connected, Sharon's "a good girl will write in the lines" section links to critical essays and research where she directly identifies examples demonstrating where she feels she has repressed her voice. Her "a bad girl will write in the margins" section begins with creative work and personal journal writing where she fleshes out her concept of the cipher box. And in "an eccentric girl will write in anything," Sharon examines through a hypertextual experience her visual art, sketches, designs, and dreams, leading her to see how her voice is developing from her personal experiences through her creative and academic writing. In this node, she challenges herself — as well as her electronic portfolio — "to 'write about what you know': What do I know? art? writing? myself? What do I really know about any of these?"

This quest is a journey that leads her through undergraduate courses, through her summer experiences in Spain and France, and back. And because electronic text is fluid text, she is able to incorporate the items she finds relevant.

First and foremost, assess access and experience for both students and teachers.

In this cycle, she threads her growth as a composer — a multimodal composer in text, graphics, and sound — through sketches, on computers, with pictures of notes on napkins, with photographic collages, with papers and teachers' and peers' responses and revisions. And it can be done using tools such as Word and PowerPoint. At one point, on a single page, Sharon offers connections that synchronize the journal she kept while abroad with notes about how the effect of those experiences changed her voice in academic writing, her self-portrait with how she feels different audiences view her visual art and her writing, and her remarks about how the development of characters in her creative writing changed her views on life. Her process of constructing her metatextual electronic portfolio is one of growth.

Sharon chose not to link to the Internet, but her response sections in the portfolio link to both teacher and peers. Most intranet programs enable specific people — students, teachers, administrators, parents — password-protected access to shared directories or folders, the feature that Sharon did use. Thus, when viewing Sharon's latest portfolio iteration, her audience could access this shared folder to offer ideas and suggestions synchronously or asynchronously by clicking on a link in her portfolio.

Recommendations for Getting Started

First and foremost, assess access and experience for both students and teachers. If students do not already compose in the environment their work will be shared in, a process of converting content to a different medium will be required, which may "deauthenticate" the portfolio-building process. For this same reason, it is advisable to assess students' work using the same tools with which they were composed. Your word-processing program in all likelihood can create hyperlinks to on-line and off-line files. If you are not using a presentation tool such as PowerPoint or an intranet system such as FirstClass, consider using the word-processing program and sharing portfolios by swapping disks or using e-mail.

HTML and Web pages can serve as useful cover page tools to package word-processed files, but Webfolio production may not be "common" to your students. Listservs are excellent resources for the "common" electronic portfolio model, however. For instance, students can easily create a hyperlink *mailto:* command in their teacher- or peer-response sections. By clicking on the link, a response can be sent to the entire class. Students can click on one link to go directly to the electronic portfolio's creator, another link to go to the teacher, a third link to go to a select group, or a fourth one to go to the entire class. If all students have ready access to the Internet, free resources such as eGroups.com may be used to share archived, threaded responses.

Demonstrating models of electronic portfolios to get started is a slippery teaching strategy. If you spend too much time on a model, students will invariably cater to the template, stifling their own metaphorical explorations of navigational themes. Navigation is a very rich, process-oriented component to the construction of electronic portfolios: It provides another opportunity for learning.

As for the management of electronic portfolios, it is important that students have frequent and stable access to where they store their files, whether at an on-line location or on a disk. And spend some time speaking with students about directory structures, encouraging students to keep all material in one location for easy retrieval and transfer of information later. Discussing directory structures helps begin the process of thinking about how one thing relates to another.

References

Fischer, K.M. (1996). Down the yellow chip road: Hypertext portfolios in Oz. *Computers and Composition 13* (2), 169-184.

Hawisher, G., & Selfe, C. (1997). Wedding the technologies of writing portfolios and computers: The challenges of electronic classrooms. In K.B. Yancey & I. Weiser (Eds.), *Situating Portfolios: Four Perspectives* (pp. 305-321). Logan, UT: Utah State University Press.

Yancey, K.B. (1996). Portfolio, electronic, and the links between. *Computers and Composition 13* (2), 129-133

Electronic Portfolios in a Management Major Curriculum

by Katrina A. Zalatan

Hartwick College is an undergraduate liberal arts college with a student body of approximately 1,500, about 130 of them management majors in 2000-2001. Forty-six students (mostly juniors) participated in our 1998-1999 portfolio pilot.

For many years, the management major consisted of traditional, lecture-based courses about separate management functions, for example, marketing, finance, and operations. In 1996, our approach changed: Every course in the junior and senior management major sequence was designed around a computer-based management simulation. Simulations actively involved students in decision making, enabling them to learn management concepts and interrelationships through experience.

All simulations in our curriculum basically follow this five-step implementation process:

1. During the first week of class, students are assigned to "company teams" (at least three teams per course), and they stay with those teams throughout the semester.
2. Each team is given financial and other information about its firm, with all teams starting at about the same position.
3. Students are given a list of management decisions they could make for their firm; company teams make these decisions confidentially, independent of the other teams, who become their "competitors."
4. Decisions are forwarded to the instructor, who inputs them into the computer-based simulation, and the software "runs" the decisions, generating a set of reports that show the result of each team's decisions in the context of all teams' decisions in the class (the "industry").
5. Each team receives the confidential report for its firm, and they repeat the decision-making process.

This process is repeated many times in every course, typically resulting in up to two simulated "years" of decision making. Course instructors facilitate the process and provide ongoing coaching and instruction.

Katrina Zalatan is an assistant professor in the Department of Management and Accounting at Hartwick College. Her research interests include nontraditional pedagogy and the assessment of learning in business education. She led the electronic portfolio pilot in her department as part of a College project funded in part by a grant from the William and Flora Hewlett Foundation.

Student computing is also an integral part of our curriculum. Because all Hartwick students receive laptop PCs, computers are used for simulation decision making, analysis, writing, and presentations in every management course. The management department also has a "laboratory" that consists of five student offices equipped with desktop PCs, monitors, and printers. During class time, student teams use these offices for decision making. We also have one classroom equipped with network ports and a variety of built-in presentation technologies.

The Rationale for Portfolios

While our approach to pedagogy changed in 1996, our approach to assessing students' learning did not. Simulation-related assessment included peer evaluation, student participation, team performance, written plans, presentations, and final "case" exams similar to the simulation. Individual student reflection and self-assessment, however, were not emphasized. Faculty observed greater motivation and critical thinking, but our assessment methods did not always capture these changes. Evaluations also tended to focus on simulation results (especially winning results), which did not necessarily measure the full extent of students' learning. Individual students continued to have little if any responsibility for assessing their own learning; and while they appeared to be learning more, their ability to articulate the scope and significance of this learning did not improve commensurately.

As we investigated alternative assessment methods for 1998-1999, several questions framed our inquiry. Could any assessment methods cause *all* students to reflect, discover, and integrate critical concepts throughout each simulation? Could they increase our students' awareness of their learning and help them better articulate these gains? And could any methods help our students see every simulation — regardless of results — as part of an ongoing, lifelong learning process? Student portfolios appeared to be an excellent solution.

Offering students the opportunity to create these portfolios electronically seemed natural, as most of the students' work was already in electronic format.

Portfolio Pilot Process

In fall 1998, we piloted portfolios as a requirement for all junior management courses. Limiting implementation to junior courses made the pilot easier to implement and support while providing enough feedback to determine whether the process should be implemented more broadly later. Two instructors were involved, each teaching two sections (20 to 24 students per section) of his or her two junior courses.

The instructors attended relevant conferences and workshops to increase their familiarity with portfolio methods, and they collaborated to design and implement the following pilot process.

Competency area lists

Brief lists of course and curricular competency areas were presented to all students on the first day of each course. *Course competency areas* included critical understandings that students should gain during each simulation (see opposite). Students were expected to use portfolios and evidence from the course to demonstrate their achievement, and as such, course competencies served as a framework to support discovery.

While each course had a functional emphasis, competencies from other disciplines were also included. In MANA I, for example, competencies were drawn from formerly separate marketing, economics, and accounting courses. Competency lists were organized using the management model taught in introductory courses.

Curricular competency areas were relevant to all courses (see opposite). Students used course portfolios to demonstrate their growth in these areas, comparing and relating experiences between (not just within) courses. Both course and curricular competency areas were left intentionally broad so students could develop meaning for these competencies throughout their courses.

Technology training and support

Course portfolio media were left to the discretion of instructors. While students had the option of submitting portfolios in an electronic medium (floppy disk, Zip disk, or compact disk) in every course, they were required to do so in MANA I and IV using Netscape Communicator as their navigational application. Netscape was chosen because it was part of the standard software installed on every student's laptop, and it could be uploaded easily to the Web for future use in career portfolios. The professor mandating electronic portfolios was proficient in Netscape and had experience using electronic portfolios in one course the previous year.

All students participated in Netscape Communicator training conducted by library staff outside regular class hours, and all had access to hard copy and Web-based self-instruction for scanning, CD burning, and Netscape. Students upgraded their laptops to include the same version of Netscape Communicator, and the management lab was upgraded to include more capable PCs, two scanners, and one CD writer. Because storage was anticipated to be an issue for students, portable Zip drives were also made available at the library reserve desk so students could use Zip disks with their laptops.

Course competency area example (excerpted from MANA I, Fall 1998)

1. Definition of marketing.
2. Philosophies of marketing.
3. Marketing Management Decision Making Process:
   a. ANALYSIS - Market situation analysis and SWOT
      (1) Customers
         (a) Needs/wants...
   b. PLANNING
      (1) Target market and positioning...
   c. IMPLEMENTATION (including "approach" to decision making)
   d. EVALUATION
      (1) Vertical and Horizontal analysis...

Curricular competency area excerpt

1. Critical thinking (about management and about yourself as a manager and a learner)

2. Communication
   a. Written
   b. Oral

3. Teamwork
   a. Specific goals
   b. Common approach
   c. Meaningful purpose...

Library staff were available for consultation throughout the semester, including the crunch time when portfolios were due.

Prescribed portfolio organization

While students had the freedom to choose what evidence supported their claims of competence, they were required to use a prescribed format for their portfolio in each course. Faculty designed these formats to ensure enough consistency between students to make assessment less time-consuming, and they presented portfolio grading criteria to students when the format was reviewed.

When electronic portfolios were required, portfolio formats and tutorials were available on the course Web sites. A standard format made grading easier for the professor and freed students to spend more time on portfolio content (see the example on the next page). Specific requirements for page layout were also provided to increase readability and enable printing.

Preliminary (formative) submission

In each course, students submitted preliminary portfolios after they accumulated enough experience upon which to reflect, typically about halfway through the simulation. All were required to be individual efforts. While portfolio assignments varied between instructors, all engaged students in selecting, presenting, and reflecting about experiences to demonstrate competence. In MANA I and IV, for example, students reflected about four examples of their experience that, together, demonstrated their achievement of the course competency areas. In MANA II and III, students were directly asked to demonstrate understanding of pivotal simulation concepts at instructor-identified points during the game, with all competency areas addressed by the end of the course.

Portfolios in all courses included reflective narratives and examples of students' simulation-related work. Faculty also provided coaching to help each student reflect about and articulate his or her learning. In MANA I and IV, the instructor also assessed each student's readiness to put his or her work into Netscape and scheduled additional training or coaching with library staff as needed.

During the entire semester, a student lab assistant cleaned students' files from the management lab PCs to prevent memory problems that could complicate scanning and other operations. Students were continually reminded to make and carefully store disk backups of their work.

Final (summative) submission

Final portfolio submissions were due on the last day of each course, typically two weeks after the last simulation decision period. For courses requiring electronic portfolios,

Example of Hartwick's standard electronic portfolio format for a management student portfolio

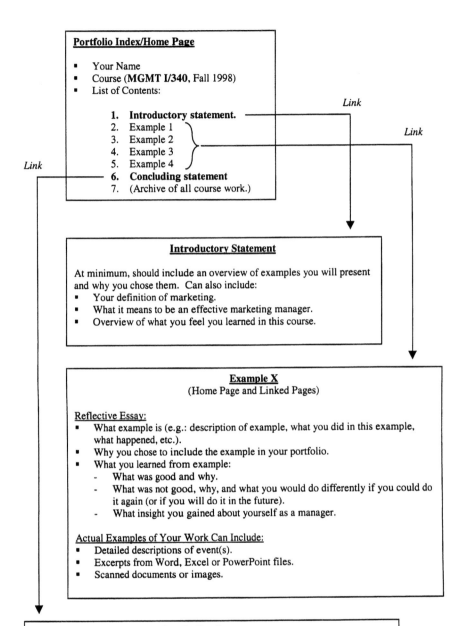

Portfolio Index/Home Page

- Your Name
- Course (**MGMT I/340**, Fall 1998)
- List of Contents:

  1. **Introductory statement.**
  2. Example 1
  3. Example 2
  4. Example 3
  5. Example 4
  6. **Concluding statement**
  7. (Archive of all course work.)

Link

Link

Link

Introductory Statement

At minimum, should include an overview of examples you will present and why you chose them. Can also include:
- Your definition of marketing.
- What it means to be an effective marketing manager.
- Overview of what you feel you learned in this course.

Example X
(Home Page and Linked Pages)

Reflective Essay:
- What example is (e.g.: description of example, what you did in this example, what happened, etc.).
- Why you chose to include the example in your portfolio.
- What you learned from example:
  - What was good and why.
  - What was not good, why, and what you would do differently if you could do it again (or if you will do it in the future).
  - What insight you gained about yourself as a manager.

Actual Examples of Your Work Can Include:
- Detailed descriptions of event(s).
- Excerpts from Word, Excel or PowerPoint files.
- Scanned documents or images.

Concluding Statement

- Summary of your most important learning(s) in this course.
- How what you actually learned compared to what you expected to learn at the beginning of this class.
- How/if you expect to use this learning in the future.
- Reflection about your overall performance in this course.

teaching assistants did a virus check and a quick check of navigational links for every disk or CD submitted before forwarding the work to the instructor. Problems found were usually corrected quickly, preventing significant headaches for the instructor later. Electronic portfolios were not submitted via the Web, because many of the students' reflections about their team interactions required confidentiality.

Students were also asked to sign a form that indicated whether they would permit their work to be copied and shared with others in future sections of the course or in the instructors' communications about the portfolio pilot. If permission was granted, excerpts could also be used on the course Web site to help students conceptualize portfolios in an electronic format.

Portfolios were returned after each course, and instructors provided feedback on paper or disk to help students understand that even summative works are formative parts of their larger curricular portfolio.

Grading

In fall 1998, portfolios in MANA I and II accounted for 20% of each final course grade. By spring 1999, the weight for portfolios increased to 30% of the course grade for MANA III and IV. This increase paralleled the increase in responsibility that students were taking for their own learning and their increasing ability to do reflective self-assessment.

As a department, faculty shared and discussed students' reactions, students' work, and instructors' reactions to workload and process variations. Because students' perceptions were also critical, we administered a portfolio project survey on the last day of spring term to all 46 participating students. The survey was anonymous, and it consisted of three sections: *technology* (eight items of various formats that measured self-reported use of various technology resources and students' satisfaction with them); *general perceptions* (seven questions on a five-point scale that collected perceptions about the pilot's objectives and assumptions); *comments and suggestions* (three open-ended questions that asked for suggestions for improvement, whether junior portfolios should be continued, and for expectations about portfolios in their senior year 1999-2000).

Results

We observed several anticipated results:
- *Portfolios developed the ability to reflect among the majority of students.* Because portfolios were not team projects, all 46 students were required to reflect. Interestingly, many students reflected about their learning from the challenges and failures they experienced during the simulation, and they appeared to appreciate the opportunity to treat these events as positive learning experiences.

As the year progressed, we observed improvement in students' reflective works. Students earned higher portfolio grades in all spring sections. Students' responses to the survey also strongly supported that portfolios fostered reflection: 91% agreed that portfolios increased their awareness of what they learned and gained from each course, 89% agreed that portfolios provided an opportunity for them to reflect about their development as managers, and 83% agreed that portfolios helped improve their understanding of course experiences.

Overall, both electronic and paper portfolios appeared highly valued despite the extra work required, clearly supporting our shift to an active learning culture. Of the 36 (out of 46) students who answered the open-response question "Should we continue to use portfolios to assess student learning in our junior courses next year?" all responded affirmatively. Of the 27 students who wrote explanatory comments, 70% supported the use of portfolios because of the reflection they fostered. Students' rationales included that the portfolio enabled them to reflect and comprehend and to truly convey what they learned.

- *Students became more involved in assessing their own learning.* In the survey, 91% of the students agreed that portfolios gave them the opportunity to assess their own learning in each course. Given the strong realism of each simulation, students appeared to perceive authenticity, and they took both simulations and portfolios very seriously. Students also appeared to be motivated by the direct link they perceived between classroom learning and future job requirements (competencies).

- *Students felt more prepared for seeking jobs.* Students perceived that their course portfolios would eventually contribute to career portfolios. Of the 27 students who had given reasons to continue using portfolios, 41 percent cited being able to better convey what they learned and being prepared for the future. And 81% of all student respondents agreed that portfolios will be worthwhile in job interviews.

Other findings pertained to the pilot instructors and portfolio-related technology:

- *Most students found content more arduous than technology.* Most students seemed to accept the need to produce, store, and communicate their work electronically, and some even saw having technology and visual communication skills as a competitive edge for future employment. Even though electronic portfolios were not required in all courses, the survey revealed that students stored an average of 79% of their management course work electronically. In courses requiring electronic portfolios, those few who reported problems with the technology also submitted poorer portfolios overall.

- *Students used and were satisfied with the technical support available outside class.* Among students in courses requiring electronic portfolios, 61% used the portfolio tutorial available on their class Web sites. Students suggested adding actual sample portfolios to the sites, which will be possible during the second year of implementation. Most reported that they used the instructional documentation for

81% of all student respondents agreed that portfolios will be worthwhile in job interviews.

Netscape (72%) and scanning (67%), and their satisfaction with both was also good. Students were also highly satisfied with technical support, though we were pleasantly surprised to learn that 20% used "friends" as their primary technical resource.

- *Of the electronic portfolio media available, Zip disks were the most used, write-once CDs the least.* Students appeared to prefer the ease and convenience of editing Zip disks, even though most students had to use labs or equipment on reserve to use Zip disks with their laptops. Storage capacity was critical when portfolios included multiple, simulation-related scanned images. Very few students used CDs, even though the CDs were inexpensive and writers, self-instruction, and technical support were available. We believe this happened because the CDs could not be edited, and students were generally unfamiliar with using CDs for storage.

- *Instructors worked harder, but they also had more information to coach teams and assess individual students.* Portfolios gave instructors detailed insights into each student's learning and self-assessment, and they helped instructors discern the extent to which individual students were really involved in their team. Portfolios also gave instructors more detail to facilitate students' discovery in the simulation. Instructors perceived that they worked harder, especially in the formative submission stage of the process, but that the benefits outweighed the extra work. Instructors in all courses reported that the time to grade final portfolios appeared comparable to the time previously required to grade case exams — if the portfolio was submitted in hard copy. If the portfolio was submitted electronically, it took longer to grade, especially if the instructor first printed its content.

- *While each instructor had slightly different approaches to portfolio assignments, most students appeared to accept these differences.* Only 13% of survey respondents suggested increased consistency. Instructors found that their approaches converged to some extent, as they shared assignments and results with each other throughout the year.

Future Challenges

Portfolios have been a significant step forward in our assessment of students' learning, but we faced two major challenges for electronic portfolios in 2000-2001: growth and inexperience, and resources.

Coordination of the portfolio pilot was relatively easy, because just two faculty members were involved and they had worked well together in situations, including team teaching, in the past. Since 1998, however, the number of management majors has increased. The number of faculty and course sections have also increased, to maintain the small class sizes necessary for our pedagogy and portfolio process. In 2000-2001, the number of faculty teaching junior courses increased to five, only two of whom had experience with electronic portfolios. While all five will implement portfolios, most will require paper versions and offer electronic media as an option. The faculty member with the most experience with electronic portfolios will coordinate meetings for department colleagues to learn more about the pilot and the technology, resources, and implications of electronic portfolios.

Because the numbers of students and course sections have increased, we expect that the demand for departmental computing and technical support resources will also increase. Making electronic portfolios optional in every course will ease demand as we consider future support needs.

Conclusions

Overall, the results of our portfolio pilot were positive, encouraging, and strongly supportive of the active learning culture so critical to our simulation-based management curriculum. While portfolios did require more time and effort from faculty and students, we believe that portfolios raised the quality and totality of students' learning experiences from simulations — raising reflection, learning, and assessment to levels not achieved with traditional evaluation methods. Portfolios also improved our rapport with students.

While portfolios did require more time and effort from faculty and students, we believe that portfolios raised the quality and totality of students' learning experiences.

Although electronic portfolios appeared to offer benefits, our department will not mandate their adoption. Rather, we will discuss, debate, and consider their adoption as a faculty team. While this process may be tiring for the faculty who participated in the portfolio pilot, it is hoped it will help us build a stronger faculty team as we educate each other, share ideas, and seek to reach consensus. Such reflection mirrors the portfolio process we require of students, helping us all learn and improve. In all, we foresee that our ability to expand to full implementation of electronic portfolios will be limited only by the availability of resources, class sizes, and each instructor's time, priorities, and technological proficiency.

Note

I would like to extend sincere thanks to my colleague Doug Mayer for his partnership in this pilot. I would also like to thank Margaret Schramm, professor of English and Hewlett Project coordinator, and Marilyn Dunn, college librarian and director of information resources, for their support. This project was funded in part by a grant from the William and Flora Hewlett Foundation.

A Major Redesign of the Kalamazoo Portfolio

by Emily Springfield

Kalamazoo College, one of Michigan's most selective private residential colleges, has since the 1960s offered the "K Plan" to its students, a varied curriculum including coursework, internships, study abroad, and senior projects. Created in 1996, the Kalamazoo Portfolio was designed to help students view these activities — as well as cocurricular activities such as sports, volunteer work, jobs, and membership in student organizations — as a cohesive whole with all parts contributing to their education.

Original Design: A Reflective Portfolio

The Kalamazoo Portfolio has always been conceived as a reflective document. The college wanted a record of students' thoughts: a place for them to articulate what was important to them about their college experiences, a place where they would be able to see their own growth and change over time.

The Kalamazoo Portfolio was originally designed around five dimensions (lifelong learning, intercultural understanding, social responsibility, career readiness, and leadership) and four skills (written expression, oral expression, quantitative literacy, and information and computer literacy). These dimensions and skills describe Kalamazoo's vision of an educated person and reach across the boundaries of academic and nonacademic areas. For example, one could develop leadership skills in a class or during an internship, and one could improve oral expression through a theater production or a group class project.

The portfolio was intended, in part, as a vehicle for planning managed by students together with academic advisers. Students would prepare for advising by drafting a list of courses and alternates and by writing in their portfolios. Instead of spending 25 out of 30 minutes selecting courses from the catalog, students and advisers could use the advising session to focus on weightier questions, such as "Why do you want to major in X?"

Students were required to begin their portfolios on-line. During orientation week, students were introduced to the concept of the portfolio, and over the course of the first quarter each student attended a workshop with his or her first-year seminar. In these

Emily Springfield is an educational technology and portfolio consultant. She has helped several institutions, most notably Kalamazoo College, begin electronic portfolio programs.

workshops, students learned more about the purpose of the portfolio, what to include in it, and how to use Netscape Composer to create the portfolio on the Web. Students had the option of switching to a paper format after the first two years.

Evaluation/Project Results

For all students, a major issue centered on reflection. We discovered a continual need to explain "reflective writing" to both students and faculty members. Most students began by describing (but not necessarily analyzing) experiences: basic who, what, where, when writing. The two questions that prompted the most meaningful responses, however, were "How did that come to pass?" and "Why was it significant?"

The college wanted a record of students' thoughts: a place for them to articulate what was important to them about their college experiences, a place where they would be able to see their own growth and change over time.

In spring 2000, seniors were asked to discuss two topics as final portfolio entries: their most significant experiences during their time at Kalamazoo College and their growth in each of the five dimensions and four skills over the previous four years. Students in this class, the first to be required to create portfolios, however, thought these requirements so challenging that they proposed waiving the requirement for their year. After careful review, the Educational Policies Committee and the faculty determined that the requirements for the portfolio were valid for graduation. Students were, however, given the option of submitting reflections on paper rather than via the Web.

By and large, the portfolios submitted by the seniors were excellent. Most students commented on study abroad, internships, and personal relationships with one or more professors as major factors shaping their education. Most were able to trace the development of their interests throughout their college years and project that path into the future through graduate study or employment. We foresee these reflections becoming useful to college administrators as a type of senior exit interview.

In addition, many students gave excellent illustrations of their development in dimensions and skills, though 30-35% of them sounded more like "the party line" than indications of a deeper understanding of lifelong learning, intercultural understanding, social responsibility, career readiness, or leadership. One consistent disappointment was the almost universal equation of intercultural understanding with study abroad or interaction with non-Americans. Although we had emphasized the expectation that students would include race, ethnicity, religion, gender, regional identity, and so on as part of their discussion of intercultural understanding, almost no students used such a broad definition of "culture." For example, a male student who had written a basic things-are-fine-and-women-and-minorities-should-quit-whining letter to the school newspaper devoted six or seven pages in his "overview" reflections to the letter, the response, his counterresponse, and his reactions after rereading all his materials six months after the fact. Although they were excellent reflections, he did not mention the issue in terms of his growth in intercultural understanding.

Portfolio Results for Freshmen, Sophomores, and Juniors

In 1999-2000, we modified the previous requirements, which had been different for each class standing, by instituting a general set of tasks. Underclass students were asked to discuss three topics: (1) growth since the previous year (in the form of a transition-to-college essay for first-year students or reflections on the previous year's goals for sophomores and juniors); (2) reflections on the main events of the current year; and (3) goals for the future.

The quality of underclass students' writing has varied significantly between fall 1996 and spring 2000. Each year's freshmen have written better portfolios than the previous year's freshmen. With the college's expectations rising each year, students have met those expectations, especially when faculty have incorporated portfolio requirements into courses or have asked students to rewrite portfolio entries as part of the advising process. Some students have written excellent reflections on their growth in the dimensions and skills. Students have also used their portfolios to make sense of tragedies, such as deaths on campus.

Sophomores and juniors generally add fewer, longer pages to their portfolios, probably because the portfolio is emphasized in orientation and the first-year seminar but not so much in the next two years, and because students in the first year need several short pages to create a navigational structure. To distinguish what sophomores and juniors have added to their freshman portfolios, students date each page.

The class entering in 1999 produced both exceptional portfolios and a number of incomplete portfolios. Some portfolios that looked incomplete on the Web, however, could have been written on paper. Because nearly 50% of advisers did not report officially on their advisees' portfolio completion, we cannot be sure. This lack of participation by some advisers continues to be the largest stumbling block in developing the Kalamazoo Portfolio.

Advisers' Participation

The faculty approved the portfolio as part of a curriculum reform that had been under discussion for about three years. Most advisers saw the advantages of the portfolio: Students would think more about their experiences and plans rather than simply hurtling from one class or cocurricular experience to the next. Advising could skip the mechanical creation of a schedule and move toward a deeper discussion of students' goals and choices.

Over the next three years, 25-30% of advisers advocated this "developmental" advising model facilitated by the portfolio as the only worthwhile form of advising. Most of these advisers were new to the advising pool, either as new faculty or, more strikingly, as Student Development staff advisers. (Advisers with the rank of "staff" rather than "faculty" do the academic advising for the first year or two; most students then move to an adviser in their major.) These advocates say advising sessions last 15-45 minutes (traditional advising appointments usually last 30-45 minutes), and if they expect students to come to the advising session prepared, the students for the most part comply.

A second group of advisers (perhaps 15-20%) think the portfolio is a good idea, but they do not have the time to spend in the advising session. These advisers are faculty members with up to 30 to 40 advisees. Many of their students do not bring to their advising session at least a preliminary list of courses on paper. Although techniques for shifting responsibility to students for coming prepared and reducing time in the advising session have been made available, these faculty believe that students will not arrive prepared and that they cannot make time to reschedule appointments.

A third category of advisers, a small, very vocal minority, describe the portfolio as "touchy-feely hand holding" that "has nothing to do with teaching or advising." They seem to prefer the puzzle of scheduling and dealing with logistical questions. They are accustomed to a method of advising that they believe has worked for 25 years, and will probably never change their minds.

In a fourth category, the remaining advisers are ambivalent or confused about the portfolio. With more outreach, they would probably join the "enthusiastic supporters" group. Current inertia, however, prevents the kind of systematic outreach needed for encouraging enthusiasm. Nevertheless, it is important to articulate the success of the program.

Electronic Format

The electronic format worked for most students at Kalamazoo. About 80% of students were able to compose functioning Web pages after one required workshop. Some of these students attended additional workshops and, we assume, made use of the manual (both print and on-line) and advice from computer lab assistants and friends. The level of Web design ranged from very basic (those who just wanted something on-line) to overly complicated (those who wanted to try as much "neat stuff" as possible) to exquisite (generally artists and computer science majors or enthusiasts). We refined workshop delivery significantly in the first two years, and we attribute students' high rate of success to these workshops and to the ever-increasing computer skills the students bring with them to college.

After the first two years, we settled on a very effective workshop structure. Most people, we discovered, can pay attention in a workshop for about an hour and learn about three new things in that hour. We learned about these capacities after a year of experimentation. Our first year, we explained what the portfolio was (and in some cases, explained what the Web was!). Then students copied templates from the hard drive of the lab computers to floppy disks, opened the templates, made changes to the templates, made links, added colors, copied images from the Web, and inserted the images on pages they created. This was far too much information to learn in an hour, especially an hour during orientation week. In subsequent years, we trimmed the workshop down considerably.

The final workshop format was usefully repetitive:
- explain the purpose of and suggest content for the portfolio (25 minutes);
- have the students make a page and save it;
- make another page and save it;
- make a link between those two pages;
- make a third page (without instruction) and link to it (at this point, about 40 minutes into the workshop, students were pretty good at the basics and were clamoring to know about colors and pictures);
- upload and unlock the portfolio (most people did not remember this bit of information, so we always reminded them where to find the information when they should need it).

A surprisingly large percentage of students found Web design to be a significant barrier.

It was vital that each student attended a workshop with a class, because few students would attend subsequent evening workshops.

The Other 20%

A surprisingly large percentage of students found Web design to be a significant barrier. We had assumed that as students entered college with more and more computer experience, Web design skills would be a given. To a great degree, it is the case; but about 20% of our students found the Web format to be a hindrance. Some could not understand the software, some were classically "computer-phobic," and some, although they understood the software, spent an inordinate amount of time (20 or more hours in some cases) struggling with the software to produce any pages at all. These students were frustrated by broken links, missing or misaligned pictures, and a simplistic look to the pages that did not adequately reflect their abilities as students. Even advanced users had trouble defining the kind and source of their problems. Malfunctioning software often turned out to be the culprit.

When we realized our difficulty with the software, our first thought was to change to a different product. All software packages pose problems, however. For example, Microsoft

FrontPage is difficult to understand. Because Claris Home Page is no longer in production, its code-rewriting bugs will never be fixed. Microsoft Word, though acceptable for translating long text documents into HTML, allows users to create documents with so much "bad form" that links can break, images disappear, and documents become unreadable. Although Macromedia's Dreamweaver has fewer problems, it sports a less than intuitive user interface.

In our final evaluation, the chief advantage of the electronic format was its portability. Students did learn something about the mechanics of making Web pages, but creating links did not necessarily increase students' recognition of connections among their experiences. Because the electronic medium posed such challenges to many students, we made the electronic format optional — though highly encouraged — for the 2000-2001 academic year.

Dimensions

The jury is still out on the five dimensions (lifelong learning, intercultural understanding, social responsibility, career readiness, leadership) that students are to document in their portfolios. Two limitations were restrictiveness and a lack of understanding of the dimensions. Although some students wrote excellent reflections on the dimensions, some complained that the dimensions were too restrictive for discussing all their experiences. Students and advisers both sometimes misunderstood the dimensions, from a student's claiming "I've been socially responsible because I always host the parties" to most students' omitting racial, religious, gender, and other cultural differences in their representation of intercultural understanding. When the dimensions were better understood, students produced effective portfolios. Some students worked well within the dimensions, which they could explain in relation to their work. Other students wrote excellent reflections attached to dimensions, although they did not explain completely why the experience fit the dimension.

It could be that the dimensions just need more time to become part of campus culture. Venues need to be added that encourage discussion of the dimensions. Clarifying the relationship between reflection on the dimensions and reflection on the experiences exemplifying the dimensions would also be useful. Students need help in selecting significant experiences and analyzing them in terms of the dimensions.

Summary

The Kalamazoo Portfolio has been successful or very successful for about half the student body. About a quarter of advisers consider the portfolio a valuable addition to advising at

Kalamazoo College, but a quarter reject either the time the portfolio takes or the portfolio concept. Many other advisers are uncertain about the virtues of the program.

Recommendations

Alterations to the current Kalamazoo Portfolio could increase its use and benefit. Other colleges can learn from our experiences.

- *Decide the purpose of the portfolio — and stick to it.* The goals of your project should be easy to remember, self-explanatory, and few in number. When students and faculty ask, "Why are we doing this?" the answer should be exact, consistent, and self-explanatory. Portfolios can easily be seen as multipurpose tools. I recommend choosing one function and establishing that function firmly before adding other purposes.

  When using dimensions, competencies, or other categories, be sure that faculty members, advisers, and students have sufficient common understandings about the terms and about their relationship to the primary purpose of the portfolio.

  Everyone involved should know exactly the goals of the portfolios, and every part of the program should help achieve those goals.

- *Keep requirements consistent.* Make the requirements the same for all classes.

- *Use a portfolio program to implement agreed upon objectives.* Kalamazoo, for example, originally developed the five dimensions and four skills as bases for a revised curriculum, but the dimensions and skills were shifted to bases for a portfolio system that would break down barriers between academic and nonacademic areas. Confusion about objectives related to the dimensions and skills created problems for the portfolio program.

- *Develop campus support before requiring student portfolios.* Because portfolios take both time and intellectual work, faculty members, advisers, and others need to understand and be committed to the program. Students will benefit from this consistent understanding and support by producing effective, useful portfolios.

Using On-Line Portfolios to Assess English Majors at Utah State University

by Christine Hult

Utah State University, a comprehensive research land-grant university, began a systematic review of campuswide assessment practices in 1997, following an assessment recommendation received after an accreditation review from the Northwest Association of Schools and Colleges. The recommendation identified a clear direction: "While the committee found assessment activities are evolving in a generally positive direction, institutional efforts are uneven and coordination is lacking. Methodologies [that] assess outcomes rather than inputs, and quality rather than quantity, need to be improved in some cases and implemented in others."

Two years later, in a response to the accreditation committee, the newly appointed director of university assessment cited the English Department as a model for its assessment practices: "This is not to say that quality assessment practices do not exist at USU. On the contrary, they do. One need look no further, for example, than the very thorough practices of the English Department or of the Department of Health, Physical Education, and Recreation, which are models to other departments."

The assessment director was referring to the English Department's systematic assessment of students, programs, and teachers. This assessment process has evolved over a number of years, motivated in large part by a total reevaluation of our curriculum in preparation for a calendar change from a quarter to a semester system between the 1997-1998 and 1998-1999 academic years. But our assessment plans really came to fruition in 1998 when the department instituted a Web-based system that allowed for easy storage and transmission of assessment documents. The system consists of two major parts: (1) a Web-based classroom, in which students can store their on-line portfolios, and (2) a department intranet, by which all members of the department can easily share documents and information over the Internet. We found that both of these on-line systems were crucial to the development of a coherent assessment program for the entire department.

Christine Hult is professor of English, associate department head, and director of the Center for On-Line Education (COLE) at Utah State University. She coordinates an English department effort to evaluate English majors in the various major tracks through the use of capstone portfolios.

Writing the Outcomes-Based Program Competencies and Course Objectives

As we revised our programs and courses for the semester calendar, we began to see the need to define very specifically the competencies we wanted students to acquire before graduating. To assess how well students were achieving the competencies and to provide students with an opportunity for self-assessment, we decided to include a capstone experience for our students in each major track in the department: Literary Studies, Technical/Professional Writing, and English Teaching.[1] The required capstone courses (three semester credits to be taken during the senior year) were designed to assess how well students were achieving each program's specific competencies as well as to provide students with an opportunity to reflect on their intellectual development. The departmental Web site provides a detailed description of the programs in our department and their various competencies.

Competencies for three tracks in the USU English Department are posted on the department's Web site

Program Competencies for Literary Studies Majors

The mission and philosophy behind the Literary Studies option are realized in terms of the specific competencies students are expected to acquire. Students completing the program will know **about**
The fundamental concepts, questions, and approaches within literary theory and history
The traditional periods and basic canon of British, American, and world literature
The literary conventions, techniques, and styles that enable them to demarcate texts and understand their formal working
Some of the debates and concerns over canon formation
Historical and cultural contexts for literary texts
The kinds of pleasure to be had in literary and cultural analysis

In addition, the Li
Construct and sup
Write critical essa
Apply critical app
Place literary text

Program Competencies for Technical/Professional Writing Majors

When students complete the Professional and Technical Writing option, they will **know about**
The relationship between client, audience, text, and writer
The importance of teamwork in the writing profession
Current hardware and software in all levels of text production
Theoretical issues in perception and reading
Rhetorical theory and strategies
The natures of different texts

Program Competencies for English Teaching Majors
The following Competencies are expected of all graduates in the English Teaching option.

Characteristics of Professional Teachers
The graduate will
Understand that American society is culturally diverse
Understand professional and political issues in English education
Be prepared to be a leading participant in the school, professional, local, and national educational communities

Disciplinary Competencies
The graduate will
Know about literary periods and genres
Know about major British, American, and world writers
Know about a variety of critical approaches to literature
Know about multicultural American writing
Understand the structure and diversity of the English language
Know about the principles of creative and transactional writing
Know and be able to use research skills
Be a competent writer

Pedagogical Competencies
The graduate will

http://english.usu.edu/dept

Program competencies for each of the three tracks in our program were written over the course of a year by the three curriculum committees. In addition to the more general program competencies, the committees also wrote specific course objectives for each course offered. The competencies and objectives form the heart of the assessment process. Unless a program has spelled out in very specific, measurable terms the "outcomes" expected from students in the program, assessment is difficult, if not impossible. Many times faculty members, especially in the humanities, resist such codification of their teaching or learning objectives. After much encouragement and many heated discussions, however, we were able to convince faculty that putting the outcomes in terms of competencies that students could achieve — and dividing those competencies into the categories of "students will know about" and "students will know how to" would be something everyone in the department could do.

Incorporating the Competencies in the Departmental Culture

English majors are first introduced to our departmental programs in general and to the specific competencies for each major track when they are freshmen and sophomores in a required one-credit course called "English Orientation."[2] In that course, students are also told about the need to save written work from the various courses they take in the English Department. They are apprised of the fact that when they are seniors, they will need to take the appropriate capstone seminar for their track. They learn that the seminar will provide them with a way to systematically reflect on their English Department coursework and to analyze their intellectual progress over time. They are encouraged to save their written work in electronic form — either on their own computer disks or on the English Department's Web server. Because many of the courses in the department take advantage of the department's Web-based classrooms to store coursework, students are able to keep their writing from year to year on-line with easy access at any time in the future. This easy access to the students' stored writing is one of the key features of our assessment process.

Subsequent to the English Orientation course, students are frequently reminded by their professors of the overall program competencies and the specific course objectives. The Literary Studies professors, for example, have all agreed to provide students with the specific course objectives at the outset of each course in the program, either by using an overhead transparency or by posting the objectives on their class Web site. Professors have also agreed to write a very brief "self-assessment" of each syllabus, explaining to the curriculum committees how their individual courses reflect the program's competencies. Discussions of program competencies and course objectives are thus becoming part of the overall culture of the English Department.

Designing the Capstone Seminars

Once the competencies were in place, we turned to designing the capstone seminars for each track. The three capstone courses, although they evolved a bit differently depending on the personalities of the faculty members teaching them and the needs of specific student populations, nevertheless contain many common themes. They all provide for an on-line class component that makes it very easy for students to store their work electronically and for other faculty members involved in assessment to read the portfolios. The course description of the Professional Writing Capstone Seminar demonstrates the kind of work called for in the capstone:

> Your primary work is to develop a professional portfolio of at least seven high-quality documents (electronic and print) of various types. These documents may be documents you have completed during your internships, in your coursework, from on-the-job experience, or new documents you develop. The specifications for documents in your portfolio include color, black and white, short, long, marketing, informational, print, and electronic. Lectures on resumes, interviews, and work group management, for example, are also included.

Assessing the Portfolios

The portfolios generated during the capstone courses are subsequently read and evaluated by members of the appropriate curriculum assessment committees (in addition to the evaluation that had been done by the capstone course instructors in conjunction with the courses themselves). The capstone portfolios are placed at a specified location on the department's Web site so that all committee members can read the portfolios on-line at their own convenience. In the case of the Technical/Professional Writing track, some portfolio documents (e.g., brochures or newsletters) need to be produced in print format, as the instructor and the committee must also evaluate the physical "look" of certain pieces. The print components are gathered in notebooks that are made accessible to the curriculum committee for their review. The majority of students' work across all the major tracks, however, can be evaluated by committee members on-line rather than in print.

Some committees use a fairly formal evaluation worksheet (see the sample worksheet reproduced at the end of this chapter); others use an informal reading and discussion of impressions. Data gathered by reading the portfolios are formulated into an annual assessment report that is submitted to the department head and posted on the Web site. These reports can be seen at http://english.usu.edu/dept/assessment/index.htm. (See the sample on the next page.)

One of the English Department assessment reports created from the review of student portfolios

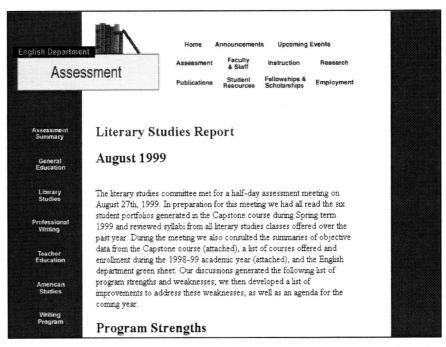

http://english.usu.edu/dept/assessment/literary/report99.htm

Technical Assistance in the Assessment Process

Many times departments face insurmountable obstacles that prevent the systematic gathering and dissemination of assessment information. How can students be encouraged to keep their work throughout their undergraduate years? What if they forget to keep some crucial writing? And, on the other end, once student portfolios are collected, where can they be stored, and how can all the faculty who need to access them do so? The sheer magnitude of the paperwork has often discouraged systematic, comprehensive assessment efforts in many departments. Enter the computer. Using the Internet as the storage and distribution mechanism has solved many of these logistical nightmares.

Our department developed its own Web-based classroom system called SyllaBase (http://english.usu.edu/online), but any Internet classroom system, such as WebCT or Blackboard, should be able to facilitate the collection of students' work into on-line portfolios. At the same time we developed SyllaBase, we also developed a departmental intranet, a communication network that included both a public and a private site. The public site can be seen at http://english.usu.edu/dept. We use the public site to disseminate information to our various constituencies, including the University Assessment Team and its director, who found out about our assessment practices through the descriptions on the departmental Web site. Faculty members use the private site as a place to store and disseminate important information in-house, such as guidelines for tenure and promotion or requests for travel authorization. Because needed assessment information can

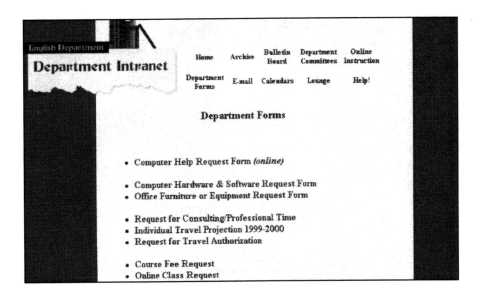

be accessed on the Internet by everyone involved in the assessment process, the entire mechanism flows smoothly.

What We Have Learned From the First Portfolio Assessment

The first year of the capstone portfolios (1998-1999) was assessed by the appropriate curriculum committees in half-day faculty workshops just before the beginning of fall semester 1999. Before the workshops, the committees sampled portfolios or read all the portfolios on-line, depending on the number of graduating seniors in the track (i.e., 15 for Literary Studies, 34 for Professional Writing, 27 for English Teaching). During the workshops, committee members discussed what they had learned from reading the portfolios and considered potential programmatic changes in light of what they discovered. Any suggested curricular changes were scheduled for implementation in the subsequent academic year and once again would be assessed at the next preterm assessment meeting.

After the workshops, the committee chairs wrote reports describing the results of the assessment. The reports from the various committees can be found at the department's assessment Web page, accessible to all constituencies, including students: http://english.usu.edu/dept/assessment/index.htm. Each committee was gratified to find that most program goals were reflected in the students' work, but each also discovered some ways in which the program could be improved based on the data gathered in the portfolios, as shown in the excerpt from the Literary Studies report on the next page.

Selected Strengths, Weaknesses, and Planned Solutions

Strengths

Students feel that we do an excellent job of teaching critical, analytical reading; Students feel that at higher levels of the curriculum we do an excellent job in teaching critical, analytical writing; Students like our program's emphasis on teaching literature in its historical and cultural context; Students praise the rigor of our program . . .

Weaknesses

A major problem identified in the Capstone portfolios was the lack of clear guidance from faculty and advisors; Students felt they were floating through the program, with little sense of how their courses fit together; Students said they were mostly not aware of program and level objectives until the Capstone course; Students often were not able to take courses in proper sequence. This was caused both by difficulty enrolling in the perennially full 2000 level courses, but also because the advisor was not strongly advocating taking courses in sequence; Transfer students seemed to feel the lack of guidance particularly acutely. . .

Solutions

1. Advising, Guidance, Counseling

A. Foregrounding Program and level objectives

The faculty felt that many of the problems our students identified in our program would be alleviated if we began to make our level and program objectives a more prominent feature of our courses. We feel that in some cases students are in fact learning what we want them to learn, but that they haven't been schooled in the terminology they need to identify those skills. So, for example, we seem indeed to be teaching students how to "analyze the relationship between form and meaning" in our 2000 level classes, but students don't understand that this is what they're doing because we haven't labeled it as such. To give another example, one of the Capstone students who most adamantly denied he had developed his "own critical voice" was a student who, we all agreed, had developed an extremely strong critical voice: he just hadn't been taught what a "critical voice" was . . . .

http://english.usu.edu/dept/assessment/index.htm

The other two curriculum committees, Technical/Professional Writing and English Teaching, also completed analyses similar to the Literary Studies description, available on the department's assessment Web page.

Students' Perceptions of the Digital Portfolio

Students' reaction to the first assessment process was uniformly positive. The capstone seminars all received rave reviews from students in their course evaluations. They were extremely appreciative of the opportunity to reflect on and make sense of their education and the chance to see more clearly what the department defined as the "guiding intelligence" behind a specific program. In the case of the Technical/Professional Writing and

English Teaching tracks, the students actually came away from the program with very tangible evidence of their skills and employability in the form of their portfolios. Many of these students made print copies of their portfolios to take with them for job interviews. Students reported that their portfolios helped them to be more confident during an interview and to field questions more readily by referring to specific documents found in the portfolio. In follow-up surveys of our graduates, we hope to learn how they have applied the skills acquired in our program to their professional and personal lives.

I opened this chapter with a mandate from the Northwest Association of Schools and Colleges to improve assessment processes at Utah State University. We in the English Department feel that we are well on the way to making data-based decisions, as the accreditation team recommended. We have also learned that the Internet can provide the way this process can be accomplished openly and with a minimum of hassle for everyone involved.

Notes

1. The English Teaching capstone originally resided in the College of Education as part of its certification requirements. The English Department decided, however, to institute its own capstone seminar, effective fall 2001. Because the seminar has resided with Education for the past two years, I was unable to attain very much assessment data from this track, other than that reported by the curriculum committee.

2. Unfortunately, transfer students do not always take the English Orientation course, as they may have transferred in as juniors with an associate's degree from another college. Transfer students present thorny articulation problems for all major tracks that we have not entirely solved but are working to address through advising.

One fairly formal portfolio evaluation used by the English Department

---

Technical/Professional Writing
Portfolio Description and Evaluation Worksheet

Student Portfolios

a. The Portfolio Contents. The portfolio should consist of at least seven finished documents done during coursework at USU (including material done as part of the Professional Writing Capstone course). These seven documents should be a mix of types and should contain representatives from each of these eight paired categories:

1. Color
2. Monochrome or Two-Color
3. Large (>= 5 pp)
4. Small (< 5 pp)
5. Marketing
6. Informational
7. Print
8. Electronic

b. A 10-pg proposal out of the Proposal Writing class, for example, would count as large, marketing, print, and either color or monochrome. A foldout brochure would count as small, marketing or informational, print, and color or monochrome. Each of the eight categories must have two documents representing it and no two documents can fulfill the same suite of categories.

c. Resume. Each student will have a high-quality resume in their final portfolio.

d. Physical Format. As part of the Professional Writing Capstone course, the student will prepare a professional portfolio to give to employers. In addition, they will prepare a file copy of their portfolio for evaluation purposes.

1. A three-ring binder with top-loading page protectors for print documents and zippered pouches for electronic media with the student's name on the binding and front cover
2. A resume
3. Seven documents (as described above)
4. Photocopies of one-of-a-kind documents
5. Electronic documents must include a copy of the file on electronic media (3.5" floppy, 100M Zip disk, or CD-ROM) and representative screen shots

e. Portfolio Evaluation. Two instructors will evaluate each portfolio. The instructor of the Professional Writing Capstone course will evaluate each portfolio as part of the grading process and will write a summary. The portfolios will then be equally divided among the remaining Technical Writing faculty on campus during the following semester and each of them will evaluate the portfolios given to them.

f. Portfolio Evaluation Tool. Each evaluator will fill out one of these worksheets for each portfolio which is evaluated by them. The Portfolio Assessment Tool is divided into sections so that each of the above eight categories can be evaluated separately and so that other factors may be considered in the overall program evaluation.

Instructor Evaluation Data

An Instructor Evaluation of Course Tool will be used at the conclusion of every Technical Writing course to assess how the instructor feels the course was conducted, how the students responded to various aspects of the course, and the success or failure of particular projects undertaken during the course. This data will become part of a reference archive for future instructors of the same course.

Portfolio Evaluation Tool
Professional and Technical Writing Program
English Department
Utah State University

Mark the most appropriate answer for each question based on student's entire portfolio. If the question asks for a 1-5 response, circle the most appropriate response. 3 is "Just Right," 1 is "Student Didn't Know or Care," 5 is "Student Is Truly Creative and Innovative." Some responses are "Circle All That Apply." If you circle a 1 or 2 on any question, you MUST either circle a reason or write a comment. If you circle a 3, 4 or 5, circling a reason or writing a comment is optional.

Professional Capstone Instructor (only): The first page asks you to list the evaluated documents and check which categories they fill. Each document will only fill four categories (one each from Graphic Content, [Color or Black & White/Two Color {B/W}], Size [>5pp or <=5pp], Format [Print or Electronic {Elec}], and Purpose [Marketing {Mark} or Informative {Inf}]).

Student's Name: _____

(B/W = Black and White or Two Color, Elec = Electronic, Mark = Marketing, Inf = Informative)

Document	Color	B/W	>5pp	<=5pp	Print	Elec	Mark	Inf
1								
2								
3								
4								
5								
6								
7								

Note: Students must have at least seven representative documents. Each of the eight subcategories must have two representative documents. No two documents can fulfill the same suite of subcategories.

Note: These ratings are for the Portfolio as a whole, not for individual documents
Note: If you score a 1 or 2 on any item, you must circle a reason or write a comment, otherwise circling a reason or writing a comment is optional

Presentation
The portfolio binding and presentation were professional (rate 1-5):   1 2 3 4 5
Check all that apply: ☐ Binding was cheap
                        ☐ Page protectors were: ☐ cheap ☐ not used properly
                        ☐ Documents were not properly identified
                        ☐ Portfolio was unorganized
                        ☐ Electronic documents had no accompanying screen shots
Other comments:

The document summaries were enlightening (rate 1-5):   1 2 3 4 5
Check all that apply: ☐ Summaries were: ☐ vague ☐ too short ☐ too long ☐ poorly written
Other comments:

Portfolio Evaluation Tool, cont.

Graphic Content

Graphics were effective (rate 1-5): 1 2 3 4 5
Check all that apply: ☐ Graphics: ☐ did not support text ☐ contradicted text
☐ Graphics: ☐ were improperly sized ☐ improperly placed on page
☐ Graphics: ☐ were overdone ☐ were too scarce
Other comments:

Color was used appropriately (rate 1-5): 1 2 3 4 5
Check all that apply: ☐ Colors: ☐ were clashing ☐ did not provide enough contrast
☐ Grayscale or two-color graphics did not provide enough contrast
☐ Use of color detracted from text
Other comments:

Document Size

The appropriate document size was selected (rate 1-5): 1 2 3 4 5
Check all that apply: ☐ Text was: ☐ too long for document ☐ redundant
☐ Graphics were crowded
Other comments:

Text was well-written (rate 1-5): 1 2 3 4 5
Check all that apply: ☐ Text was: ☐ too verbose ☐ too terse
☐ Spelling was not checked properly
☐ Grammar was not natural
Other comments:

Publishing Format

The documents were designed with the format in mind (rate 1-5): 1 2 3 4 5
Check all that apply: ☐ Electronic documents: ☐ looked like paper documents
☐ exceeded average screen capabilities
☐ had too much "eye candy"
☐ Print documents were: ☐ not easy to use ☐ not well-organized
☐ not appropriately bound
Other comments:

Electronic documents were easy to use (rate 1-5): 1 2 3 4 5
Check all that apply: ☐ Hyperlinks were: ☐ not logical ☐ not relevant ☐ not well-marked
☐ Text could not be followed linearly
☐ Effort expended to use exceeded usefulness of electronic format
Other comments:

Document Purpose

Documents addressed the Customer appropriately (rate 1-5): 1 2 3 4 5
Check all that apply: ☐ Marketing documents: ☐ did not link features with Customer benefits
☐ showed no knowledge of Customer requirements
☐ Informative documents were: ☐ hard to use ☐ not clearly written
☐ boring to look at
Other comments:

Development of Electronic Portfolios for Nursing Students

by Peggy Jenkins

As a result of a grant from the Hewlett Foundation in 1997, Hartwick College focused on the development and use of student electronic portfolios. At the time, the Nursing Department was searching for a method to increase our students' use of technology and to create a way for students to display their accomplishments to graduate schools and/or employers. Thus it was that during spring 1998, the Nursing Department began to expect senior nursing students to create electronic professional portfolios in the required Trends and Issues course.

Electronic Professional Portfolios

The student professional nursing portfolio is a selection of works that documents personal and academic accomplishments during a student's college years. To begin, a list of possible artifacts that can be included in the portfolio is distributed in class. That list includes a required *reflection-in-presentation* essay; this culminating text demonstrates (1) the student's comprehension of the influence of baccalaureate education on professional practice, (2) synthesizes the information presented in the portfolio, and (3) provides a clear description of how to navigate the portfolio. The professional portfolio is worth 20% of the final grade for the course.

The professional portfolio has been well received by students as a culminating project of their college career. A few students have taken their portfolio with them to interviews for employment, and potential employers have been extremely impressed with the use of technology and students' documentation of accomplishments. To the Nursing Department's knowledge, each candidate for employment who has used a clinical portfolio has been offered a position.

Issues related to the development of the professional portfolio are centered about three main themes: (1) technology, (2) time, and (3) reflective thinking. Technology issues such as compatibility of systems and platforms, software, and equipment needs were handled by

Peggy Jenkins is associate professor of nursing at Hartwick College. In her role as a co-coordinator of a grant from the William and Flora Hewlett Foundation, she introduced electronic portfolios burned onto CDs to enable nursing students to develop critical-thinking skills and to increase their marketability to the health care world.

staff from the Center for Learning, Teaching, and Technology. Potential technology concerns were recognized and handled efficiently before they affected students' ability to complete the portfolio.

A learning curve related to the technology of developing electronic portfolios, however, existed for both faculty and students. For instance, faculty changed from expecting a CD as the outcome to accepting either a CD or a Zip disk. (Zip disks provide students an opportunity to be more independent and grant them more flexibility to change their portfolios.) Write-once CDs, the original choice, are inexpensive but do not allow for revisions or updates as the student's career evolves. Read-and-write CDs permit additional material to be supplemented, but were considered too expensive to require the students to purchase.

Time spent reading and navigating through the portfolios varied considerably, largely because students' organizational abilities were so diverse and the medium was so new. Although hints were provided to students about artistic presentation and organization of their portfolios, the end product was totally of their own creation. The list opposite contains many of the tips designed to help students improve the artistic presentation of their portfolio.

Reflection

Our purpose is to help students develop into reflective clinical practitioners, and reflection is seen as the key to this process. More particularly, as the clinical practitioner's expertise grows, reflective learning can help to define clinical knowledge. Reflective learning has been depicted as a process in which a student responds to a lived experience and then cognitively and metacognitively reviews and investigates the experience so as to create and clarify the meaning of the experience within himself or herself. This process increases critical-thinking skills, contributes to self-awareness growth, and leads to the development of new knowledge (Boyd & Fales, 1983). Nursing students need to acquire the ability to critique their own clinical practice across a variety of situations if they are to develop into the lifelong learners needed in the profession.

Initially, the reflective essays for the professional portfolios needed many iterations. After the first year, examples of portfolios with the reflective essays were provided for students to review before creating their own portfolio. Students were instructed to write their reflective essay in a format that would highlight their personal accomplishments and abilities, including how the students learned and future implications for their delivery of nursing care. Links could be used to connect to documentation that would support the students' assertions.

Artistic Presentation Hints

▶ Remember content
▶ Use pale or neutral background
▶ Organize chronologically, alphabetically, or topically
▶ Links should move logically & clearly through portfolio
▶ Keep it simple
▶ Limit excessive "bells & whistles"
▶ Check documents after scanning for clarity
▶ Be contained on one Zip disk or CD
▶ Use action verbs
▶ Use few pictures to emphasize ideas or portray student

Clinical Portfolios

By fall 1998, the Nursing Department had initiated using portfolios at an earlier stage — with junior students, who would create a clinical portfolio. The clinical portfolio provided students with more opportunities to practice writing reflectively in preparation for creating their professional portfolio. In addition, junior-level faculty were searching for a method to value students' clinical work and thought the portfolio might foster a higher level of reflection about clinical praxis. The expected outcomes of the clinical portfolio were to improve students' reflective ability and demonstrate to students the faculty's valuing of their clinical work. In addition, faculty decided that given the evidence of clinical work as documented in the portfolio, they would begin giving grades for it.

Throughout the semester, students are expected to hand in weekly work demonstrating the nursing process in action, as well as a journal addressing three components of our curriculum: (1) therapeutic nursing interventions, (2) communication, and (3) professional practice. With each journal entry, students write a narrative about a clinical experience related to one of the above curricular components and evaluate their critical-thinking ability during that clinical experience through double-entry journaling. What we expected from the students was *reflection-on-action*, a process that takes place after a situation, in which the individual reviews the situation and considers how to project or revise his or her thinking for a similar situation in the future (Schön, 1987). A previously assembled list of 26 questions guided students in the writing of their weekly reflective essays. These questions became too cumbersome and were not always relevant to the student's clinical experience. Faculty narrowed the guiding questions for the weekly journals to three: (1) What did you learn? (2) How did you learn it? and (3) How will what you learned affect your future nursing practice?

With the use of these three questions, the weekly journals improved. Students addressed the specific clinical experience with greater depth. And students began to be more aware of their own learning process and to consider possible ways to change their nursing practice based on their learning.

At the end of the semester, students submit a clinical portfolio. The clinical portfolio is written with a reflection-in-presentation view of their learning. The specific context for this reflection-in-presentation essay is for the students to demonstrate their development and achievement throughout the semester in their use of the nursing process. The audience for the clinical portfolio is the clinical instructors for the course and possibly employers for summer externships.

The list opposite documents the contents of the clinical portfolio. For each nursing care plan, the student writes a one-paragraph to one-page reflective statement about the best work, the one needing the most improvement, or the one most valued for the learning the student attached to that experience. Students are also asked to choose two journal entries for each curriculum component that they believe will demonstrate evidence of their achievement, development, and reflection. In addition, students select three clinical practicum criteria, for each one of which they write a two- to three-page self-reflective essay addressing achievement and development by answering the above three questions related to their learning throughout the semester.

Electronic portfolios were unable to be implemented in the creation of clinical portfolios; instead, students created print portfolios. A lack of computers at bedside in local health-care facilities was the major impediment. Faculty felt that requiring students to copy notes later on the computer would not contribute substantively to students' learning.

Reading and evaluating clinical portfolios is randomly assigned to three clinical faculty, who evaluate the portfolios based on achievement of clinical outcomes, development through the semester, and reflective thinking. Each clinical portfolio is graded using a standard scoring guide, as shown below. Students receive a grade worth 10% of the final grade for the course.

Contents of Clinical Portfolio

▶ Teaching Plan

▶ 3 Nursing Care Plans with a Reflective Paragraph
— Best
— One needing most improvement
— One most valued for learning by student

▶ 2 Journal Entries for each Curricular Component
— Therapeutic Nursing Interventions
— Communication
— Professional Practice

▶ Reflective Essays for 3 Clinical Outcome Criteria

Criteria For Clinical Portfolio Evaluation

Are all exhibits present? ☐ Yes   ☐ No. If any exhibit is missing, clinical portfolio should not be submitted until completed.

	Little Evidence	Satisfactory Evidence	Significant Evidence
Achievement	☐	☐	☐
Development	☐	☐	☐
Reflection	☐	☐	☐

Results

No quantitative or qualitative data have been accumulated about this experience yet, but the impressionistic picture reveals clear patterns. Students are increasingly self-aware of their strengths and areas needing improvement, they can articulate the variety of resources available and used, and they have begun to recognize changes in thinking about their nursing practice. In addition, students appreciate receiving a grade and acknowledgment of their hard work in the clinical arena.

Portfolios are often criticized for the time required of students to create them and faculty to provide feedback. Before clinical portfolios, the clinical faculty reviewed all the students' clinical paperwork at the end of the semester. Since the initiation of clinical portfolios, the amount of time spent reading and grading work at the end of the semester has decreased. More important, students' overall thoughts about and insight into their own behaviors have improved.

Faculty are generally pleased with the reflection-in-presentation essays written by students in their weekly journals and at the end of the semester in their clinical portfolios. Clinical portfolios will continue to be implemented in junior-level courses.

Changes continue to be made each year in response to faculty evaluation of the process and the outcomes and student comments on both professional and clinical portfolios. Plans are currently being developed to systematically evaluate the outcomes of the implementation of both clinical and professional portfolios.

Note

Thanks to my colleagues who contributed to this work: Theresa Turick-Gibson, Penny Boyer, Sharon Dettenrieder, Margaret Schramm, and Louise Netreba.

References

Boyd, E., & Fales, A. (1983). Reflective learning: Key to learning from experience. *Journal of Human Psychology 23* (2), 99-117.

Schön, D. (1987). *Educating the Reflective Practitioner* (1st ed.). San Francisco: Jossey-Bass.

Comparing Electronic and Paper Portfolios

by Emily Springfield

If you are starting a portfolio program from scratch or if you already use a paper portfolio, you may be wondering about differences between the electronic and paper formats. To help answer that question, I talked with three directors of established paper-based portfolio programs who are considering switching to an electronic format. In addition, I have included some insights I gained in four years as the portfolio coordinator for Kalamazoo College.

Because all three directors manage portfolio programs already well established at their institution, it is easier to separate the challenges of developing a portfolio program from the challenges associated with potentially tricky media.

- Bernita Quoss, associate professor of child and family studies, directs the University of Wyoming Family and Consumer Science portfolio, which was launched in 1997. Students use it during their sophomore year to set goals and make action plans for developing four generic skills (communication, thinking, community practice, and professional practice) as well as writing a statement of professional goals.
- Michael True, director of the Internship Center at Messiah College, says that students have been completing career-oriented portfolios as part of their internships since 1995. The internship program focuses on teaching students how to direct their own meaningful learning experiences, and the portfolio helps them assimilate the knowledge gained during those experiences.
- Carol Dean, director of Academic Support Services at Samford University, oversees the senior professional portfolio, which has been completed by teacher education students since 1992. The project provides preservice teachers with a venue for reflection on and presentation of their various teaching-related skills.
- I was the portfolio coordinator at Kalamazoo College from the inception of the program in 1996 until the end of a FIPSE grant in summer 2000. The Kalamazoo Portfolio is a reflective tool students use for academic planning.

Emily Springfield is an educational technology and portfolio consultant. She has helped several institutions, most notably Kalamazoo College, begin electronic portfolio programs.

Advantages of the Electronic Format

These administrators give two primary reasons for considering an electronic portfolio: (1) easy storage and retrieval of information and (2) the development of students' technology skills. The benefits of electronic storage and retrieval are quite simple: Paper portfolios are awkward to store and share, especially with multiple audiences. Either a department needs a large room full of shelves, or students keep their own portfolios and the department has no access to them after students graduate. Even while a student is on campus, reviewers may not have easy access to paper portfolios. In contrast, electronic portfolios (especially those stored on the Web) are easy to share with multiple readers simultaneously, including off-campus audiences such as future employers. With students' permission, Web-based portfolios can even be shared with underclass students as a form of student-to-student mentoring. At Kalamazoo College, however, our primary reason for requiring a Web format was actually quite different: We thought creating the navigational links in the portfolio would help students see how their experiences interrelate.

As employers demand more and more technology skills of new hires, students who can demonstrate adequate computer skills have the advantage over those who cannot. Simply by putting their thoughts onto a Web page or into another electronic structure such as a PowerPoint presentation, students demonstrate their level of proficiency with that software. "Demonstrating technology skills" can reach far beyond the obvious ability to design a PowerPoint presentation or Web page, however. Students seeking work in jobs without an obvious computer component can illustrate technology skills specific to their prospective field. Including a sound clip, for instance, demonstrates a music major's performance talents and skills in recording, mixing, and formatting samples for the Web. Theater majors can include audio or video of performances they directed or acted in or for which they designed set, lights, or sound. Biology, chemistry, or physics students can present graphs of results of their lab work demonstrating that they can use both the lab equipment and the software needed to display the results.

Disadvantages of the Electronic Format

The directors I interviewed listed three concerns about the electronic format: (1) time needed to master the software, (2) compatibility of the audience's computers, and (3) privacy. Chief among these concerns was the time needed to learn to use the software. Most students want to add graphics, photos, and other multimedia elements to their portfolios, and each task requires learning to use new hardware and software. An electronic portfolio is therefore indicative of a very broad set of skills — writing and organizing text, designing page layouts, creating graphics, scanning and optimizing photos, and creating and editing videos and/or sound clips — and experience shows that students may not acquire sufficient technological skill to showcase their work properly. For example, a student with excellent piano performance skills but only basic Web audio skills might produce a poor-quality sound clip. Accordingly, even though an interviewer (say, for admission to graduate school) is interested in the student's performance skills, it might be difficult to assess them. Does the clip sound bad due to the student's lack of facility with the sound editing equipment, or due to the student's musical skills at the piano?

Such a problem illustrates key issues. Do students need to master all the skills necessary to produce a top-quality electronic portfolio? Will the demands on their skills increase, or will we reach a point where it is acceptable to outsource Web presentation materials? Is it more advantageous to demonstrate rudimentary computer skills by including imperfect elements in the portfolio, or are students better off including only items that demonstrate perfected skills? Finally, all this preparation takes time, even if students know what they are doing. Is the time spent on creating a portfolio worth the effort? In some cases, such as interviewing for a Web design job, the answer is an unequivocal "yes." In other cases, such as explaining educational goals, reflecting on an internship, or demonstrating learning in a particular subject area, development of an electronic portfolio — when it requires considerable technological skills — may not be an effective use of time.

We thought creating the navigational links in the portfolio would help students see how their experiences interrelate.

Another possible drawback is lack of portability. Especially with PowerPoint, HyperStudio, or Macromedia Director (software packages for electronic presentations that are not Web-based), system and file compatibility can be a real problem. Thinking about the use of portfolios for employment, Michael True of Messiah College reminds us that "incompatible . . . fonts and images may be an issue, and some personnel in nonprofit organizations (and some businesses) are not as technologically proficient as we might want to believe, so a paper-based portfolio works better." Carol Dean, from Samford, whose students use their portfolios in interviews for teaching positions, agrees. She suggests that even though most school systems have reasonably up-to-date and standardized computer systems, "Interviews are not always conducted in a place with easy access to technology. The paper format is more accessible to take anywhere to an interview." In addition, some employers may simply choose not to take the time to view the portfolio. Even for those with a ready computer and an inclination to view the portfolio, the reader must know how and be able to access it. Proprietary software such as Blackboard or WebCT requires training for all users, including those simply viewing material, thus making a digital portfolio including such files suddenly less, not more, accessible to all readers. Bernita Quoss cites this training as a main obstacle to the conversion of the University of Wyoming Family and Consumer Science portfolio to an electronic format: "The university now has WebCT, but the learning curve for many of us is long, and time and resources are limited. For some distance education courses, ECollege can do much of the work, and we hope our course will receive this support. Otherwise, we will stay with a paper format for some time to come."

An additional concern is privacy. Who will have access to the portfolio? Can students determine who gets to see which pages? It is relatively simple for students to lock or unlock Web pages on a standard Web server, but the only two settings are usually "open to the world" and "completely closed from view." Password protection would be ideal, but many institutions find it difficult and time-consuming to implement. Some institutions have students keep their portfolios on a disk. But this option is not completely secure, either, because disks are easily stolen or lost, and students often share hard drives with roommates. Disks also have the disadvantage of becoming damaged or losing data because of their short shelf life.

Should the Electronic Format Be Required or Optional?

When I asked my group of portfolio practitioners whether they would migrate completely to an electronic portfolio or leave it open as an option, reactions were mixed. Quoss answered, "A complete switch would be preferable, as it gives some reluctant students another push into developing their technical skills." Dean agreed: "If we switch, we will probably switch completely. We will want to maintain a certain level of consistency in portfolios." But True disagreed:

> We would leave the electronic format as an option. The point is not the medium but that students follow our prescribed guidelines for self-directed learning and good content. It seems to me that the format they use is part of their self-expression as well as comfort level. Organizational abilities and creativity, among other skills, can be demonstrated on paper as easily as with an electronic format.

At Kalamazoo College, we decided four years into the project that making the electronic format an option was a good choice for us. Some students — not just the computer-phobic ones — were having so much difficulty with the software that it was hard to justify the amount of time they were taking. Because our main goal was encouraging students to discover connections among experiences, we decided it best to allow students to pick the format that best suited them.

What Specific Technology Are You Considering Using?

A comparison of some of the different choices these schools have made attests to the importance of design issues. (See the table on the next page.)

Maintenance, Training, and Documentation

Any portfolio shared over a network (either the Web or a proprietary program on an intranet) needs to be designed in conjunction with college- or university-wide informa-

Institution	Software	Advantages	Disadvantages
University of Wyoming	WebCT	Robust, used campus-wide. Can handle Web-based courses, not just portfolios.	Steep learning curve; individual faculty members would be responsible for designing and maintaining course materials online and training students.
Messiah College	Netscape Composer or Microsoft FrontPage	Simple system. Easily transferable skills. Netscape is free, and many campuses already own FrontPage.	FrontPage can be hard to learn and support, especially if it's not already in place on a campus.
Samford University	Web design software	Simple system. Easily transferable skills.	Every software package has disadvantages ranging from unintuitive user interface to code writing problems.
Kalamazoo College	Netscape Composer	Very easy to learn.	Netscape rewrites code under some very specific circumstances, which can lead to broken links and considerable frustration. Also, Netscape only makes Web pages; most new software allows management of Web sites as a unit, which is very helpful.

tion technology staff. The program directors I interviewed said they expected the college or university to maintain the necessary machinery; in fact, the hardware and software needed were already in place on their campuses. All agreed, however, that they would play at least some role in training students to use the software. Dean said Samford's School of Education already has a person who teaches technology to the education students, and Dean expects that person would also teach students how to make portfolios. Quoss said that once individual faculty members are trained in using WebCT, it is their responsibility to teach students how to use the system. True says that though Messiah's Information Technology Services staff would probably provide the workshops for a mandatory electronic portfolio, he would author the manual in conjunction with them. At Kalamazoo College, the portfolio coordinator writes the manuals and gives the workshops.

These experiences all point to a very important practice: "Portfolio people" need to teach students how to *make* portfolios, even if information technology staff teach them how to use the software. In addition, both a manual of "how to make a portfolio" and instructions on "how to use the software" are necessary. Through collaborative writing by portfolio developers and information technology staff, both dimensions of the portfolio can be addressed. In addition, information technology staff may already have good instructions for the appropriate software. If they do not, one option is to borrow from another institution (Kalamazoo College's instructions are free for the taking; see, for example, http://www.kzoo.edu/pfolio/manual). In either case, including every step in a task and testing the instructions by having a rookie follow them without help are essential.

Who should teach the introductory computer workshops? Although information technology staff members seem obvious choices, a person does not have to be a computer wizard to teach a good workshop. In fact, very advanced computer users may conduct workshops too quickly because they forget how much thought beginners need to put into basic tasks such as navigating among windows, reading dialogue boxes, and finding the correct button on the screen. And in a single workshop, students will not learn everything there is to know about a software package or a portfolio template. At Kalamazoo College, we learned it is far better to have students learn a small amount of information thoroughly than to be swamped with too much information. Once students have mastered the basics, they go on to learn more advanced techniques on their own. If they need instruction in more advanced skills, they can consult the Computer Science department, Web tutorials, or classmates.

Financial Concerns

The cost of implementing electronic student portfolios depends on the model planned. If a college already makes Web accounts available to students, owns some type of Web creation software, and has staff dedicated to a portfolio program, the monetary costs of going electronic can be negligible, though staff time will probably increase somewhat. Using a proprietary software system such as WebCT, ECollege, or Blackboard can be much more costly, though this option may be the only one available for colleges developing portfolios as part of Web-based courses. Quoss's observations about the potential costs of the system in the 2000-2001 academic year at Wyoming are illustrative:

> The university's Center for Teaching Excellence has the technology and support. . . . For a few faculty members, the university secured a Hewlett Packard grant to fund ECollege support; the company takes care of technology for the faculty member, as much as is desired. In addition, I have been granted a sabbatical for one semester. Counting everyone's time plus materials and so on, I would estimate it would cost between $30,000 to $35,000 for

a WebCT-developed course and much more for ECollege support, at least $50,000. These costs are for an entire two-hour course, not just the portfolio.

Crucial Considerations

To help make a decision about moving to electronic portfolios, instructors and institutions should consider the following questions:

- Who are the audiences for this portfolio? Will that audience have the hardware, software, skills, time, and inclination to access the portfolio electronically?
- Does the institution have the hardware and software in place to create these portfolios electronically? If not, what will it cost, and who will install it?
- What is the current level of computer skill of the students and faculty members involved with this project? Who will teach them how to use the technology necessary to create and view electronic portfolios? Will students use the portfolio long enough to refine their computer skills to an acceptable level?

This book and its companion Web site (http://www.aahe.org/electronicportfolios/) can also serve as resources for contacting institutions with established electronic portfolios to discuss effective planning of such programs.

General Patterns and the Future

by Kathleen Blake Yancey

Where student electronic portfolios have worked, why have they worked? Perhaps most obvious, they solve the problem of storage, although at a cost. They provide a new kind of space for intellectual work and opportunities to connect and represent that intellectual work in new ways. Less obvious, digital portfolios can bring pedagogy and assessment into alignment. And still less obvious, they fill a need for connections across classes, experiences, and even life itself. And finally, perhaps also less obvious but no less important, student electronic portfolios rest on the assumption that *the engaged learner, one who records and interprets and evaluates his or her own learning, is the best learner.*

What will the digital portfolio of the future look like? This question is, of course, impossible to answer, but it can be framed in two interesting ways, one based in practice and the other in theory. As Barbara Cambridge suggests in the introduction to this book, Peg Syverson, a Carnegie Scholar[i] working at the University of Texas at Austin, has developed the next stage of on-line student portfolios — the Online Learning Record — that revolutionizes the curriculum. It relies on five ways of understanding students' work and asks students regularly and systematically to evaluate their progress in those terms. Like the Alverno model, Syverson's on-line portfolio seems as least as interested in the analysis and interpretation of performance and progress as it is in the performance itself.

The second way we might consider the future is by thinking in terms of the options and tensions the digital format raises, as explained in *Interface Culture: How New Technology Transforms the Way We Create and Communicate.* The author, cofounder and editor of *Feed*, an on-line cultural magazine, suggests that there are multiple dimensions along which interface design — the kind of design, linking structures, and pathways we see in portfolios — will be developed (Johnson, 1997). On the one hand, he says, we have the

Kathleen Blake Yancey, editor of this section on student portfolios, is R. Roy Pearce Professor of Professional Communication at Clemson University, where she also directs the Roy and Marnie Pearce Center for Professional Communication. Yancey is editor of *Portfolios in the Writing Classroom: An Introduction* (NCTE, 1992) and coeditor of *Situating Portfolios: Four Perspectives* (Utah State University Press, 1997).

impulse for a standardized model: interfaces that are singular (one per vehicle such as a portfolio), conventional, synthetic, and simulational. In tension with them are interfaces with a more aesthetic sensibility, where the values are competing: multiple interfaces in a single vehicle, avant-garde, fragmented, and metaphorical. It may be, of course, that the design issues here fall out into disciplinary fields, with a more conventional approach appropriate for some and a more experimental approach suitable for others. But Johnson's title is telling: The new technology we see in digital portfolios does not change only the way we communicate; it changes the ways we create and how we know.

A Heuristic for the Design and Creation of Student Electronic Portfolios

Given the many portfolio options discussed here, it may be difficult to know when, where, and how to begin — or whether to begin at all. Two vehicles can provide some assistance in this effort: a heuristic that can be used in thinking through the possibilities and a set of recommendations deriving from the experiences of portfolio stakeholders of all kinds.

An electronic portfolio needs to have an authentic purpose, needs to be social, and needs to be integrated into the academic and intellectual lives of both students and faculty.

The heuristic that follows moves from the concepts of portfolio and purpose to the nature of the medium to the kinds of resources that are required:

- *What is/are the purpose/s?* As is the case in both curricular design and assessment, it is wiser in general to limit one's purposes, at least initially, to selected intents. Given a review of the functionality of the original plan, other purposes can be designed into the model later.
- *How familiar is the portfolio concept? Is the familiarity a plus or a minus?* If students and faculty are already using portfolios, then migrating to a digital form may be a relatively simple process. On the other hand, if campus stakeholders are satisfied with a print version, there may be little incentive to migrate. And if the technology — both resources and skills — is not already in place, the transition will need to be an elaborated one requiring support.
- *Who wants to create an electronic portfolio, and why?* A lesson that seems very obvious across even very diverse experiences is that to work well, an electronic portfolio needs to have an authentic purpose, needs to be social, and needs to be integrated into the academic and intellectual lives of both students and faculty. Thus, attending to the "who" of the portfolio — the composer as well as its audience — and to why they want to use it and how it fits into or will enhance what they already do is likewise foundational.
- *Who wants to read an electronic portfolio, and why?* Regardless of model, one answer to this question is *the student* — to review, to reflect, to synthesize, to connect, to plan. In fact, many portfolio advocates suggest that this reading experience, of one's own work, is among the most important reading experiences of the undergraduate curriculum, precisely because it allows students to connect

what they have learned, in multiple settings, with previous knowledge and curricular competencies and within curricular frameworks. Other readers — faculty, advisers, potential employers — may have quite different needs.

- *Why electronic? What about electronic is central to the model? And is sufficient infrastructure (resources, knowledge, commitment) available for the electronic portfolio?* The electronic portfolio brings with it opportunities for new kinds of learning: linking structures that can help students connect many different kinds of experience and the design of pathways for multiple audiences, to name two. But the learning does not happen just because the portfolio takes an electronic form: It needs to be designed into the model and provided for in terms of the curriculum writ large. Likewise, we hear repeatedly about the importance of the infrastructure, and ensuring that it is in place and up-to-date is also central. And finally, the infrastructure will not be the same for all, as we see in the different choices of media.

- *What processes are entailed? What resources are presumed?* Basic to portfolios, both print and electronic, are the processes of *collection, selection,* and *reflection.* Collection may be made easier with a digital portfolio. But reflection continues to be a process in search of enhancement, which is not really surprising given how new reflection's role is in the curriculum. But it does mean that even in cultures where portfolios have been introduced, the process of reflection will continue to need to be defined, practiced, and integrated into the curriculum. Likewise, certain resources, both human and digital, are presumed. To ensure they are provided, it is best to build them in from the beginning.

- *What faculty development component does the model assume or include?* Some faculty may bring both knowledge about and practice in portfolios, others may bring technological expertise, and still others may be informed about program assessment. Most faculty will probably find, however — as did those at Hartwick College and Utah State University — that faculty development is part of the process of using digital portfolios. It is therefore useful to think about electronic portfolios through these three lenses: (1) portfolios as a *curricular* tool; (2) *electronic* in terms of skills and pedagogy; and (3) *assessment* in terms of its potential for curricular enhancement. What learning will faculty need to undertake? And what kinds of support can be provided to them?

- *What skills will students need to develop?* Interestingly, no one here suggests that electronic portfolios are business as usual. Students will need to control basic software, like word-processing programs and spreadsheets, as well as software enabling the compilation and design of the portfolio itself. Moreover, the lesson of Kalamazoo is that if the technology is not well provided for, even a worthy program may be harmed. Planning the software that is essential to the model and how it is to be provided are other considerations for a well designed model.

- *What curricular enhancement does the model assume or include?* In some cases, such as Donna Reiss's and Rich Rice's, the electronic portfolio was created to match a curricular enhancement already in place. In other cases, such as that of Utah State and Kalamazoo, the intent of the portfolio, at least in part, is itself to enhance curriculum. A key question, then, is whether curricular enhancement is an intent or an outcome of the portfolio. It is axiomatic among those who use portfolios, however, that simply reviewing portfolios, given their inclusion of multiple kinds of exhibits and student voices, tends to lead to curricular enhancement of some kind.

- *How will the portfolio be introduced?* If the portfolio model operates in the classroom, it is safe to assume that the faculty member teaching the class will introduce it. If, on the other hand, it is a program portfolio, other kinds of structures, introductory and maintenance, will need to be designed into the model. Also important, as Springfield suggests, is providing a standardized introduction to the skills that the digital portfolio requires; it too is an introduction that needs to be planned. A final element here that might be considered is the use of the Web itself to provide directions to students, sample entries, and an opportunity to talk to others about their portfolios.

- *How will the portfolio be reviewed?* Portfolios need readers, and for each type of model, readers seem obvious. All portfolios will be read and reviewed by the student composer, and some may be read by other students. Classroom portfolios will have individual faculty readers. Program portfolios will have collective faculty readers. Career portfolios will have employer reviewers. But all these models could enjoy more than one type of reviewer. Without them designed into the portfolio model, as we saw with Steve, my student majoring in packaging science, it is unlikely that it will be read. In other words, Steve remembered the portfolio when an occasion for its use arose, but as curriculum designers, we might think about ways for those occasions to be planned. Several key questions then arise: Who will the reviewers be? Do we provide guidelines or suggestions in the portfolio as to ways of reading and reviewing it? How do different audiences read and review digital portfolios? Do they value them similarly?

Recommendations for Designing a Digital Portfolio

Student survey information, reflective observations, and formal program assessments point to a number of recommendations for the design of a digital portfolio:

- *Think rhetorically.* Who is creating the portfolio and why? Who is reading and reviewing it and why? Think not only in terms of how it *could* be used but also how it *will* be used.

- *Consider how the electronic portfolio needs to be electronic.* How will it be interactive? What relationships and connections does the digital form make possible? One common element among successful developers of student portfolios is their invitation to students to link their work in one classroom to work in other classrooms and other contexts. It may be that as electronic portfolios become more common, this feature will be increasingly required or strongly suggested.

- *Consider how the portfolio will be interactive socially.* The experience of the portfolio designers here, as elsewhere, is that the portfolio needs to be part of a social process. Designing the social process that situates the portfolio seems to be as important — another kind of interactivity — as designing the format.

- *Develop some key terms that you can associate with your model of an e-portfolio, and use them consistently.* If assessment is a central concern, then terms such as Rice's — *scale, sustainability, reliability* — are useful. Other terms, such as the process terms of *collection, selection,* and *reflection,* seem central regardless of the type of model. And as Springfield at Kalamazoo suggested, the terms need to be well defined and consistently used.

- *Be realistic about how long it will take to introduce the model and the skills that faculty and students will need.* It might be best to think in terms of phased implementation. Doing so allows those ready now to begin and provides them with support while permitting other faculty and students time to become ready.

- *Be realistic about the difficulty that teachers may have in designing reflective texts, that students may experience in writing reflections, and that teachers may have in responding to and evaluating those reflections.* This issue is not particular to digital portfolios, as we have seen. Still, given the potential for hyperlinks of electronic portfolios — that is, their potential to link *inward* to a student's own text and *outward* to external texts — it seems especially important to e-portfolios.

- *Perhaps more than other innovative practices, the development of e-portfolios calls for a collaborative process of development.* In the case of student portfolios, students may be our best collaborators. Likewise, the electronic portfolio for students is focused on learning much more than on teaching, and it is focused on learning writ large: learning for both faculty and students. What it means, of course, is that in this endeavor, faculty do not hold all the expertise; they do not have all the answers. This position can be new for many faculty, and it is one worth introducing carefully.

Note

1. A "Carnegie Scholar" is a participant in The Pew National Fellowship Program for Carnegie Scholars, one component of The Carnegie Academy for the Scholarship of Teaching and Learning (CASTL). The other two components of CASTL are a program for scholarly societies and the AAHE-directed Campus Program, the latter open to all campuses that foster the scholarship of teaching and learning. CASTL is a major initiative of The Carnegie Foundation for the Advancement of Teaching; for more information, visit http://www.carnegiefoundation.org/CASTL.

Reference

Johnson, S. (1997). *Interface Culture: How New Technology Transforms the Way We Create and Communicate.* San Francisco: Harper.

Faculty Portfolios

Ambassadors With Portfolios: Electronic Portfolios and the Improvement of Teaching

by Daniel P. Tompkins

Why Portfolios?

"Portfolio" is a capacious term, describing any collection of "leaves" or papers, sometimes portable, generally accessible, intended for display to others. Because they are so flexible and adaptable, because they provide more substantial evidence of teaching activity than other devices, and because they fulfill some current needs at American universities, portfolios are being used increasingly by faculty in American higher education.

Faculty portfolios are collections of evidence intended to document a teacher's classroom practice and to allow various sorts of comment by colleagues or superiors. Faculty portfolios generally fall into two categories: teaching and course. *Teaching portfolios* collect evidence from a wide range of activities, often over a number of years. They can be used both "formatively" and "summatively," that is, either to improve performance or for assessment before promotion, merit, or employment decisions (Seldin, 1997, pp. 15-17). The intended audience is often a mentor or superior (pp. 10-12, 20, 26).

Course portfolios, on the other hand, were developed primarily to support the "formative" process of reflection, discussion, and improvement. Peers, not decision makers, make up their usual readership, although several national projects are developing readers' abilities to assess course portfolios in high-stakes situations. These portfolios deal with particular courses, often posing a research question about them: As Mills Kelly remarks in his chapter that follows, his portfolio sought to answer the question "how was it that I knew using the Web in my teaching was improving students' understanding of the past?" William Cerbin of the University of Wisconsin La Crosse, credited with first proposing course-based portfolios, says, "In a nutshell, I am trying to understand how students

Daniel P. Tompkins, editor of this section on faculty portfolios, is director of the Intellectual Heritage Program at Temple University. He coordinated the Temple University team in the AAHE Peer Review Project.

come to 'think with' important disciplinary knowledge and not just 'think about' it" (interview, August 2000). Pat Hutchings and other authors in Hutchings's seminal collection *The Course Portfolio* (1998a) touch on other functions of the portfolio: It can be an "aid to memory," an escape from pedagogical isolation, a "way of bringing recognition," an argument for a certain teaching technique, a tool for evaluating the "scholarly work" of a teacher or for helping to "sort through the teaching issues that currently consume" a professor (Hutchings, 1998b, pp. 17-18; Martsolf, 1998, p. 26; Huber, 1998, p. 32; Langsam, 1998, p. 58). But the underlying theme in this volume, repeated in chapter after chapter, is *purposeful inquiry*.

Family resemblances, individual differences

Summative and formative portfolios can take different forms. But a basic tripartite structure obtains with both genres: material from oneself, materials from others, and products of teaching. To build a composite outline listing the contents of a portfolio, I used Seldin's discussion (1997, pp. 4-9) and Mills Kelly's electronic course portfolio.

Material from oneself could include:
- An executive summary — Kelly introduces his course; provides a detailed course design; mentions learning outcomes, the process of "unfolding" the course, and his evaluation criteria; and summarizes the conclusions he reached after studying students' performance and responses
- An introduction or cover letter
- An index of the portfolio's contents
- Teaching responsibilities (important when a reader desires a picture of the faculty member's overall workload)
- A statement of teaching philosophy, especially useful when matched with students' work
- Teaching strategies and objectives
- Course design — Kelly carefully lists the skills and knowledge he expects students to acquire
- A description of course materials
- Efforts to improve teaching
- Essays about the portfolio — Kelly includes a set of reflective essays that grew out of the teaching experience
- A summary of what was learned from the portfolio.

Materials from others could include student ratings; analysis and critique by colleagues based on the syllabus, comparison with other courses, discussion of learning goals, and class visits (Kelly provides a helpful response form that can be used by anyone reading his portfolio); and unsolicited student statements, letters, and e-mails.

Western Civilization: A Course Portfolio
T. Mills Kelly, Department of History, Texas Tech University

By chance or by design you have arrived at a website that contains the course portfolio for two sections of one particular course--Western Civilization--which I offer in the Department of History at Texas Tech University. This portfolio is the core of an even larger project, **Wired for Trouble?**, which is an investigation of the impact of hypermedia pedagogy on student learning in history courses. **Wired for Trouble?** is generously supported by the Carnegie Foundation for the Advancement of Teaching, whose Carnegie Scholar program makes it possible for me to pursue this contribution to the scholarship of teaching.

As you travel around within this site you will find many opportunities to move back and forth between the course and the larger project, and I hope you will take advantage of those opportunities to explore connections between the two.

Because the Western Civilization course described here served as the laboratory for my investigation of the impact of hypermedia on student learning, this portfolio is organized around the same question that animates that larger project:

How does the introduction of hypermedia into a history course influence student learning in that course?

I approached this question by using my tw[...] laboratory. In the fall semester both sect[...] hypermedia (although it is specifically not[...] on-line). In the spring semester, one sect[...] the students in the second section receive[...] hyper" formats (books, overheads, video[...]

Executive Summary

I. **Introduction:** The portfolio begins with a brief introduction to course portfolios as a contribution to the scholarship of teaching. Links to samples of other course portfolios by historians and those in other disciplines are also included in the introduction.

II. **Course Design:** This section of the portfolio tells the story of my Western Civilization course as it has evolved over the past six years at five different institutions from a fairly standard "coverage" course to its present incarnation. In its current form, History 1301 is a reflection of several specific objectives. Most of my objectives for the course center on a set of student learning outcomes which I believe are susceptible to measurement. Of course, much that goes on in a history class cannot be quantified, so I also describe several objectives that might more accurately described as hopes or intentions. These two types of expectation drove the design of the course and its emphasis on assessing the impact of hypermedia on student learning.

III. **Unfolding:** This fourteen week course is divided into six discrete two-week blocs and so this portfolio includes seven linked narratives of how each bloc unfolded. Imbedded in these narratives are my own reflections on what happened (or did not happen) along the way.

IV. **Evaluation of Student Learning:** Throughout the semester there are several specific points of [...]valuations are performed by me, some by my students, and [...] semester I also asked my students to reflect on the entire [...]d not, and how much we all learned along the way. In addition [...]partment of History also evaluated the course as part of our

[...]his section of the portfolio will include information on student [...]mple, I will be collecting data on how many students in this [...]w they did in those courses, and so on.

[...]lio is a reflection on the totality of the course in which I draw

Objectives

For the purpose of discussion, I separate learning objectives for the students into two categories--skills and knowledge. I recognize and accept at the outset that my objectives for student learning in this course are probably not ones well synchronized with my students' objectives when they arrive on the first day of class. However, because Western Civilization at Texas Tech University is primarily intended to be a freshman/sophomore course, my discussions with students around this question have convinced me that their objectives are so unformed (and generally instrumental--learn some history, pass the class, see if I might want to be a history major, etc.) that any dissonance between our respective agendas is largely one way. I simply need to communicate mine to them in a clear and concise fashion and they are generally willing to sit back and see what I can do. And so, what follows is a brief discussion of what *my* objectives are for the course.

Skills: By the end of the semester there are several fairly specific skills I hope my students have acquired, in whole or in part. Without these skills they have no where to go when they begin to try to make sense of the welter of content that their readings throw at them. All of the[...] under the general heading of "how historians think":

1. I want them to be able to distinguish between a primary an[...]

2. I want them to be able to analyze a primary source within i[...]

3. I want them to be able to locate the thesis or argument in a[...] able to offer an informed evaluation of that argument. To do t[...] secondary source within its particular context as part of a larg[...] etc., that are its main concern.

4. I want them to be able to construct a thesis/argument of th[...] discussions, that is informed by what they find in whatever th[...]

Essays

From this page you can access several useful essays that relate to the subject of my portfolio. The first of these is a paper I presented at the American Historical Association national conference in Chicago (January 2000) which offers my interim results after one semester of work on the project. Because the scholarship of teaching and learning should be equal parts public dialogue and scholarly exchange, I hope you will take the time to read this paper and send me your comments and criticisms.

As of today, I am still collecting the URLs of the essays I intend to post here, so the list below is quite short. More resources will appear in the months ahead. If you know of one or two that you think merit inclusion in my list, by all means, let me know and I will look them over.

T. Mills Kelly, *For Better or Worse? The Marriage of the Web and Classroom*, paper presented at the American Historical Association national conference, January 2000. [Now published in the *Journal of the American Association for History and Computing* as *For Better or Worse? The Marriage of Web and the History Classroom*, III/2, August 2000.]

[...] of this panel were: Paula Petrik, *"We Shall Be All"*,
[...]. Knox, *The Rewards of Teaching On-Line*.

[...]nd David Pace, *PAST IMPERFECT: Historians and the*
[...] presented at the American Association for Higher Education
[...]n, March 29-31, 2000.

[...] *Electronic Journal of Australian and New Zealand History*,

[...]o the History Survey Course using Multimedia Techniques,

Conclusions

Students Who Access Learning Resources on the Web Display a Higher Level of Recursive Reading

Given the current debates about how the web influences student learning, for good or ill, one of the questions I was especially interested in answering is whether at later points in the semester students returned to primary source documents assigned earlier in the semester. Good historians return to the same pieces of evidence over and over again, considering many possible meanings of their sources before finally committing themselves to one interpretation. Therefore, we hope that our students will learn this skill, not only because it is an example of what we like to call "critical thinking," but also because it is one very important way that they develop a stronger sense of the interrelatedness of historical evidence and of change over time. In my surveys with students I asked them very specifically whether or not they had gone back to primary sources used earlier in the semester and, as Table 1 indicates, in the three web sections, approximately three-fourths of them said they had done so. The final papers turned in by the students in the sections taught through the website bear out their answers on the surveys because the essay[...] recursiveness. [Go to survey data]

Students in the course section taught via print did not display th[...] Only one in four reported going back to materials assigned earlie[...] bore out this finding, displaying a much lower use of sources ass[...] essays...under construction]

In the interviews I conducted with a selected sample of the stud[...] work patterns in more detail and all of the students I interviewe[...] the documents they looked at from earlier in the semester were [...] likely to use them. When I asked if they would have done the sar[...] pack, all but one demurred, saying that, as one student put it, "h[...] not be as immediate as a hyperlink. Or, as another student said[...]

Examples of Student Work

This page contains selections from the work submitted by students in History 1301 during the 1999-2000 academic year. From this page you can access both samples of student writing as well as samples from the on-line discussion forums in the sections taught via the course website. Hyperlinks in the text of the student work presented here generally were added by me to make it easier for the reader to determine which assignments, source materials, etc., the students are referring to. Where a hyperlink was included by the student, I have added [st] after the link to indicate that fact. Each of the student essays includes comments by one or more of the external reviewers who read them for me.

Samples from Discussion Forum	Examples of Student Essays
Discussion of Silver Blaze (historical methods)	Fall 1999 Assignment #1
Discussion of Darwin	Fall 1999 Assignment #2
Discussion of the Holocaust	Spring 2000 Assignment #1
	Spring 2000 Assignment #2

http://www2.tltc.ttu.edu/kelly/Pew/Portfolio/welcome.htm

Products of teaching would include evidence of students' learning, with the teacher's responses. In both teaching and learning portfolios, it is essential to provide examples of students' learning, which are important in decisions about awards and promotion and serve as evidence in the "research" activity of course portfolios. In her chapter in this collection, Elizabeth Barkley says that the research for her course portfolio "moved me beyond intuition and anecdote to a culture of evidence." Kelly records samples of students' work and comments on them.

Examinations and classroom assessments could also appear there. For examples of classroom assessments, see Angelo and Cross (1994).

Overlapping contexts

Teaching and course portfolios are both recent innovations: The teaching portfolio blossomed with the first edition of Peter Seldin's book and with AAHE's book (Edgerton, Hutchings & Quinlan), both in 1991; the course portfolio in 1992, when William Cerbin first proposed it (in Hutchings, 1998b, pp. 15-16). It is worthwhile to glance briefly at the intellectual tendencies nurturing "the portfolio movement," the loose alliance of university faculty who believe that portfolios can benefit their teaching. On the one hand, the last two decades of the 20th century brought a growing desire for evidence of achievement. Teaching portfolios answered this need by providing a wider ranging and more nuanced basis for promotion decisions than ratings alone allowed (Seldin, 1997, p. 16). But accountability was hardly the only goal of the portfolio movement, which also advanced a new model of faculty improvement emphasizing peer collaboration and shared knowledge. Schön's advocacy of "reflective practice," Barr and Tagg's article on the "learning paradigm," Boyer's classification of teaching as a form of scholarship, Cross and Steadman's studies of classroom research, and Shulman's insistence on making teaching "community property" all struck a chord among faculty who sensed that their solo activity, however diligent or polished, was affecting students' learning less than it might (Barr & Tagg, 1995; Boyer, 1990; Cross & Steadman, 1996; Schön, 1984, 1990; Schön & Rein, 1995; Shulman, 1993).

The portfolio movement provided a tool for reflective practice, an instrument for focusing on learning, a stimulus to communal work.

The portfolio movement provided a tool for reflective practice, an instrument for focusing on learning, a stimulus to communal work. Faculty were encouraged to study their classes, to gather samples of students' work, to treat the classroom as an arena for research activity. As Mills Kelly's chapter reveals, strikingly few ground rules existed for this activity: Faculty truly did set out on their own to build research schemes. The lines between course and teaching portfolios in the early years blurred, with some individuals working in both realms. Shulman's appointment as president of The Carnegie Foundation for the Advancement of Teaching in 1997 gave new force to what was now called the "scholarship of teaching and learning," in which portfolios play a major role. Shulman (1998, p. 5) remarks that all scholarship is public, "susceptible to critical review" by professional peers, and "accessible for exchange and use by others in the future." (For examples, see Cerbin's, Kelly's, and Barkley's portfolios discussed in this chapter, along with others on the Carnegie Web site at http://kml2.carnegiefoundation.org/gallery/general/, which must be accessed by first signing up at http://kml2.carnegiefoundation.org/kml/login/.)

These concurrent movements owed some of their credibility and momentum to even wider trends, especially to the movement toward "organizational learning" and "learning organizations" that Schön and his colleagues at MIT were promoting. Rooted in a Deweyan link of theory and practice and marked by a taste for metaphor, the writings of the MIT school cut a wide swath in the 1990s.

The advent of electricity

In the early 1990s, then, a confluence of forces converged to open pedagogical activity to outsiders, whether for formative or summative purposes. The latter half of the decade was marked by the rapid spread of the World Wide Web, which assisted the promulgation of portfolios.

Portfolio writers quickly recognized that the flexible and often nonlinear format of the Web site was congruent with the loose organization of many portfolios. Information can be inserted at any place in the Web portfolio with only minimal effect on its overall structure, comments can be invited, and links can be created between any two items that seem to have a connection. Faculty began to put work onto the Web, using the Web first to support and then to interrogate their classroom teaching. The examples from Kelly's portfolio illustrate how congenial the portfolio structure is with the resources available on the Web.

In preparing this section, I conducted interviews with a number of scholars who have done important work on electronic portfolios. I read portfolios and selected four for further discussion here. And I solicited chapters from portfolio authors.

Introduction to the Chapters

In this section, four university teachers have written about their portfolios. At first glance, these chapters may seem to have little in common. The academic homes of the authors could not be farther apart (Texas, California, Alaska, and Pennsylvania). They represent four different academic disciplines. One teaches at a two-year institution; another has graduate students. Some write their own HTML code throughout; others have built powerful partnerships with design teams. But these differences are superficial compared with the vast differences in purpose and philosophy among the authors.

It is precisely this vastness that inspired the choices. If the portfolio movement is to move forward and gather adherents, it will have to remain open to a range of approaches. One could go on at length about the sometimes destructive debates between collaborative and cooperative educators, or between different approaches to student learning communities, or the many other contemporary pedagogical activities. These debates often force participants to clarify their thinking but perhaps equally often lead to a sectarianism that undermines common goals — especially when a movement is struggling to move beyond its current, relatively narrow band of adherents and win over colleagues and administrators.

Marc Stier: thinking about teaching on the Web

Marc Stier, a political theorist, teaches in a program that introduces students at a large urban university to the Western intellectual tradition. He constructed his Web site on his own and has refined it regularly over the years.

I chose his site (http://www.stier.net/teaching/teaching.htm) precisely because it does *not* conform to the standard definition of a portfolio. It contains information about a number of courses. The pages for Intellectual Heritage 51 show that the teacher has thought carefully about each class in the semester, has provided students with a summary of these classes and notes on the readings, and in general has produced a thorough "public" statement about his course. He has not written a reflective statement or included examples of students' work, although his chapter shows that he would have no trouble doing so. (Note that in this chapter he shares the interest of William Cerbin and others in helping students make the "conceptual leap" to a "new way of thinking.")

The Web turns out to hold many documents similar to Stier's. My own favorites include Robert Wood's impressive site for his sociology courses at Rutgers University Camden (http://www.camden.rutgers.edu/~wood/), Robin Mitchell-Boyask's classical mythology site at Temple (http://www.temple.edu/classics/mythdirectory.html), and Janice Siegel's Illustrated Guide to the Classical World (http://www.drjclassics.com/drj/indexdrj.htm). In each case, the teacher has deliberated about the shape of the course. After developing a calendar and syllabus, the teacher gathered information to support student learning at each stage, gradually adding bibliography, hints, and mini-lectures to guide the student. Often, they have gone on to develop review sheets for examinations or detailed comments on writing papers. Increasingly, professors accept, grade, and return papers on-line, sometimes using Blackboard or other course software as well as the tools in Microsoft Word.

What is significant and promising is precisely this: None of these sites was developed under the guidance of the portfolio movement, yet the existence of the Web has encouraged behavior that leads in the direction of portfolios. These teachers have all gathered substantial "material from themselves," and their Web sites have encouraged them to

Three interesting faculty portfolio sites by Robert Wood, Robin Mitchell-Boyask, and Janice Siegel

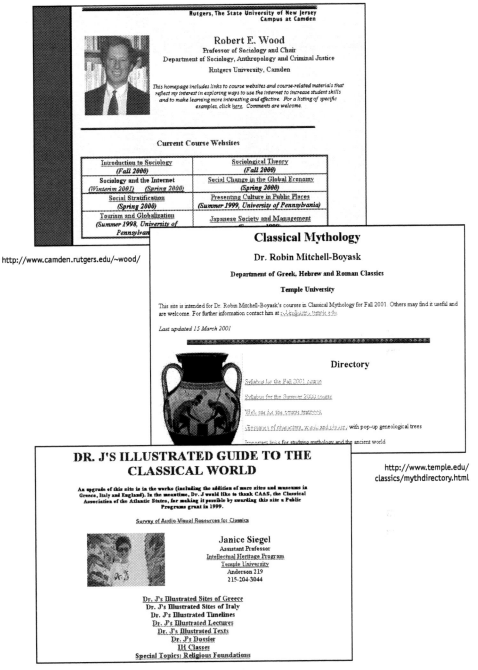

http://www.camden.rutgers.edu/~wood/

http://www.temple.edu/classics/mythdirectory.html

http://www.drjclassics.com/drj/indexdrj.htm

build incrementally on that material. Course design, materials, and teaching strategies are all there.

In short, the Web has encouraged these teachers, and others all over the country, to take their practice public — perhaps the crucial step in portfolio development. Their work is "public, susceptible to critical review, and accessible for exchange and use," thus meeting

Shulman's three standards of scholarly work. Stier, Wood, Mitchell-Boyask, and Siegel all report receiving correspondence from around the nation and from foreign countries, usually to acknowledge the assistance their sites have provided. Stier insists on the public quality of his course Web site and on its benefits for him while recognizing that such openness may upset others: "To make this process most useful, faculty members have to overcome their reluctance to expose their teaching to a wide audience."

The authors I have just mentioned are skillful Web practitioners and committed teachers. They do not yet regard themselves as portfolio authors. Could their proto-portfolios or potential portfolios become "full" portfolios? They could, if the authors added reflective statements (as Stier now has), gathered student ratings and other comments, displayed students' work, and perhaps posed research questions.

Now we can turn to three examples of conscious portfolio construction, each with its own merits. Helen Barrett worked independently and creatively to develop a substantial source for portfolio developers. Elizabeth Barkley used a portfolio to trace a change in the style and content of her teaching. Mills Kelly concentrated on what was happening in a single course. The technology of these three portfolios is as instructive as the authors' comments on teaching. Barrett and Kelly were both self-taught. Barkley received substantial assistance from the staff at The Carnegie Foundation, which has developed an impressive set of portfolio displays.

In short, the Web has encouraged these teachers, and others all over the country, to take their practice public — perhaps the crucial step in portfolio development.

Helen Barrett: portfolios for teachers

> I decided that, after talking and writing about electronic portfolios, I had better practice what I was preaching. . . . I decided to change my focus from student portfolios to teaching portfolios: If we expected students to have e-portfolios, teachers needed to model that activity, which they can then share with their own students. Now, when I make presentations on this topic, the first portfolio I usually show is my own. . . . As I developed my portfolio, I found that it fulfilled another purpose: validating my professional growth over time. (interview, July 2000)

This response to an interview question is significant. Student portfolios and student electronic portfolios are fairly common in colleges of education, but extended reflections about portfolio creation seem relatively rare, and detailed instructions on portfolio development, carefully keyed to different levels of technological sophistication, are even less common. One influence on Professor Barrett's work was the movement toward standards-based teaching, which seemed to support a greater emphasis on teaching portfolios:

> I propose that a portfolio without standards is just a multimedia presentation or a fancy electronic resume or a digital scrapbook. There is a place for that type of format in class-

rooms or in employment searches, but a savvy administrator will look for evidence that the candidate meets the teaching standards that have been set for the district or state; a savvy teacher will look for evidence that a student's portfolio demonstrates achievement of at least one of the district/state/national standards. Without standards as the organizing basis for a portfolio, the collection becomes just that . . . a collection, haphazard and without structure; the purpose is lost in the noise, glitz and hype. High technology disconnected from a focus on curriculum standards will only exacerbate the lack of meaningful integration of technology into teaching and learning. (Barrett 1998)

One merit of Professor Barrett's chapter here and publications elsewhere is to point to bodies of scholarship that are slightly different from those followed by the school of portfolio development begun by Cerbin and associated with Hutchings, Shulman, and The Carnegie Foundation. Her Web site includes not only a lengthy bibliography of sources but more than 20 articles and presentations of her own. Her chapter reviews a number of technical topics (such as the utility of PDF) that are not often mentioned in the literature about portfolio development, with careful guidance about each step of the process.

The two planes on which Professor Barrett operates — her own portfolio development and that of the student teachers she trains — are both reflected in her chapter. One reason for including this chapter is that it is far more deliberate about technology than some other studies of electronic portfolios; another is that it reveals how active student teachers have been in this area.

Elizabeth Barkley: a record of change

A professor of music in a two-year institution, Elizabeth Barkley responded energetically to the changing tastes and declining interest of students, revising her curriculum and emphasizing active learning. Her portfolio (http://kml2.carnegiefoundation.org/gallery/ebarkley/), compiled with Toru Iiyoshi of the Knowledge Media Laboratory at The Carnegie Foundation for the Advancement of Teaching, describes the transformation of her course Music of Multicultural America, with an abundance of data in PDF files and substantial narrative material. In her chapter for this volume, Professor Barkley reflects on that transformation and on the power of the portfolio to describe this change: "I believe that a portfolio offered the fullest and most nuanced way to share this transformation with other teachers, disciplines, and institutions." This is a statement of discovery: At moments, Elizabeth Barkley resembles an explorer in a forest, seemingly surprised by the emerging benefits of her portfolio experience. Interestingly, both she and Mills Kelly now plan to write portfolios for all the courses they teach.

T. Mills Kelly: in search of historical thinking

> I wanted to better understand how the introduction of hypermedia into the survey course changed students' understanding of course content, whether hypermedia improved or detracted from students' ability to acquire a greater facility with historical methods, and whether using hypermedia might give students new or different insights into something we historians like to call "historical thinking."

Mills Kelly, assistant professor at George Mason University, compiled his electronic portfolio on his own at Texas Tech University. What is fascinating about his portfolio (which can be found at http://www2.tltc.ttu.edu/kelly/Pew/Portfolio/welcome.htm) is that in it we see a historian at work, posing a research question, using evaluations and "instructional diagnoses." The "Conclusions" section lists a set of intriguing, evidence-based findings:

1. Students Who Access Learning Resources on the Web Display a Higher Level of Recursive Reading.
2. The Hypermedia Revolution Signals the Doom of Conventional History Survey Courses.
3. The Web Does Encourage Independent Investigation, But Not as Much As We Would Like.

The first finding confirms that Web-based research involves students in an activity the author considers essential to historical work: Students using the Web were far more likely than others to return repeatedly to a central text while constructing an argument. The second finding reflects Kelly's conviction that students using the Web will do more recursive and "self-directed" research than others, thus undermining the "coverage-oriented" bias of traditional survey courses. Finally, the third finding reports that contrary to the grand claims made for Web-based learning, "less than half (44%) actually ever left the class Web site to go poking around on the Web, despite being encouraged to do so" and that "students in my courses . . . remain disinclined to apply any sort of critical analysis to the sites they visit."

Kelly's chapter reveals that his historian's inquisitiveness remains keen: He is planning new projects that will involve his students even more intensively in using the Web.

Criticism of Portfolios

The portfolio movement comes at a particularly tense moment in the history of higher education. On the one hand, concern with student learning is growing. On the other, the burgeoning of short-term nontenured contracts, along with occasional frontal assaults on the institution of tenure, has contributed to faculty feelings of powerlessness; Gary Rhoades's term "managed professionals" captures these anxieties nicely (Rhoades, 1998).

In this context, any evaluation of teaching may seem threatening. *Academe,* the magazine of the American Association of University Professors, has run its share of attacks on student ratings but was also the source of a negative appraisal of the entire portfolio movement. The most revealing feature of this attack was its assured binarism: Noting a correlation between teachers' enthusiasm and students' ratings, the author concluded that teaching is most effectively improved through consultations on "key teaching characteristics, such as enthusiasm and clarity, . . . " while portfolios are both wasteful and dangerous, as they provide administrators with information that might be used against professors (Burns, 2000).

If teaching improvement were really, as Burns avers, a matter of behavior modification and learned enthusiasm, the way to pedagogical improvement would be smooth, without the dark nights of the soul so many of us experience. One function of portfolios is to facilitate extended reflection on and collegial discussion of how we teach. The teacher ratings Burns prizes figure importantly in most portfolios, but they become objects of analysis, probed and unpacked as practitioners explore the relationship among ratings, student learning, and other topics, or discuss the tensions between local experience and meta-analytic claims. The virtue of portfolios is to reframe confident statements — "Enthusiasm improves learning" — as research questions — "What has raised learning in my own setting, and why?"

More measured concerns about the administrative use of portfolios can be found in other quarters. In the interviews I conducted as background for this chapter, several faculty members criticized summative portfolios as unreliable and spotty. Some disagreement exists as to whether it is wise to be frank and open about one's teaching in a public setting such as the Web. Interestingly, several interviewees mentioned that colleagues (not administrators) have sometimes sought to use portfolio information against them in cases involving promotion. Each of these demurrers, however, is balanced by a report that the portfolio experience was successful and deeply meaningful. According to Mills Kelly:

> I had to think much more deeply about my own discipline, about what the scholarship of
> teaching and learning is or is becoming, and about the multiple audiences for my work
> and how it might resonate with them. In other words, I faced a series of decisions that
> overlapped with those we all face when we prepare to publish the results of our discipli-
> nary research but that also included many new questions I had not considered previously.

The Current Status of Electronic Faculty Portfolios

Faculty portfolios are now being used in a wide range of academic fields, as we can see from the multiple contributors to the second edition of Seldin's book (1997) and the six electronic portfolios (each from a different discipline) at The Carnegie Foundation for the

Advancement of Teaching Web site (http://kml2.carnegiefoundation.org). Electronic portfolios are also gaining a foothold in some disciplines, such as the American Historical Association, which published William Cutler's portfolio in the "Teaching" section of its Web site in 1999 (http://www.theaha.org/teaching/aahe/aahecover.html). The AHA is also planning to publish Mills Kelly's portfolio (Cutler, 1999).

Is this activity matched by equivalent depth on the campuses? Or is the electronic portfolio movement a "religion of the highways" with only a few outposts at important sites? The answer, for both summative and formative portfolios, remains unclear. In the thousands of postsecondary institutions in the United States, teaching is treated with varied degrees of seriousness, and "student learning" is only sometimes included in the evaluation of teaching. When we turn to the use of portfolios for teaching, we find a huge variety of practices. Teaching portfolios for promotion and tenure seem to be relatively widely accepted, while formative portfolio development remains somewhat marginal, and electronic portfolios of both sorts — summative and formative — are even rarer. Without attempting to quantify the degree of electronic portfolio use, it is clear from interviews, surveys, and personal experience that formative electronic portfolios have substantial potential but that continued missionary work is still necessary to win over a cautious academic audience.

The Samford University Problem-Based Learning Project

An example of a project that contributes to an information base for portfolio users and potential users is Samford University's problem-based learning project. Samford, in Birmingham, Alabama, has been a leader in the development of problem-based learning for undergraduates. Faculty participants in the Samford project have recorded and reflected on their work in course portfolios that have circulated in the American academic world. With a grant from The Pew Charitable Trusts, Samford is establishing a national center for peer review of problem-based learning courses, using course portfolios and exploring the potential of on-line storage and display of the documents. The project has an outstanding design and assessment team that includes, in addition to experts in problem-based learning, Daniel Bernstein, Randy Bass, and Pat Hutchings, all leaders in the portfolio movement. Building on a strong background in portfolio construction and the study of student learning, this project is likely to yield results useful across the nation (see http://www.samford.edu/pbl/).

Positive and Problematic Features of Electronic Portfolios

The potential gain that Web use provides portfolio builders is impressive, though attaining it requires some work. Often, educational presentations (including portfolios) on the Web begin by simply putting reports, syllabi, or other documents into HTML format and placing them on Web sites. It is a natural first step, the best many of us are capable of at the outset. But, like the stage mannerisms that early screen actors refused to shed, "uploaded paper" barely begins to exploit the potential of the new medium. Faculty building portfolios will be interested in information about exploiting the medium further. One such example is a short article that suggests including links to other Web sites, samples of electronic materials, and animations (Lieberman & Rueter, 1997, pp. 46-48).

The following features distinguish electronic from paper portfolios:

- *Nonlinearity*. Faculty regularly praise this feature, which is a major strength of electronic portfolios and enables links of all sorts. Portfolio creators are no longer locked into linear organization. If intelligence works by association, so can a Web site.
- *Direct and unmediated contact with evidence*. Sometimes this feature is called "transparency," by which I mean access to information on university computers or other local sites without an intermediary. An example in a university is the ability to access a faculty member's class enrollments, records of students dropping a class, and similar data. Similar immediacy is available in some educational settings. California State University's institutional portfolio, described later, directs us to a sample department, Sociology, and summarizes students' comments on the department's success, with percentage figures (http://www.csus.edu/soc/ portfolio/goalsdata.html). It is not absurd to imagine portfolio pages that directly access university computers, automatically adjusting the data from day to day. Institutions and individuals will have to struggle with the issues of publicity, access, and mediation of such direct access.
- *Interactivity*. A Web site can be set up with e-mail communication devices permitting direct connections to a chair or program director, facilitating and speeding communication. In the examples in this section, both Kelly and Barkley used such a tool. (Barkley with characteristic flair called hers an "issue bin.")
- *Integrated audio and video displays*. Electronic portfolios can give learning a face and a voice by integrating audio and video displays. As William Cerbin notes, "It is now possible to *show* (not just describe or explain) teaching and learning by integrating audio and video with text" (interview, August 2000).
- *Portability*. Once they are on the Web, electronic portfolios are far more "portable" and accessible than paper.
- *Power*. The sheer volume of data available on the Web, or capable of being stored on the Web, dwarfs most other media. In this sense, the Web is simply a more powerful tool than its competitors.

But some potential problems are involved as well.

- *Too much information*. Paper and electronic portfolios alike invite faculty to pile data on a problem. Careful editing of print portfolios and careful development of

What could be more transparent than posting all of my evaluations, copies of student work, etc., for the whole world to see? I'm trying to be as transparent as I possibly can with my teaching and we'll let the chips fall where they may.

A faculty member (interview, July 2000)

pathways through information in electronic portfolios aid readers in making sense of information.

- *Form without substance.* Electronic media provide a fertile ground for flashy but unproductive use of electronic media: Frames, blinking lights, streaming, and so on become meaningless without good content.

Conclusion

At this point, it is worthwhile to consider how much the Web has opened up for us. One indication may be a wholly worthwhile phrase found at various pedagogical sites: "to capture and document the scholarship of teaching." Web-based work brings a linguistic and conceptual shift: When portfolios become interactive and transparent, our relationship moves from that of the predator ("capture") viewing the prey to that of partner engaged in a dialogue in process — perhaps across continents — aimed at improving pedagogy. In a sense, Web-based work enables us to move from "capturing and documenting" to "sharing, collaborating, and benefiting," from viewing to participating. Consider the language of Kelly's opening statement of his portfolio (www2.tltc.ttu.edu/kelly/Pew/Portfolio/welcome.htm):

> An essential element of all published course portfolios is that they open up the author's teaching to public scrutiny and the possibility of formal or informal peer review. Whether you want to engage me in a more extended discussion of my project, my conclusions, or my course, or if you simply want to offer a comment (or criticism), I hope you will contact me. I have included a comment form as part of this site. E-mail is also a very efficient way to reach me, and good old snail mail works just as well.

Note the pronouns: It is worth considering whether this "I-thou" relationship could have been established before the Web.

References

Angelo, T.A., & Cross, P. (1994). *Classroom Assessment Techniques: A Handbook for College Teachers.* San Francisco: Jossey-Bass.

Barr, R.B., & Tagg, J. (1995, November/December). From teaching to learning: A new paradigm for undergraduate education. *Change* 27 (6), 12-25.

Barrett, H. (1998). Electronic portfolios and standards. http://transition.alaska.edu/www/portfolios/TelEd98Abstract.html.

Boyer, E. (1990). *Scholarship Reconsidered: Priorities of the Professoriate.* Princeton, NJ: Carnegie Foundation for the Advancement of Teaching.

Burns, C.W. (2000, January-February). Another perspective. Are teaching portfolios a scam? They're time-consuming to put together, and we don't know if they improve teaching. *Academe,* 44-47.

Cerbin, W. (1996). Inventing a new genre: The course portfolio at the University of Wisconsin-La Crosse. In P. Hutchings (Ed.), *Making Teaching Community Property: A Menu for Peer Collaboration and Peer Review* (pp. 52-56). Washington, DC: American Association for Higher Education.

Cross, K.P., & Steadman, M.H. (1996). *Classroom Research: Implementing the Scholarship of Teaching.* San Francisco: Jossey-Bass.

Cutler, W. (1999). History 67. A course portfolio 1996 and 1997. http://www.theaha.org/teaching/aahe/portfol1.html.

Edgerton, R., Hutchings, P., & Quinlan, K. (1991). *The Teaching Portfolio: Capturing the Scholarship in Teaching.* Washington, DC: American Association for Higher Education.

Huber, M.T. (1998). Why now? Course portfolios in context. In P. Hutchings (Ed.), *The Course Portfolio: How Faculty Can Examine Their Teaching to Advance Practice and Improve Student Learning* (pp. 29-34). Washington, DC: American Association for Higher Education.

Hutchings, P. (1998a). *The Course Portfolio: How Faculty Can Examine Their Teaching to Advance Practice and Improve Student Learning.* Washington, DC: American Association for Higher Education.

Hutchings, P. (1998b). Defining features and significant functions of the course portfolio. In P. Hutchings (Ed.), *The Course Portfolio: How Faculty Can Examine Their Teaching to Advance Practice and Improve Student Learning* (pp. 13-18). Washington, DC: American Association for Higher Education.

Langsam, D.M. (1998). A course portfolio for midyear reflection. In P. Hutchings (Ed.), *The Course Portfolio: How Faculty Can Examine Their Teaching to Advance Practice and Improve Student Learning* (pp. 57-63). Washington, DC: American Association for Higher Education.

Lieberman, D., & Rueter, J. (1997). The electronically augmented teaching portfolio. In P. Seldin (Ed.), *The Teaching Portfolio: A Practical Guide to Improved Performance and Promotion and Tenure Decisions* (2nd ed., pp. 46-58). Bolton, MA: Anker.

Martsolf, D. (1998). A course portfolio for a graduate nursing course. In P. Hutchings (Ed.), *The Course Portfolio: How Faculty Can Examine Their Teaching to Advance Practice and Improve Student Learning* (pp. 26-28). Washington, DC: American Association for Higher Education.

Rhoades, G. (1998). *Managed Professionals: Unionized Faculty and Restructuring Academic Labor.* Albany: State University of New York Press.

Schön, D. (1984). *The Reflective Practitioner: How Professionals Think in Action.* New York: Basic Books.

Schön, D. (1990). *Educating the Reflective Practitioner* (2nd ed.). San Francisco: Jossey-Bass.

Schön, D., & Rein, M. (1995). *Frame Reflection: Toward the Resolution of Intractable Policy Controversies.* New York: Basic Books.

Seldin, P. (1991). *The Teaching Portfolio: A Practical Guide to Improved Performance and Promotion and Tenure Decisions* (1st ed.). Bolton, MA: Anker.

Seldin, P., & Associates. (1997). *The Teaching Portfolio: A Practical Guide to Improved Performance and Promotion and Tenure Decisions* (2nd ed.). Bolton, MA: Anker.

Shulman, L.S. (1993, November/December). Teaching as community property: Putting an end to pedagogical solitude. *Change* 25 (6), 6-7.

Shulman, L.S. (1998). Course anatomy: The dissection and analysis of knowledge through teaching. In P. Hutchings (Ed.), *The Course Portfolio: How Faculty Can Examine Their Teaching to Advance Practice and Improve Student Learning* (pp. 5-12). Washington, DC: American Association for Higher Education.

Teaching Great Books on the Web

by Marc Stier

The Web is a wonderful tool for teachers. But if we are to use it properly, we have to think through the connection between what appears on our Web sites and what we do in class. So the first half of this chapter is not about the Web at all but about what I teach and my assumptions about how this material should be taught. Then I turn to an account of my own way of using the Web in the two great books courses that I teach in the Temple University Intellectual Heritage Program.

Intellectual Heritage is a two-semester sequence of courses required of all undergraduates at Temple University. The first semester begins with Thucydides, Sophocles, and Plato and includes texts drawn from the Hebrew Bible, the New Testament, and the Qur'an as well as works by Galileo, Machiavelli, and Shakespeare. The second semester begins with John Locke and romantic poetry; continues to Marx, Darwin, and Freud; and concludes with Gandhi and a contemporary novel.

The central assumption of my way of teaching these courses is that all learning that transforms the way we think and understand ourselves is, somewhat paradoxically, rote learning. The greatest mistake beginning teachers make — the greatest mistake I used to make — is to assume that one teaches students by telling them something. When I teach about the various ways in which power can be centralized and decentralized in a legislative body and the political consequences of these different forms of organization, I cannot simply tell them. To understand the importance of different distributions of power, students have to take a conceptual leap. They have to develop a new way of thinking and acquire a new vocabulary.

What is true for studying power in a legislative body is even more true for studying great books. To understand each text, our students must come to think in a new way. They have to address problems they have not considered with ways of thought that are foreign to them. Learning this material is not so much an accumulation of information as it is a second acculturation. My Intellectual Heritage students learn a new way of talking and writing by repeatedly hearing and then using a new set of concepts and ideas.

Marc Stier teaches The Great Books and The Western Intellectual Tradition in Temple University's Intellectual Heritage Program. He has created an extensive Web-based portfolio for his own courses, and will become Web master for the whole program in the fall of 2001.

Critics of rote learning forget that students do not learn to use new ideas and concepts in one step. Most of our students come to use new ideas in small and halting steps with frequent, and necessary, backsliding and detours. A new concept or idea is but one element in a network. Students slowly come to grasp the interconnections of these different elements crisscrossing from one part of the network to another many times and from different directions. As Wittgenstein once put it, learning a new way of thought is like learning one's way around a city. Only when we have come to the same intersection from many different routes will we confidently know how to make our way through it to our destination.

Socratic Dialogue and Its Limits

In most ways, I am a very traditional teacher. I am convinced that the best way for me to teach students classic texts is through Socratic discussion. My class sessions consist almost entirely of discussions in which our aim is to interpret some text. I ask my students to focus on questions that are meant to elucidate the meaning or meanings of particular passages. As time goes by, we try to put these passages together, which involves considerable rethinking and reevaluating the conclusions we have already reached.

Socratic discussion has many advantages. I can lead students step by step into new ideas. I can model new forms of thought. By responding to my questions, students can begin to think in a new way. But it creates difficulties as well. Some students get entirely lost. Even after a good class, most students have to do work on their own to master the material. Most students feel that, even though they have followed the discussion from beginning to end, they will have difficulty in putting the material together as a whole. They can answer narrow questions but cannot begin to give a coherent account of the central ideas of the text we are studying.

How the Web Helps

My solution to all these difficulties is to use the Web to provide a variety of aids for my students that help them to review the material we discuss in class and to make it their own. I provide students with:

- *Introductions to assignments.* Before every class, I try to provide a brief review of where we have gone and an introduction to the topics for the next day. These remarks largely replace in-class summaries of the material.
- *Notes on the texts.* These notes are, I think, the most valuable material for my students. I provide them with very detailed and highly structured notes on the text.
- *Overviews of the course.* In addition to notes on specific texts, I provide my students with an overview of the course. In these notes, I try to emphasize broader

Marc Stier's Intellectual Heritage course portfolio: His notes on the texts that students read in his class

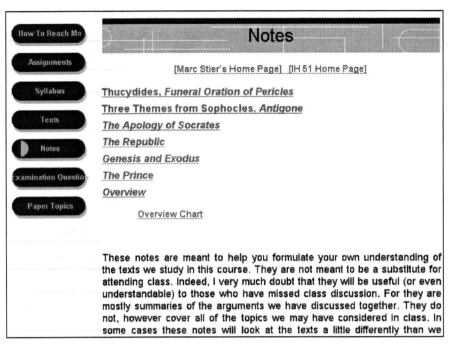

http://www.stier.net/teaching/ih51/ih51.html

themes and help students see key points of comparison and contrast between the texts.

- *Paper topics and examination questions.*
- *On-line discussion.*

Moreover, for the last few years, I have required students to hand in their papers in electronic form. I then grade them using the revision marks and footnote functions in Microsoft Word.

Students very much enjoy having all this material available to them. By providing it, I am in effect more than doubling the time I spend with them. The notes and overviews on the Web are essentially the lectures I would give if I taught Intellectual Heritage as a lecture course. Rather than resenting the material on the Web because it makes additional demands on them, most students are eager to have help in working through our class discussions. At the same time, students very much value those discussions because they can ask questions, express their own take on the texts, and actively learn how to think in the ways demanded by the texts.

About 85% of my students use the material on the Web; probably 65% use it extensively. I have no doubt that students who use this material receive higher grades and enjoy the course more. As my Web site has expanded, the quality of students' work has improved steadily.

I have used the Web largely as a means of helping my own students. But as the amount and variety of material on my Web site grow, other kinds of uses become possible. I shall mention just one: It enables us teachers in the Intellectual Heritage Program to look more closely at the different approaches of our colleagues.

Possible Problems and Solutions

Providing students so much material on the Web entails two possible dangers. One is that students will rely on the material on the Web and not come to class or read the texts. So I explain that taking part in class is a common good that is available to us only if we all do our part in providing it. Moreover, because my notes are written at a fairly high level, students have difficulty understanding them if they have not read the text or come to class. For this and other reasons, students cannot succeed using my Web notes alone.

A second possible difficulty posed by the volume of material I put on the Web is that students will simply repeat what they find there in their own examinations and papers. Somewhat to my own surprise, I have not found that to be a problem at all.

It takes a great deal of effort to make all the material I put on the Web available to my students. But it is not an overwhelming task, because I can reuse much of this material from one semester to another and because the Web helps so much in preparing my introductions to texts, notes, and overviews. I could not work so close to deadline if it were not possible for me to post material to the Web the evening before each class.

For this traditional teacher of a traditional course, the Web has proved to be an extremely useful tool, one that reinforces but does not replace my efforts in class.

To make this process most useful, faculty members have to overcome their reluctance to expose their teaching to a wide audience.

Once that reluctance is overcome, the possibilities expand for moving to additional uses for the teaching materials. Constructing a teaching or course portfolio, for example, would involve reflection on and analysis of materials and choices of materials to include based on the purpose of the portfolio. Possible content or evidence, however, is already available, and it is available on-line so that an electronic portfolio would be a natural.

Note

This essay is also available at http://www.stier.net/writing/great/frame/htm.

Electronic Portfolios = Multimedia Development + Portfolio Development: The Electronic Portfolio Development Process

by Helen Barrett

This essay is intended to be more practical than philosophical, drawing on my own and my students' experiences and focusing on the questions often asked about electronic portfolios: Where do I start? What software should I use? What strategies seem to work well? I view portfolios as a process rather than a product — a concrete representation of critical thinking and reflection used to set goals for ongoing professional development.

An electronic portfolio constructed for this purpose includes technologies that allow the portfolio developer to collect and organize artifacts in many formats (audio, video, graphical, and text). A standards-based electronic portfolio uses hypertext links to organize the material, connecting artifacts to appropriate goals or standards. Often, the terms "electronic portfolio" and "digital portfolio" are used interchangeably. I make a distinction, however: An electronic portfolio contains artifacts that may be in analog (e.g., videotape) or computer-readable form. In a digital portfolio, all artifacts have been transformed into computer-readable form (Barrett, 2000).

My framework for the development of electronic portfolios derives from two bodies of literature: portfolio development in K-12 education and the multimedia or instructional design process. These complementary processes are both essential for effective electronic portfolio development. Understanding how these processes fit together and how standards or goals contribute to the development of electronic portfolios, faculty gain a powerful tool for demonstrating growth over time.

The multimedia development process usually covers the following stages (Ivers & Barron, 1998):
1. *Decide/Assess:* determining the needs, goals, and audience for the presentation;
2. *Design/Plan:* determining the content and sequence of the presentation;

Helen Barrett is assistant professor of educational technology in the School of Education at the University of Alaska Anchorage. She has been researching electronic portfolios since 1991 and publishing a Web site of technology and alternative assessment since 1995 (http://electronicportfolios.com). She is the assessment coordinator for the International Society for Technology in Education's National Educational Technology Standards for Teachers.

Using Technology to Support Alternative Assessment and Electronic Portfolios

| References & Links | On-Line Publications | Conference Presentations | Workshop Training Sessions |

This set of web pages will describe and discuss the use of technology to support alternative assessment from a number of perspectives. Developed and maintained by Dr. Helen Barrett, Assistant Professor, Educational Technology, School of Education, University of Alaska Anchorage.

- **Announcing** a Listserv devoted to issues related to Electronic and Digital Portfolios, beginning July 15, 1998.
- **Announcing** an online class covering Electronic Portfolio Development for Anchorage School District teachers, beginning October 15, 2000 through April 15, 2001.
- **For UAA students:** Draft Reflective Portfolio Instructions using Microsoft Word. Optional instructions for converting to Acrobat.

References & Links

- Favorite Internet links on Alternative Assessment & Electronic Portfolios
- Books and Articles on Portfolios, Alternative Assessment and Tools for Developing Electronic Portfolios

Dr. Barrett's On-Line Publications on Electronic Portfolios

- **Tutorial - How to Create a Standards-Based Electronic Portfolio using a variety of software** (based on the Electronic Portfolio Development Process) by Helen C. Barrett *(under development)*- Course Instructions: ED 320 (Foundations) - ED 626 (Foundations) - ED 655 (Endorsement)
- Electronic Portfolios = Multimedia Development + Portfolio Development: The Electronic Portfolio

http://transition.alaska.edu/www/portfolios.html

3. *Develop:* gathering and organizing multimedia materials to include in the presentation;
4. *Implement:* giving the presentation;
5. *Evaluate:* evaluating the presentation's effectiveness.

The portfolio development process covers the following stages (Danielson & Abrutyn, 1997):

1. *Collection:* saving the artifacts that represent the day-to-day results of teaching and learning;
2. *Selection:* reviewing and evaluating the artifacts saved and identifying those that demonstrate achievement of specific standards or goals;
3. *Reflection:* reflecting on the significance of the artifacts chosen for the portfolio in relationship to specific learning goals;
4. *Projection (or Direction):* aligning the reflections against the standards or goals and performance indicators; revising learning goals for the future;
5. *Presentation:* sharing the portfolio with peers and receiving feedback.

A faculty portfolio can be one of three types: *formative,* usually employed on an ongoing basis to support professional development; *summative,* for formal evaluation; and *marketing,* used for seeking employment (Hartnell-Young & Morriss, 1999).

The Electronic Portfolio Development Process:
Five Stages and Five Levels

In addition to the stages of portfolio development are at least five levels of electronic portfolio development, each with its own levels of expectation. These levels are closely aligned with the technology skills of the teacher portfolio developer:

1. No digital artifacts; some videotape artifacts;
2. Word-processing or other commonly used files stored in electronic folders on a hard drive, floppy disk, or LAN server;
3. Databases, hypermedia (e.g., HyperStudio), or slide shows (e.g., PowerPoint) stored on a hard drive, Zip disk, floppy disk, or LAN server;
4. Portable Document Format (Adobe Acrobat PDF) files stored on a hard drive, Zip disk, Jaz, CD, or LAN server;
5. HTML-based Web pages created with a Web authoring program and posted to a Web server;
6. Multimedia authoring program, such as Macromedia Authorware or Director, pressed to CD or posted to the Web in streaming format.

The Stages of Electronic Portfolio Development:
Matching Tasks and Tools

A participant in my dissertation research stated, "When learning new tools, use familiar tasks, and when learning new tasks, use familiar tools." Creating an electronic portfolio can seem daunting, but it becomes less arduous if viewed as a series of stages, each with its own goals and activities and requiring different types of software.

Stage 1: defining the portfolio's context (multimedia development: decide/assess; portfolio development: purpose and audience)

In this first stage of developing an electronic portfolio, the primary tasks are to identify the assessment context, including the purpose of the portfolio, and then to identify the goals to be addressed in the portfolio. If the portfolio is summative, the goals should follow from university standards for promotion and tenure and from standards set by relevant professional associations. This important step sets the assessment context and helps frame the rest of the portfolio development process. Knowing the primary audience for the portfolio helps in deciding the format and storage of the formal or presentation portfolio.

Before making any decisions about the development software, identify the resources available for electronic portfolio development. What hardware and software do you have? What technology skills do you have or want to develop?

Stage 2: the working portfolio (multimedia development: design/plan; portfolio development: collect)

This stage of electronic portfolio development occupies the longest span of time and is the stage I call "Becoming a Digital Packrat." Knowing which goals or standards you are trying to demonstrate should help determine the types of portfolio artifacts to be collected and then selected.

Select the software development tools most appropriate for the portfolio context and the resources available. Just as McLuhan said, the medium is the message. The software used to create the electronic portfolio will control, restrict, or enhance the development of your portfolio. Form should follow function as well, and the electronic portfolio software should match the vision and style of the portfolio developer.

Use whatever software tools are currently available to collect artifacts, storing them on a hard drive, a server, or videotape. Set up electronic folders for each standard to organize the artifacts (any type of electronic document) and use a word processor, database, hypermedia software, or slide show to articulate the goals/standards to be demonstrated in the portfolio and to organize the artifacts.

Microsoft Word, Microsoft PowerPoint, Adobe Acrobat, and Web pages created with HTML editors are the most common software packages used in my field for electronic portfolio development. The primary advantage of Word and Acrobat is ease of use, and Acrobat files can be created from any application. Creating a portfolio in HTML, even with the many tools available, takes greater effort to convert documents and organize the large number of files usually generated. Creating a portfolio in PowerPoint can emphasize the portfolio as a "multimedia presentation" rather than as a reflective tool.

Identify the storage and presentation medium most appropriate for the situation.

Gather the multimedia materials that represent your achievement. You will want to collect artifacts from different points in time to demonstrate growth and learning. Write short reflective statements with each artifact stored to capture its significance at the time it was created. You might convert significant documents into Adobe Acrobat format and attach electronic "sticky notes" with your immediate reflections.

Use word-processing, slide show, hypermedia, or database programs to list and organize the artifacts placed in the working portfolio.

Convert your work into digital format.

Add style and individuality to your portfolio by using the multimedia you find appropriate. Save your work in a format that can be easily used. Throughout the year, I convert a variety of files — word-processing files, Web pages I create, e-mail messages I might want to include — in my own working portfolio into Adobe Acrobat format (attaching electronic "sticky notes" with my reflection) and store them in a "new items" folder for later use. Use a scanner, microphone, and video camera as called for to prepare artifacts.

Stage 3: the reflective portfolio (multimedia development: develop; portfolio development: select, reflect, direct)

This stage in the development of portfolios is for evaluation or employment applications. In formative portfolios, reflections are typically added throughout the learning process. Reflection on one's work is requisite if the portfolio owner is to learn from the process: As John Dewey said, we don't learn from experience; we learn from reflecting on experience. One challenge in the development of summative and marketing portfolios is the need to keep these reflections confidential. The personal, private reflections of the learner need to be guarded and not published in a public medium, such as the World Wide Web.

In formative portfolios, reflections are typically added throughout the learning process.

Record feedback on work and achievement of goals. I have found several strategies useful with my students' portfolios:

- Review the reflective statements written for each artifact as it was stored, elaborating on its meaning and value and why you are selecting it for your presentation portfolio.
- Refer back to the goals or standards identified in the first stage and write general reflective statements on your related achievement.
- Select the artifacts that represent achievement of the standards or goals.
- From the reflections and feedback, set learning goals for the future.

Three simple questions clarify this reflective process: "What?" "So what?" and "Now what?" (Campbell, Melenyzer, Nettles & Wyman, 2000, p. 22).

This process of setting future learning goals turns electronic portfolio development into a powerful tool for professional development. That is why "Now what?" becomes important. As Burke (1996) insists, quoting Kenneth Wolf, a professional portfolio system invites "teachers to become the architects of their own professional development" (p. 37).

Stage 4: the connected portfolio (multimedia development: implement; portfolio development: inspect, perfect, connect)

To some degree, this stage is unique to the electronic portfolio because of the capability of the software to create hypertext links between documents, either locally or on the Internet. At this stage, if you have not done so, convert word-processing, database, or slide show documents into PDF or HTML and create hypertext links between goals, work samples, rubrics, and reflections. Insert appropriate multimedia artifacts. Create a table of contents to structure the portfolio; I recommend using the outlining capabilities of Word or PowerPoint or the graphical organizing and outlining capabilities of Inspiration.

The process of creating a portfolio with hypertext links contributes to the summative assessment process. When using the portfolio for assessment, the transformation from "artifacts" to "evidence" is not always clear. Linking reflections to artifacts makes this thinking process more explicit. The ability to create links from multiple perspectives (and multiple goals) also overcomes the linearity of two-dimensional paper portfolios, permitting a single artifact to demonstrate multiple standards (i.e., national technology standards, a state's teaching standards).

Use the portfolio evidence to make decisions about instruction/learning or professional development. This process effectively brings together instruction and assessment, portfolio development and professional development.

Stage 5: the presentation portfolio (multimedia development: present, publish, evaluate; portfolio development: respect (celebrate))

At this stage, record the portfolio to an appropriate presentation and storage medium, which will be different for a working portfolio versus a formal or presentation portfolio.

Present the portfolio before an audience (real or virtual) and celebrate the accomplishments represented. This strategy will be very individualized, depending on the context, and an opportunity for professionals to share their teaching portfolios with colleagues for meaningful feedback and collaboration in self-assessment. This "public commitment" provides motivation to carry out the professional development plan of a formative portfolio.

Evaluate the portfolio's effectiveness in light of its purpose and the assessment context. In an environment of continuous improvement, a portfolio should be viewed as an ongoing learning tool, and its effectiveness should be reviewed regularly to be sure that it meets the goals set.

Post the portfolio to a Web server, write the portfolio to a CD, or record the portfolio on videotape.

Skills for Developing an Acrobat Portfolio

I use Adobe's Acrobat for publishing my portfolio because this software emulates the three-ring binder most often used in paper-based portfolios. In my opinion, PDF files are the ideal universal container for digital portfolios. In fact, John Warnock, cofounder and

CEO of Adobe Systems, defines the Acrobat PDF as "an extensible form of paper, a hyper-media that is device independent, platform independent, color consistent and . . . the best universal transmission medium for creative and intellectual assets."

What else is a portfolio but a container for our creative and intellectual efforts? If Adobe Acrobat is chosen as your development software, the following skills are important:
1. Convert files from any application to PDF using PDFWriter or Acrobat Distiller.
2. Scan/capture and edit graphical images.
3. Digitize and edit sound files.
4. Digitize and edit video files (VCR —> computer).
5. Organize portfolio artifacts with Acrobat Exchange, creating links and buttons.
6. Organize multimedia files and premaster CD using Jaz disks.
7. Write a CD-recordable disk using appropriate CD mastering software.

Conclusions

Many tools can be used to develop electronic portfolios. The value added from creation of an electronic portfolio should exceed the efforts expended, and faculty members should approach their use of technology conservatively. Keep the process simple by using famil-iar software as you begin the process. (My students have made very creative, reflective portfolios, complete with hyperlinks to their digital artifacts, with nothing more compli-cated than Microsoft Word.) Above all, the electronic portfolio should showcase your achievements and your growing capabilities in using technology to support your own life-long professional development.

References

Barrett, H. (2000, April). Create your own electronic portfolio. *Learning & Leading With Technology.*

Burke, K. (Ed.). (1996). *Professional Portfolios.* Palatine, IL: IRI/SkyLight Training & Publishing.

Campbell, D.M., Melenyzer, B.J., Nettles, D.H., & Wyman, R.M., Jr. (2000). *Portfolio and Performance Assessment in Teacher Education.* Boston: Allyn & Bacon.

Danielson, C., & Abrutyn, L. (1997). An introduction to using portfolios in the classroom.

Hartnell-Young, E., & Morriss, M. (1999). *Digital Professional Portfolios for Change.* Arlington Heights, IL: Skylight Professional Development.

Ivers, K., & Barron, A.E. (1998). *Multimedia Projects in Education.* Englewood, CO: Libraries Unlimited.

From Bach to Tupac: Using an Electronic Course Portfolio to Analyze a Curricular Transformation

by Elizabeth F. Barkley

"Sometimes I feel like a partner in an unholy alliance," commented a colleague. "I pretend to teach, and my students pretend to learn." Recalling my own early experience teaching a general education course in music history, I smiled at his understatement: In my course, the handful of students sitting in front of me weren't even pretending to learn! They stared at me with bored, apathetic faces as I struggled to engage them in a lively discussion on the structural nuances of a Beethoven symphony. Beethoven? Their music heroes were Tupac and Nine Inch Nails. This curricular crisis was the catalyst for a five-year transformation out of which I created an entirely new course. My efforts paid off. Annual enrollment increased from 45 to 782, filling my course with enthusiastic students who had enrolled on the advice of friends. Students testified not only to how much they loved the course but also to how much they had learned. This transformation created considerable attention, and it was on an exhilarating wave of success that I was selected as a Carnegie Scholar.[1]

As a Carnegie Scholar, I was challenged to design, implement, and report on a research project that would contribute to the scholarship of teaching and learning in my discipline of music. Like many of my Carnegie Scholar colleagues, I anguished over what to do. Suspicious of educational jargon, I was skeptical that I could design a research project that would tell me anything I really did not already know. Or, if it did reveal something new and significant, I worried that the methodology would not withstand scholarly scrutiny. After considering various project ideas and conversing with other Carnegie Scholars who were also struggling with documenting teaching and learning, I decided to construct a course portfolio in which I analyzed and documented the transformation of that general education music course.[2]

Why a Course Portfolio?

Course portfolios were developed as a mechanism to help faculty investigate and document what they know and do as teachers in ways that contribute to more powerful student learning. I decided on a course portfolio for three reasons. First, course portfolios

Elizabeth F. Barkley is professor of music at Foothill College in Los Altos, California. As a 1999 Carnegie Scholar, she created an electronic course portfolio that is currently housed on The Carnegie Foundation's Knowledge Media Laboratory Gallery site.

seemed to manifest the essential characteristics of scholarship: They could be made public, they were susceptible to critical review and evaluation, and they could be used and built on by others. Thus, course portfolios provided me with an almost ready-made template for delving into this new (for me) territory called "the scholarship of teaching and learning." Second, course portfolios seemed to allow for the messy complexity that I knew characterized teaching and learning. I hoped that a course portfolio might help me capture the subtle but important aspects of teaching and learning that crisper methodologies might miss. Third, I chose to do a course portfolio because I knew, deep in my heart, that over that period of five years and before any conscious concern about the scholarship of teaching and learning, I had used my intuitive sense and natural talent as a teacher to transform that music course in very deep and meaningful ways. A portfolio offered the fullest and most nuanced way to share this transformation with other teachers, disciplines, and institutions.

Once I decided to construct a course portfolio, it did not take long to move to the next step of making it an electronic course portfolio. Electronic course portfolios offered several advantages over their paper counterparts. Much of my own and my students' work was already in electronic format, an electronic portfolio could be easily accessed and disseminated, it could be layered to include multiple points of entry and ways to navigate

Elizabeth Barkley's Music of Multicultural America course portfolio

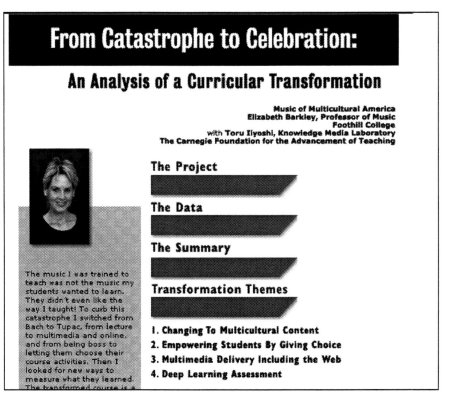

http://kml2.carnegiefoundation.org/gallery/ebarkley/index.html

through the information, it could incorporate multimedia, and it had the potential for integrating interactivity.

What Did I Learn From the Analysis of the Course Transformation?

The foundation of my course portfolio was the analysis of the course transformation, an extremely instructive analysis. Knowing that teachers are justifiably suspicious of huge enrollments, one of the first things I wanted to determine was whether the course's popularity was because it was too "easy." I decided to define "easy" in two ways: light workload or ease of achieving a high grade. Students soon assured me that the workload was not light. For example, one very high achieving mature student complained in caps, which is the electronic equivalent of shouting, "THIS COURSE IS TOO D#$@%NED MUCH WORK." And one of the student investigators wrote, "I have never, ever heard anyone say that this was an easy course." Analysis of final grades revealed that the average grade was a C, with a fairly standard bell curve distribution of both higher and lower grades on either side. So if it was not because the course was easy, why was it so popular? Self-reflection combined with analysis of students' comments revealed four curricular themes:

- *Content.* The earlier version of this course was based on European classical music. Although this curriculum remains the standard for higher education, it simply does not engage a large percentage of contemporary students who listen to popular music and have grown up in an increasingly diverse multicultural society. The transformed course uses ethnicity as a central organizing principle to trace the development of popular musics such as blues, jazz, country, Tejano, Cajun, and so on from their roots in the ethnic traditions of a specific immigrant group to their development into a uniquely American music.
- *Empowering Students to Be Architects of Their Own Learning.* The baseline course had been taught in the sequential, passive, pyramidal approach of traditional higher education. The transformed course allows students to select from a variety of activities to construct their own learning in ways that meet their individual learning styles and personal interests. Although all students do core readings and work sheets, they build on this common foundation by choosing activities from a varied menu that includes concert reports, museum and historical site visits, attendance at cultural events, Web quests, film observations, book reports, independent research, interviews, and participation in on-line academic forums.
- *Multimedia Instruction (Including On-Line).* The baseline course had been taught in the traditional lecture face-to-face format. The transformed course uses blended delivery in which students select, on an ongoing and flexible basis, where they want to be on a continuum from traditional face-to-face learning activities to entirely Web-based activities.
- *Authentic Assessment.* The baseline course had used traditional, objective, and subjective in-class testing. The transformed course uses a point accrual system in

which, within clearly articulated guidelines for both quantity and quality, students earn their final grades by submitting multiple and varied artifacts demonstrating their learning.

I investigated these themes using both quantitative and qualitative research methodologies. Quantitative data included enrollment trends, demographic characteristics, and students' success and retention rates over six years. To generate qualitative data, I conducted surveys, used various classroom assessment techniques, and enlisted 15 "student investigators" selected through a controlled random selection process to probe deeper into the learning process. The data I collected have been a gold mine of information that I continue to excavate and that lead to new course strategies. For example, one of the most interesting pieces of information was the increasingly large percentage of students of color in comparison with white students. In fall 1995, the class comprised 66% white students and 33% students of color. By fall 1999, the ratio had inverted, and students of color constituted 67%. I was thrilled with this statistic until I pulled apart the various race/ethnicities to find that there was a slight but steady downward trend in black students. Additionally, black students were at highest risk for not completing the course (only a 46% success rate, whereas black students had a 76% success rate collegewide).

I surmised that a contributing factor was probably the discomfort and resentment black students might feel at hearing a white woman discuss black history, music, and social experience. As a solution, I engaged as a teaching partner a black professor who specializes in African-American music and the historical context in which that music developed. I am going to track this trend to see whether it will make a difference, but from the qualitative data, it seems to be working. For example, one African-American student wrote, "There was so much going on in my life that I hated all of my classes, but not this one. . . . This was the only class that I wanted to go to every day."

What Did I Learn From the Creation of the Course Portfolio?

The greatest challenge for me was figuring out how best to organize and present the information. Ultimately (and after many different drafts), I decided to organize the portfolio into four major sections. "The Project" provides an overview and contains answers to the questions who, what, where, why, when, and how of the course portfolio. "The Data" consists of a series of linked PDFs so that readers can access and download information such as syllabi, tests, student comments, and enrollment trends. "The Summary" provides a brief narrative of the project, with essential information and results. The final section, "Transformation Themes," organizes the analysis into the four curricular themes identified earlier (content, empowering students, multimedia, and assessment) and then addresses these themes in four stages: baseline course, analysis, transformed course, and significant research and findings. Toward the end I added an additional component, "Issue Bin," in which I identified enduring concerns associated with that section and provided an interactive opportunity for portfolio readers to contribute their comments.

How Did the Electronic Aspects of the Course Portfolio Hinder or Help Success?

In several ways, going electronic made the course portfolio more difficult. For example, to make it electronic, every document needed first to be created as a Word or graphics file and then converted to HTML and positioned in a series of linked Web pages. This process of creation and conversion was very time-consuming and, I am sure, at least doubled the work. I was very fortunate to have had Toru Iiyoshi, director of Carnegie's Knowledge Media Lab, provide guidance on the content and be responsible for turning the materials into the Web version. Once created, an electronic site requires constant maintenance and updating if it is to remain viable — all of which not only requires knowledge of new technologies and a significant time commitment but also is physically hazardous for someone like myself who already spends a considerable amount of time on the computer and suffers from technology-based repetitive stress syndrome.

To create an appealing site requires visual literacy that includes not only aesthetics but also good choices about what verbal information is most effectively replaced by graphics.

The construction of an electronic course portfolio poses other challenges. I am accustomed to thinking in the linear mode of print media. Because of the multilayering and navigational options of the Web, constructing documents suitable for this environment forced me to think in a nonlinear manner. It also required brevity: There is only so much information that fits on a single Web page, and one needs to minimize the number of linked Web pages because the portfolio reader's computer must go back to the server to retrieve them. This back and forth process interrupts, slows down, and potentially aggravates the reader. And there is the gnawing fear that this constant distilling for near "sound bite" simplicity sacrifices significant depth, accuracy, and nuance. Finally, Web site construction requires attention to visual appeal to sustain readers' interest. To create an appealing site requires visual literacy that includes not only aesthetics but also good choices about what verbal information is most effectively replaced by graphics. For example, although Toru and I had together created an informative site, initial readers felt that the entry page was too verbal, confusing, and uninviting. At this stage, having input from a professional Web designer was extremely helpful to improve the design of the Web site's welcoming page.

Certainly, many of these negatives have their flip side. For example, I suspect that logical, linear thinking can only be enhanced and enriched by the creative connections and "genius solution" flashes of insight that come from nonlinear thinking. In this era of information overload, it may be important to keep distilling information to its essentials. If we wish to continue to communicate effectively in the contemporary environment (especially with our students who have come of age in a visual and digital milieu), we may need to constantly update our visual literacy and our technological knowledge.

The electronic portfolio has other benefits. First, the Web has emerged as the current communication medium of choice. By creating my portfolio on-line, I had the glorious self-satisfaction that I was up to date with contemporary trends. Second, the multimedia capabilities provide a much richer and more complete picture of the course, because graphics and video and audio clips allow nuances impossible to achieve through conventional print media. In addition, I could make accessible to readers an extensive number and variety of documents through PDFs that would have been much too cumbersome as print attachments. Third, through the multilayered and navigational qualities of the Web, readers can customize and hence pursue efficiently those aspects of my course portfolio in which they are specifically interested. Finally, the Web-based electronic portfolio allows me an exportability and interactivity that paper portfolios simply cannot possess. The portfolio for this course has already attracted attention all over the country, and I no longer need to say, "I'll mail you information." Because of the electronic portfolio and its location on the World Wide Web, readers can investigate numerous aspects of my course at any time they wish and with minimum additional effort on my part.

How Has the Course Portfolio Helped Students?

Again, I need to separate the course portfolio from the electronic course portfolio. There is no question in my mind that the thoughtful and reflective analysis of my course was, and continues to be, highly beneficial to my students. But I was already doing that during the five years of course transformation that antedated the portfolio. The added value of the course portfolio was that it moved me beyond intuition and anecdote to a culture of evidence. For example, now when skeptical colleagues challenge my course's popularity because it is "easy," I have an informed response. The course portfolio also created a framework that organized the investigation in such a way that I was forced to gather data that *did* teach me things that I did not know. Although I had a general sense that enrollment was growing and that racial and ethnic diversity was increasing, I did not know the specifics until the portfolio framework required that I investigate it. Students have been helped because, as a result of this information, I have identified new interventions that I hope will improve instruction.

The electronic aspect of the course portfolio is less obvious, but I can see at least three advantages for students. First, constructing the Web-based portfolio has forced me to learn to think in the digital and visual ways that I believe dominate many of my students' ways of seeing and knowing. Narrowing the gap between us must certainly help clarify communication and enrich their learning. Second, I plan to use the Web-based portfolio to provide students with an easily accessible and much richer "picture" of my course than I can currently provide them with the conventional paper course syllabus. Third, the public nature of the course portfolio has put me in touch with teachers of similar courses, enabling us to share materials and strategies that strengthen and enrich all of our courses.

Conclusion

Would I do it again? Absolutely. When I was finished, I felt that the portfolio really did provide a framework to analyze, capture, and represent the reality of the course transformation. And, like all good research, it raised issues that pointed me toward additional research. For example, in fall 2000, I took much of the information I have learned from the course portfolio and applied it to a resurrected version of my old course on Western European classical music, planning to investigate to what extent the three noncontent curricular interventions (empowering students, multimedia delivery, and more authentic assessment) will affect students' enrollment and engagement in the original baseline course. I will construct another electronic course portfolio to document and analyze this process. An issue that is still being explored is the capacity of the portfolio to communicate clearly and significantly with readers. I feel hopeful that the portfolio is effective in this area, although it is something that I will be able to assess only after I have shared the portfolio with different audiences.

One thing remains clear: Six years ago I found myself wondering whether trying to teach today's students had become my worst nightmare. Most of the students were different not only from me but from one another — in race and ethnicity, in their preparation for college education, in the music they listened to, in their world view. Transforming my course into one that bridged the gaps while not compromising academic integrity seemed an impossible dream. Too young to retire, however, I began the process of change. My electronic course portfolio attempted to analyze and document that transformation. The analysis has perhaps raised as many questions as it has answered, but I believe I am moving in the right direction. Teaching no longer feels like an "unholy alliance" but a healthy and invigorating partnership in which my students, colleagues, and I work together to achieve more powerful learning.

Notes

1. A "Carnegie Scholar" is a participant in The Pew National Fellowship Program for Carnegie Scholars, one component of The Carnegie Academy for the Scholarship of Teaching and Learning (CASTL). The other two components of CASTL are a program for scholarly societies and the AAHE-directed Campus Program, the latter open to all campuses that foster the scholarship of teaching and learning. CASTL is a major initiative of The Carnegie Foundation for the Advancement of Teaching; for more information, visit http://www.carnegiefoundation.org/CASTL.

2. My course portfolio is located at http://kml2.carnegiefoundation.org/gallery/ebarkley/index.html. It was developed as part of my work with the higher education program of CASTL. I was responsible for conceiving of the project, conducting the research, compiling the documents, and writing the Web site text. Toru Iiyoshi, director of Carnegie's Knowledge Media Laboratory, provided guidance on the content and was responsible for turning the materials into the Web version. Carnegie Senior Scholars Tom Hatch and Pat Hutchings gave important feedback in the later stages of the process. From Foothill College, Kurt Hueg, Robin Reynolds, Janet Covey, Mike Sult, and Paul Aguilar assisted in acquiring digital materials and in certain aspects of site design.

Wired for Trouble? Creating a Hypermedia Course Portfolio

by T. Mills Kelly

My course portfolio is a direct outgrowth of, and therefore inextricably linked to, the research project I conducted during the 1999-2000 academic year during my tenure as a Carnegie Scholar.[1] That project is an investigation of the influence of hypermedia learning resources on student learning in introductory history courses. When I began the project, I wanted to better understand how the introduction of hypermedia into the survey course changed students' understanding of course content, whether hypermedia improved or detracted from students' ability to acquire a greater facility with historical methods, and whether using hypermedia might give students new or different insights into something we historians like to call "historical thinking."

When I first conceptualized the research project that the portfolio describes, I had never heard of course portfolios — or of the scholarship of teaching and learning, for that matter. Instead, I hoped to answer a question that began to vex me in spring 1998. That question was posed to me by a colleague at Grinnell College, Dan Kaiser, who asked me one day how it was that I knew using the Web in my teaching was improving students' understanding of the past. In retrospect, Dan's question was an obvious one but one that I simply had not asked when I began migrating my courses onto the Web the year before. Given the amount of time and effort being consumed by the "ramping up" of my courses, I suddenly began to worry that I might be spending many, many hours creating hypermedia for my courses to no avail, or worse, that my students might actually be learning less — or at least not as well — when they encountered the past in my courses via hypermedia.

Because I did not know the answer to Dan's question, I did what any good historian would do: I went to the library and began to search for answers to my question. When I began that search, I assumed that historians had already spent a fair amount of time thinking through these matters and that at least a few would have published something. Instead, what I found was that, with the exception of Samuel S. Wineburg, an educational researcher at the University of Washington who has spent his career thinking and writing about how students understand history, not only did historians not know anything

T. Mills Kelly is an assistant professor of history at George Mason University and director of education programs at the Center for History and New Media. He developed his portfolio (http://www2.tltc.ttu.edu/kelly/Pew/Portfolio/welcome.htm) during his year as a Carnegie Scholar.

about how hypermedia might influence student learning in our courses, they also do not know very much about how students learn in those courses at all. To be sure, an extensive literature exists on teaching history, but that literature falls almost entirely into two categories — musings on what ought to be taught in history courses or extended discussions of "best practices" in the teaching of history. Only Wineburg has investigated how students acquire a deeper understanding of the past, and one of his more interesting conclusions is that historical thinking is a fundamentally "unnatural act."

When confronted with this lacuna in the literature, I became somewhat depressed, especially because it seemed to me that if I were going to answer my question, I could not do so within the framework of some larger discussion about historical learning. The following year I was fortunate enough to become a Carnegie Scholar, and, with the assistance and encouragement of The Carnegie Foundation for the Advancement of Teaching and my colleagues in the Carnegie Scholars program, I learned a tremendous amount about how students learn and how scholars who are not educational researchers or cognitive psychologists by training can pursue answers to questions such as mine. At the same time, I learned about course portfolios as a means of representing the scholarship of teaching to a broader audience, so I decided to create a portfolio. Because my project is all about hypermedia, it was only natural that my portfolio would be a hypermedia document.

What Problems Emerged?

The first problem I faced when I began to think about how I might create a course portfolio was figuring out exactly what mine might look and feel like. Because those of us creating course portfolios are still defining the parameters of an emerging genre, it is still unclear what a course portfolio ought to look like, what it ought to include, and how one might go about creating one. Of course, this lack of clarity is an advantage in one sense, because it means that there is no wrong way to create a course portfolio. This same freedom comes at a price, however, because it means that I had to make my own decisions about what ought to be included in mine without any sense of where the limits might be, what might be appropriate to include, and what was better omitted.

A second difficulty I faced was determining how best to present the information I was collecting to my most important audience — other historians. As a group, we historians are a skeptical bunch, obsessing as much about what we do not find in an archive as we do about what we actually locate. For this reason, I knew that if my portfolio were to resonate with my colleagues, I had to provide them with everything I learned, including the data I had collected, without cluttering up the portfolio site. If I required readers to plow through several hundred pages of text to find out about my research, the project was doomed. Here, the Web offers possibilities that a more linear text does not, because with hypertext the reader can move easily between various portions of a site, following his or her own path through the material. Any visitor to my site can read it either way — as a linear text or as a hypertext.

My decision to provide the visitor with everything from my course — syllabus, assignments, samples of students' work I had analyzed, students' every survey, evaluation, and comment — also required me to consider certain risks. Teaching is normally a very private activity, not only closed off from peers by the four walls of the classrooms but also often jealously guarded behind the wall of academic freedom. A course portfolio such as mine that exposes the entire course to public view tears down those walls and invites the entire world to pass judgment on my teaching. Because not everyone is in a professional situation like mine that makes it possible to be quite so open about what is happening in his or her classroom, the level of disclosure evident in my portfolio is not for everyone.

Finally, I faced the difficulty that everyone who is not a Web designer by training faces when creating a relatively large and complex Web site, namely the dual constraints of time and ignorance. Everything I know about Web design I have learned through the brute force method, that is, by picking up a manual and puzzling out for myself how to get the HTML to do what I want it to do. Because creation of a Web site requires one to be author, editor, designer, and publisher all at once, my lack of formal training in site design meant that I would take longer to create my portfolio as a hypermedia site than as a linear text. Moreover, because at this writing the scholarship of teaching and learning is still an emerging discipline, how the finished product would "count" in my department's calculations about tenure and promotion was unclear, so I had to be mindful of the trade-offs between time spent on the portfolio and time spent on my more conventional disciplinary scholarship.

I had to be mindful of the trade-offs between time spent on the portfolio and time spent on my more conventional disciplinary scholarship.

What Did I Learn From It?

For several reasons, the creation of my course portfolio has been one of the more professionally enriching activities I have engaged in over the past few years. The decision to represent the results of my investigations into student learning in a hypermedia course portfolio forced me to concentrate my attention not only on technical questions about how the portfolio would look and feel when it was complete but also, more important, on the very nature of hypermedia. Before this effort, my most important concern when creating course materials had been how to make them easily accessible and visually pleasing. But as I began this project, which centers on how hypermedia influence learning, I had to think about how my course site and the portfolio site would interact with each other as part of a larger whole. This issue, which might seem on the surface to be a question of design, is actually more than that, because thinking about it forced me to consider not only how my students were thinking in the class but also how my colleagues who might visit the Web site would think about the class, about my research, and about the scholarship of teaching and learning as an emerging discipline. I had to make many decisions about look and feel, about navigation, about inclusion or exclusion of information, and about which media to use to make a certain point. As I worked my way through each question, I had to think much more deeply about my own discipline, about what the scholarship of teaching and learning is or is becoming, and about the multiple audiences for my work and how it might resonate with them. In other words, I faced a series of decisions that overlapped with those we all face when we prepare to publish the results of our disciplinary research but that also included many new questions I had not considered previously.

A second lesson I learned from the creation of my portfolio is the importance of transparency in moving the scholarship of teaching and learning from its status as an emerging field to something like an established discipline. Not that long ago something called "women's studies" began to emerge on campuses across the country, but at the time few people were convinced it would ever become an established discipline. Today, there are women's studies departments at most major universities as well as at many more smaller institutions, and when someone says "women's studies" we have a ready-made image of what that discipline looks like. For the scholarship of teaching and learning to be as successful, its practitioners must open up the private space of their classrooms in ways that are mindful of the ethical considerations where students are concerned. The course portfolio is one of several ideal vehicles for creating that sort of transparency. My research project includes among its conclusions a prediction of the demise of the traditional history survey course in the very near future — certainly a conclusion that a number of my colleagues will disagree with. For me to predict such a substantive change in the way introductory history courses are taught at most colleges and universities without full transparency would be no better than the generally shallow polemicizing of the punditocracy that rules Sunday morning television. By contrast, my course portfolio offers those who want to engage the questions I raise a means to investigate my research, to read the data I collected from their own perspective, and to draw their own conclusions — which may be quite different from my own. Such alternate readings of my research offer the possibility of opening up a discussion about the nature of the survey course that is based on research into student learning, not simply opinion about what seems to offer the greatest potential to improve student learning. I hope that such a discussion will convince at least a few of my colleagues to conduct similar research along lines they think are equally or more promising than mine. If they do, we will know a great deal more than we do right now about the issues I raise in the portfolio.

A third lesson I learned in the creation of my portfolio is that there truly is no right or wrong way to create a course portfolio. The objectives of my research project are rather more grandiose than what I expect most practitioners have, so it is very important to be mindful of what the final product might look like before one embarks on such an endeavor. Were I simply hoping to document a teaching practice or to think more critically about one aspect of a course, my portfolio would be much less complex, although I suspect it would still retain a number of the elements it currently includes. Because I spent a fair amount of time at the beginning of the project thinking carefully about what I expected the portfolio to look like, I think in the end it was easier to create than I had expected it to be.

Where Do I Want to Go From Here?

Now that I have been through the process of creating a portfolio, I expect to write portfolios for all the courses I teach. Because I hope to continue my research on the influence of hypermedia on student learning, each portfolio will include at least some attention to this question and will therefore become part of some as yet undefined hypertext that weaves all my portfolios together. At the same time, these future portfolios will concentrate on other questions that vex me, such as how the use of film in teaching the history of modern East Central Europe influences student learning in that course. Certainly, I do not expect future portfolios to be as large or complex as the one I have just completed, in part because I believe it is possible for more limited projects to make important contributions to the scholarship of teaching and learning, but also because the questions I hope to address in future iterations of my course portfolios strike me as less complex than the one that is at the heart of my current project.

No matter what happens, course portfolios have become and will continue to be an essential part of my teaching practice and my scholarship in the field of teaching and learning.

I also hope to expand my Carnegie research project to include an investigation of students' interaction with hypermedia in history classes at other institutions, but such an expansion of my research depends entirely on the success of various grant applications. For the scholarship of teaching and learning to emerge as a discipline, such funding is absolutely essential, not just for me but also for the growing body of scholars engaged in research on teaching and learning. Significant scholarship rarely takes place late in the evening and on weekends: Only when the scholar has the time to think through the implications of his or her project, to develop sufficient data, and to engage in thoughtful reflection on those data will we see significant advances in the scholarship of teaching and learning. One way that I am attempting to deal with the time-consuming nature of creating course portfolios is by exploring new ways to feed students' work into a portfolio template more seamlessly so that my own task load declines. With new ways of incorporating students' work, I will be able to continue to provide the high level of documentation that is available in my current portfolio.

Finally, beginning in fall 2000, I planned to engage students in an honors section of Western Civilization in creating a course portfolio for the course they are taking. I want to know whether and how participation in creating a portfolio might enhance their learning. As I wrote this essay, I had not worked my way through all the ethical and practical considerations of this new effort, and so I cannot say with certainty exactly what that student-created portfolio might look like. Nor can I say whether I should retain parts of the process for myself. I have more questions than answers, but I think the prospect of students' participation in writing a course portfolio (as opposed to a learning portfolio) is an exciting one. No matter what happens, course portfolios have become and will continue to be an essential part of my teaching practice and my scholarship in the field of teaching and learning.

Note

1. A "Carnegie Scholar" is a participant in The Pew National Fellowship Program for Carnegie Scholars, one component of The Carnegie Academy for the Scholarship of Teaching and Learning (CASTL). The other two components of CASTL are a program for scholarly societies and the AAHE-directed Campus Program, the latter open to all campuses that foster the scholarship of teaching and learning. CASTL is a major initiative of The Carnegie Foundation for the Advancement of Teaching; for more information, visit http://www.carnegiefoundation.org/CASTL.

Ambassadors With Portfolios: Recommendations

by Daniel P. Tompkins

Because they can provide deep and nuanced evidence of effective teaching, portfolios can contribute significantly to summative reviews. Because they invite peers to engage in constructive and collaborative discussion of student learning, portfolios are a key tool in formative reviews. Finally, electronic media have enabled a display and exchange of information that is both immediate and unmediated. In short, electronic portfolios are powerful but also, if misused, threatening.

Institutions

The first steps in building a faculty portfolio, whether for summative or formative purposes, are often the most difficult: creating a template or model and choosing what to include. With electronic portfolios, the challenge can be even greater, especially if faculty must start from scratch. And without agreement among institutions, departments, and individuals about how a portfolio will be used, faculty are unlikely to engage in the process with the enthusiasm and sincerity that make it worthwhile.

Institutions, then, can advance the development of faculty portfolios by:
- *Developing templates* that faculty can use and adapt.
- *Offering hands-on faculty development workshops.*
- *Ensuring that technical support services will assist in building the portfolio.* Portfolio design is not merely an aesthetic venture: Good visual presentation of graphical information is essential to a successful portfolio. Technical support should include graphic design.
- *Establishing a network of faculty.* A strong support network can reduce faculty feelings of isolation and pointlessness.

Daniel P. Tompkins, editor of this section on faculty portfolios, is director of the Intellectual Heritage Program at Temple University. He coordinated the Temple University team in the AAHE Peer Review Project.

- *Exploring the use of institutional data.* The University of Colorado publishes and updates its student evaluations at http://www.colorado.edu/pba/fcq/by_inst/ index.html. This example shows institutional information that could be incorporated into faculty portfolios. We have just begun to drill down into such data in building local and individual portfolios.
- *Setting up procedures for feedback* on all portfolios, whether summative or formative. Faculty need feedback to know that their work is not being ignored and is being judged with dialogue, not in the "managed professionals" syndrome. Faculty must trust the process.
- *Getting agreement with key faculty units* (faculty union, senate, department chairs) on how portfolios will be used.

Departments

Portfolios are often most effective when shared with or reviewed by knowledgeable professionals, which means one's colleagues in a department or, if used beyond the institution, in a discipline. They are most effective when used with the goal of department-wide pedagogical improvement. Conversely, sharing portfolios can contribute to departmental unity by moving a discussion from the daily fare of interfaculty dialogue to the new topic of student learning.

Feedback without fear is essential in constructing departmental portfolios, particularly for untenured faculty. Developing a culture of interactivity about teaching and learning, as mentioned in this book's introduction, sets the scene for trust and learning among departmental colleagues.

Individuals

Portfolios are often viewed as "reporting" tools. Portfolios are also instruments of inquiry and intellection, used by a faculty member to pose questions and probe for answers. There is every reason for individuals seeking to improve their teaching to build portfolios on their own, whether or not an institution requires them. Portfolio creators can focus on a particular question or topic in a course, thereby continuing their own learning about student learning. Portfolios offer possibilities for intensifying the deep learning of both student and faculty member.

Institutional Portfolios

Linking Learning, Improvement, and Accountability: An Introduction to Electronic Institutional Portfolios

by Susan Kahn

Electronic institutional portfolios, the newest variation on the portfolio concept in higher education, are a logical development. Over the past 15 years, research and national discussion on higher education have emphasized the role of the entire curriculum in contributing to students' intellectual and personal development. Many institutions and their faculties have become more deliberate about designing curricula and employing pedagogies that help students work toward higher-order learning outcomes over the course of an entire baccalaureate or graduate degree program. As colleges and universities have turned to assessing the impact of the entire educational experience on students' learning, recapturing this larger work of the institution in the emerging medium of electronic portfolios began to make sense — for many of the reasons it makes sense for the work of individual students and faculty members: the accessibility of the Web environment, the ability to present new kinds of evidence of teaching and learning in this environment, and the ability to represent ongoing learning and improvement.

Like individual student and faculty portfolios, institutional portfolios feature authentic work and evidence in a context of learning, reflection, and assessment. Like other portfolios, they can serve purposes of both internal improvement and external accountability. But institutional portfolios differ from individual ones in that they address these purposes at the level of the whole institution. As such, they present a greater range of evidence and serve a different array of audiences. The process of developing an institutional portfolio also makes specific demands on an institution. Finding the right people to be involved in the process, to lead it, and to ensure that the portfolio is integrated with other, ongoing initiatives on student learning, assessment, and effectiveness is critical to the success of an institutional portfolio.

Susan Kahn, editor of this section on institutional portfolios, is national director of the Urban Universities Portfolio Project and director of programs and planning in the Office for Professional Development at Indiana University Purdue University Indianapolis. She has written and spoken extensively on electronic institutional portfolios.

The essays that follow in this section describe the work of two universities on developing, organizing, and using electronic institutional portfolios; the role of institutional research and data in institutional portfolios; an innovative variation on the electronic institutional portfolio — an electronic department or program portfolio; and the use of portfolios for institutional accreditation by a regional accrediting association. This introduction addresses basic issues and questions about electronic institutional portfolios: what they are, why an institution might want to create one, what might be included in one, and what issues to consider when beginning work on an electronic institutional portfolio.

What Is an Institutional Portfolio?

An institutional portfolio is a focused selection of authentic work, data, and analysis that demonstrates institutional accountability and serves as a vehicle for institution-wide reflection, learning, and improvement. Because institutional portfolios are so new, this definition is a work in progress, meant to provide a context for this introduction and the essays that follow but not intended as a last word. As we shall see later in this introduction and in this section, existing portfolios take a wide variety of forms and may include very different types of information and evidence; uses and applications for institutional portfolios, especially electronic ones, are in an early stage of development; and audiences for current institutional portfolios vary and may be narrowly or broadly described.

Like individual student and faculty portfolios, institutional portfolios feature authentic work and evidence in a context of learning, reflection, and assessment.

But the definition does incorporate some of the common elements and purposes of those institutional portfolios developed to date. For example, institutional portfolios aim to capture information and evidence from across the entire institution and to assess and improve effectiveness institution-wide. They focus strongly on student learning and are intended to demonstrate accountability for learning, even if only to one external audience (for example, the institution's regional accrediting association). In some cases, such as the portfolios created at Georgia State University and California State University Sacramento, they have also been deliberately designed as data and planning resources that campus leaders can draw on to make strategic decisions based on evidence. And, in some instances, they have served as important catalysts for institution-wide discussion, reflection, and improvement initiatives: The essays that follow on the portfolios developed at Indiana University Purdue University Indianapolis (IUPUI) and Portland State University discuss the dramatic impact of these universities' portfolio on the entire campus.

Web-based institutional portfolios are distinct from a campus's general informational Web site in several respects. First, unlike a campus's main Web site, the institutional portfolio is not designed as a repository of comprehensive campus information but focuses on several well defined themes or questions. Second, while most institutional portfolios communicate with external constituents of higher education, the focus of this communication is on evidence-based information about institutional effectiveness and accountability — not on "public relations" in the usual sense. At the same time, a Web-based electronic institutional portfolio may be linked to the campus's main Web site at many points for visitors who want information beyond that included in the portfolio itself.

At this writing, well developed models of electronic institutional portfolios are relatively few. (URLs for several current portfolios are provided at the end of the relevant essays in this section.) Most current portfolios were begun under two initiatives funded by The Pew Charitable Trusts: the Urban Universities Portfolio Project (UUPP)[1] and the Integrated Accreditation Standards Project of the Western Association of Schools and Colleges (WASC). As institutional portfolios are increasingly accepted by regional accrediting organizations in place of or along with self-studies, and as additional uses and audiences develop, the number of portfolios is certain to expand in the coming decade.

Why Electronic Institutional Portfolios?

The current interest in electronic institutional portfolios arises from their capacity to respond to pressing issues confronting higher education. Universities and colleges have undertaken electronic portfolios for four main reasons:

- to demonstrate accountability,
- to highlight institutional distinctiveness,
- to stimulate internal improvement, and
- to put the spotlight on student learning.

Demonstrating accountability

Today's higher education institutions are accountable to the concerns of a growing array of constituencies. The litany is familiar by now: Accrediting organizations seek evidence that the institution is setting and meeting standards and, increasingly, focus on issues of assessment and educational effectiveness. State governments institute performance measures and, in some cases, performance-based funding for public universities. Employers, as well as prospective students and parents, want assurance that graduates have mastered fundamental skills. For institutions with local or regional missions, local and regional constituencies want to know how effectively the institution is addressing their priorities.

These recent calls for enhancing accountability in higher education have increasingly emphasized performance and results — as opposed to such traditional criteria as prestige, selectivity, and resources — to ensure institutional quality and effectiveness. Web-based institutional portfolios are not only public and highly accessible to stakeholders; they are also especially useful tools for communicating evidence-based information demanded by higher education stakeholders. For example, the electronic environment allows for presentation of evidence using various media — visual, aural, and written. Unlike a written report, which can accommodate only a limited amount of information and only so many examples, the electronic format permits portfolio visitors to choose from a wide array of different types of evidence, ranging from authentic examples of individual student and faculty work to summative data on institutional trends.

The ability of portfolios to respond to a more evidence- and performance-based concept of accountability and quality has already attracted the interest of several regional accrediting associations. In fact, regional accreditors are emerging as a primary audience for institutional portfolios. Judie Wexler's essay in this section discusses WASC's experiments with using portfolios for accreditation and the association's recent decision to require institutional portfolios rather than traditional self-studies. The North Central Association of Colleges and Schools, the Middle States Association of Colleges and Schools, and the New England Association of Schools and Colleges are also exploring the potential of portfolios as alternatives or adjuncts to self-studies.

Use of electronic institutional portfolios to respond to the concerns of other external stakeholder groups is at an early, but promising, stage. Several institutions in the UUPP that have shown their portfolio to community groups to demonstrate their university's impact on improving the community's quality of life have received enthusiastic responses. Portland State University has presented its portfolio to the Oregon Board of Regents to highlight the university's urban mission and its effectiveness in carrying out this mission. Several universities, such as the University of Illinois Chicago, are experimenting with using electronic portfolios to provide substantive information on learning and effectiveness to current and prospective students. State legislatures and higher education commissions are another group that may well find electronic portfolios useful for gauging institutional performance of public universities.

As uses for accreditation and other accountability purposes become more clearly defined and more solidly established, the ability of the electronic environment to respond flexibly to the interests of different people and groups will make it an increasingly attractive vehicle for communicating with multiple publics. Rather than developing an array of different reports for its various constituencies, a university can design a single Web site that allows visitors to follow the path that best suits their particular priorities and purposes. If the institution wishes to add a new group of stakeholders, portals and pages can be created without a wholesale revision of the entire portfolio site. When institutional assessment and improvement initiatives yield new information about learning and effectiveness, the portfolio can be expanded to accommodate the additional material. In short, as higher education institutions and their various stakeholders continue to focus on evidence and performance, electronic institutional portfolios may prove to be the most convenient and compelling medium for demonstrating institutional and educational effectiveness.

Highlighting institutional distinctiveness

The growing interest in accountability among higher education stakeholders comes, not coincidentally, at a time when higher education institutions are becoming increasingly diverse. New providers of higher education are proliferating, established institutions are consolidating resources in areas of strength or need, and on-line education is challenging traditional ideas about the very definition of a university or college. Students themselves are also becoming far more diverse, as older, working, minority, and first-generation students enter higher education at an accelerating rate.

In this environment, generic standards of quality based on traditional paradigms of higher education institutions and students are no longer appropriate for evaluating or comparing colleges and universities. For example, a criterion that makes sense for a selective liberal arts college, such as entering students' test scores, may make less sense for a public regional or community college that aims to provide access to higher education for first-generation or working students. The number of books in the library is hardly relevant in evaluating an on-line, distance education university, so long as the institution ensures that students have access to the information they need, wherever they may happen to be.

Because electronic institutional portfolios have no standard structure, they can be readily tailored to an institution's particular purposes and circumstances. This flexibility makes them especially useful for institutions with nontraditional or unique missions. Portfolios can be organized to direct attention to important areas of the mission and provide documentation of activities, outcomes, and efforts to improve in those areas. As such, portfolios provide an alternative to rating and ranking approaches that focus on prestige and resources and that rely on ideas about higher education that reflect an older paradigm.

In the UUPP, for example, six urban public universities have developed portfolios that capture their distinctive urban missions and accomplishments. Student learning and the implications of the urban context for learning are a major focus. Urban public universities typically have more nontraditional, diverse student bodies than other institutions, with very high proportions of commuter and transfer students. In these circumstances, what kinds of experiences and environments are most effective in engaging students in learning? How can the institution draw on the varied resources of the urban community to enrich learning? How can urban universities assess the impact of the education they provide for students who spend only their first or last two years there, or who take many years to complete a degree while also attending to work and family responsibilities? The UUPP portfolios explore these issues, document the institutions' efforts to address them, and present evidence for the effectiveness of these efforts. The particular missions and circumstances of the universities shape the portfolios, which ask audiences to evaluate institutional quality using criteria appropriate to those missions and circumstances.

Stimulating internal improvement

While electronic institutional portfolios have great potential to help colleges and universities portray their missions and demonstrate effectiveness to external publics, their potential as vehicles for internal improvement may be even greater. For example, a portfolio can become an integral component of an institution's efforts to develop assessment, strategic planning, and institutional effectiveness processes, as do the portfolios developed at California State University Sacramento and Georgia State University. These institutional portfolio sites focus on information and evidence that support and document planning, work under way to implement plans, efforts to measure and assess progress on planning priorities (which include improving student learning), and the results of these efforts. During the second year of its portfolio work, Georgia State took the additional step of creating a discussion area in its Web portfolio that invited faculty and staff cam-

Two portfolios that help drive the institution's internal improvement effort

www.csus.edu/portfolo/

www.gsu.edu/~wwwupp

puswide to provide feedback to the committee developing a new strategic plan for the campus.

Several other campuses have used institutional portfolio initiatives even more broadly, as occasions to bring together key people and groups on campus to think collaboratively about mission and to consider how particular activities, programs, and innovations complement one another and advance the mission — or fail to do so. In these instances, campuses have found that portfolio development can help build institutional identity and community, strengthen connections among units and initiatives, and develop and reinforce shared visions and commitments.

For example, during a UUPP site visit to Portland State University, members of PSU's Faculty Advisory Committee for the institutional portfolio commented that portfolio discussion and work have broadened their perspective on the institution beyond their own departments, helped them see the institution as a coherent whole, and shown them that the institution's mission is "real." Members noted that they were surprised by how much of the mission was "really" being carried out through various campus initiatives and by the way these activities complemented one another in supporting the mission and giving it depth and breadth. They added that work on the portfolio has helped them to bridge the gap between the institution's mission and their own everyday activities, to see how their individual work relates to the mission of the institution as a whole. In this instance, portfolio development became a vehicle for faculty and organizational development, deepening faculty members' understanding of and commitment to the institution's mission and their own roles within the institution.

Portfolio development can help build institutional identity and community, strengthen connections among units and initiatives, and develop and reinforce shared visions and commitments.

In addition, as mission, structures, and activities become more widely and cohesively understood across the institution and as portfolio developers gather documentation of effectiveness, unmet needs and areas for improvement become more readily apparent. For instance, as Sharon Hamilton reports later in this section, IUPUI's work on an institutional portfolio spurred a study of how the campus's six "principles of undergraduate learning" (PULs) are taught and assessed campuswide. The results of the study, included in the IUPUI portfolio, are helping to guide planning for curriculum and faculty development to ensure effective teaching and learning of the principles for all undergraduates.

Similarly, catalyzed by work on its institutional portfolio, the University of Illinois Chicago adopted a set of learning outcomes for the baccalaureate degree and is now incorporating the outcomes into curricula and developing appropriate assessment strategies. And at California State University Sacramento, work on an institutional portfolio led to the creation of a prototype for a department-level portfolio and to a new approach to program review more directly focused on student learning. Dean Dorn's essay in this sec-

Learning outcomes for a degree program were stimulated by this portfolio's development

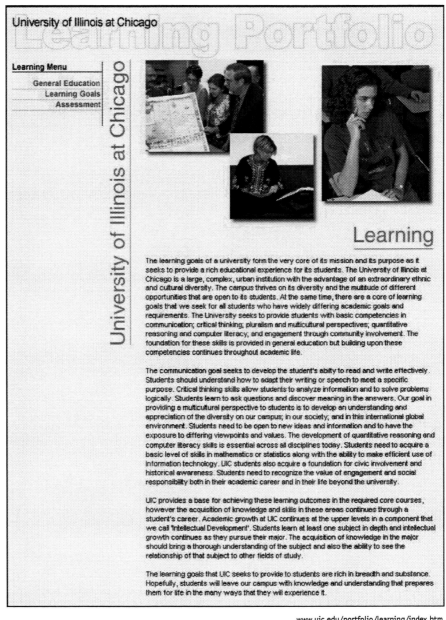

www.uic.edu/portfolio/learning/index.htm

tion discusses the department portfolio prototype and possible uses for a department portfolio.

As these instances illustrate, an institutional portfolio is more than a record of information and evidence; it also influences the policies, structures, and activities that it documents. The development of an institutional portfolio and the development of the evidence that goes into the portfolio are thus a cyclical process. As evidence is gathered for inclusion in the portfolio, gaps and weaknesses in the evidence or in the policies, structures, or activities being assessed are identified; ideally, necessary changes are made, assessment continues, and better, more complete evidence, or evidence of improvement, is generated for the portfolio.

Because of this cyclical, iterative nature, an institutional portfolio is never "finished." Portfolio development is not a discrete, one-time task but an ongoing system that allows a university to monitor and document its performance for internal and external stakeholders. An institutional portfolio Web site evolves continuously, demonstrating changes and improvements as they unfold over real time; the electronic environment is ideal for representing this ongoing evolution. Thus, the portfolio becomes both a vehicle for continuous institution-wide self-assessment and improvement, and a medium for communicating these efforts and their results to the institution's multiple internal and external publics.

Spotlighting student learning

The past decade's work on student, faculty, and course portfolios, including electronic ones, provides a wealth of models for documenting and exhibiting evidence for teaching and learning. Electronic institutional portfolios draw on these models to enrich the assessment and documentation of student learning across the whole institution. As such, institutional portfolios respond to both internal and external stakeholders' growing interest in educational effectiveness as well as to the shift in focus from teaching to learning (Barr & Tagg, 1995).

With the entire institution to draw from and with the multimedia capabilities of the electronic environment, the potential for displaying multiple types of evidence for learning in electronic institutional portfolios is enormous. In particular, the possibilities for showing primary or authentic materials that, as William Cerbin puts it, actually show (not just describe or explain) teaching and learning are vastly greater than in a paper report.

Videotaped portions of real class sessions, audio commentary by faculty and students, examples of students' written work, and samples of students' art work or students' work on the Web are a few examples of authentic evidence that might be included. Imagine a piece of student writing accompanied by video commentary by the student on what she learned from the assignment. Imagine the same writing sample accompanied by a video of the faculty member commenting on the student's work or explaining the rationale for the assignment. Such evidence that can give portfolio audiences an especially vivid and immediate sense of the work of students and faculty is a particularly valuable feature of electronic institutional portfolios.

In short, electronic institutional portfolios can use multiple media to present an array of qualitative and quantitative evidence that does justice to the complexity of teaching and learning. Just as teaching and course portfolios can document an individual faculty member's practice of the scholarship of teaching and learning, so institutional portfolios can display institution-wide scholarly inquiry and findings about teaching and learning. Pat Hutchings and Lee Shulman (1999) of The Carnegie Foundation for the Advancement of Teaching advocate just such an institution-level practice of the scholarship of teaching and learning; electronic institutional portfolios may well provide a starting point for this practice.

Getting Started: Key Questions

Given all the issues and materials that might be included in an electronic institutional portfolio, getting started can be a daunting task. Articulating specific purposes and audiences, the messages the university wants to convey to those audiences, and the ways the portfolio will be used by its audiences are essential to beginning productive work. With a succinct rationale in place, initial work might focus on the following six key questions:

- Who should be involved in developing the portfolio?
- What themes should the portfolio focus on?
- What kinds of documentation and evidence should be included?
- How should the portfolio be organized in the Web environment to communicate these themes to its audiences?
- How will the portfolio be related to the institution's main informational Web site?
- What resources will be required to develop and maintain the portfolio?

The essays by Sharon Hamilton and Kathi Ketcheson in this section discuss in detail how two institutions, Indiana University Purdue University Indianapolis and Portland State University, addressed these questions. The following general suggestions are based on these and other institutions' experiences with electronic portfolios.

Who should be involved in developing the portfolio?

The portfolios most successful as vehicles for internal improvement have been developed with wide involvement of key people and groups across the campus. Participation by (or regular consultation with) faculty governance bodies and with committees and groups engaged in assessment, teaching, and learning, curriculum development, and strategic planning is crucial to realizing genuine institutional learning, reflection, and improvement.

On the other hand, "assigning" portfolio development to a committee with other substantial work to do, even if that work is closely related to the portfolio initiative, has not been a successful approach to getting started. A more productive strategy has been to designate one or two carefully selected people — perhaps a respected senior faculty member and an administrator with expertise in assessment or data collection — to lead the effort, backed by a central working group of faculty and administrative leaders committed to working collaboratively and productively. Diverse perspectives, open-mindedness, and creativity may be more important to a successful effort than equal representation of all campus units.

A small, dedicated working group is particularly critical for developing the initial conceptual structure for the portfolio. Other groups, such as those suggested above, can be consulted or brought together at key points in the process to brainstorm about the main themes and focuses of the portfolio, to offer expertise about relevant sources of evidence, and to provide perspective on important campus issues and activities. Both Portland State University and IUPUI used this approach successfully. Later, once the overall structure of the portfolio is established, additional working groups can be convened to develop specific portions of the portfolio.

Portfolio developers should consider early on how and when they will involve external stakeholders. If the portfolio is to respond to the interests and priorities of its intended audiences, the perspectives of those audiences need to be considered at the outset. If stakeholders outside the academy are among the intended audiences, special care is necessary to avoid jargon and overly specialized language and to explain the purpose of the portfolio and the work it exhibits.

For these reasons, external stakeholders should be included early in the process of portfolio development and should be consulted regularly as the portfolio develops. Institutions have used a variety of strategies for involving stakeholders, including focus groups; presentations and discussions with key groups, such as external advisory boards and community organizations; and site visits that provide visitors the opportunity to review and give feedback on the portfolio. Again, both Portland State and IUPUI have experimented with a range of approaches to external stakeholders' participation; reports on them are included in Ketcheson's and Hamilton's essays in this section.

What themes should the portfolio focus on?

Because the portfolio's themes are its basic building blocks, all information, evidence, and exhibits in the portfolio should relate to them. The themes might be conceptualized as lines of inquiry that the institution wishes to pursue or arguments, with supporting evidence, that the institution wishes to develop. They may be drawn from components of the institutional mission statement, special priorities of the institution, elements in the institution's strategic plan, or some similar source that defines the institution's identity and key purposes. Because of the emphasis on assessment in most current institutional portfolios, teaching and learning generally make up one or more of the primary themes.

Whatever themes are chosen, they should be few in number and geared to the specific goals and audiences for the portfolio, with information and evidence carefully selected to provide a context of assessment, reflection, and improvement around each theme.

Typically, after beginning with many possible themes, institutions gradually narrow them to three to eight, depending on the institution's resources and purposes for the portfolio. Attempting to address too many themes in depth risks diluting the internal and external impact of the portfolio and can undermine the feasibility of the initiative.

For example, California State University Sacramento has organized its portfolio around the institution's eight "strategic planning themes," which include "teaching and learning." IUPUI's portfolio focuses on three main themes, including "effective student learning," selected to match the priorities of the campus as it redefines its mission and goals. As these campuses and others have found, organizing the portfolio around themes based on current planning and priorities helps ensure that portfolio work will be integrated with other, ongoing efforts to improve institutional effectiveness.

These portfolios are organized around themes: "strategic planning" for one and key questions for the other

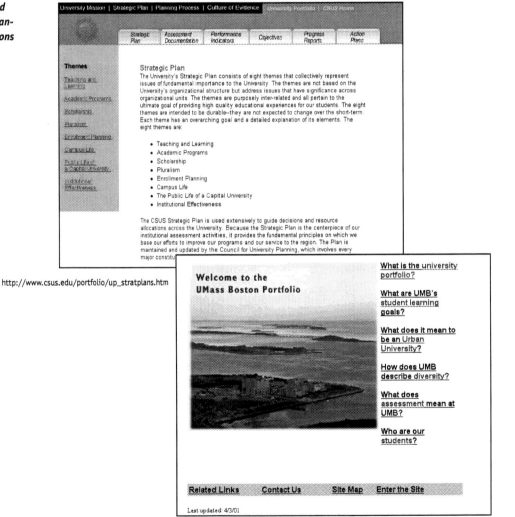

http://www.csus.edu/portfolio/up_stratplans.htm

http://www.umb.edu/about_umb/pew/

On the other hand, portfolios developed for very specific purposes or audiences may be built around themes that align with the main concerns of that audience. For example, portfolios intended for accreditation may include some mandated components and topics. Judie Wexler's essay in this section on the use of portfolios for accreditation addresses issues relevant to this more specialized type of portfolio.

Maintaining and communicating a focus on a few clear themes present special challenges for electronic institutional portfolios. A wide range of issues and materials must be narrowed; however, a visible portfolio initiative attracts people and groups on campus who will want their program or initiative represented. As a portfolio develops, deciding what to leave out and firmly adhering to this decision may well become more difficult than determining what to include. But keeping the portfolio focused is essential so that it does not become just another campus Web site with little impact on anyone in or out of the institution.

What kinds of documentation and evidence should be included?

Institutional portfolios aim to demonstrate that the institution is effective — that it sets goals, assesses results and progress toward the goals, and uses results of the assessment to improve. Institution- or other unit-wide data may be included to provide an overall context, while strategically chosen examples and exhibits of authentic evidence help portfolio visitors interpret the meaning and applications of the data in practice.

For example, the "effective student learning" theme of IUPUI's electronic portfolio includes a key section on the university's six "Principles of Undergraduate Learning," the

In demonstrating its effectiveness, IUPUI first sets context for its "Principles of Undergraduate Learning". . .

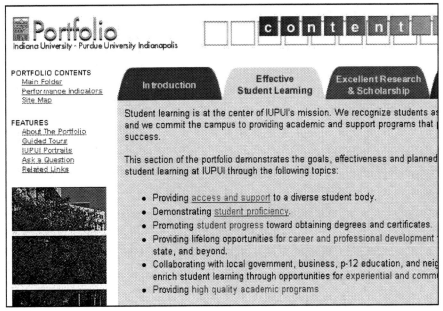

http://www.imir.iupui.edu/iupuifolio/frCont.asp

. . . explains how the principles are integrated into IUPUI's curricula, and how they are assessed . . .

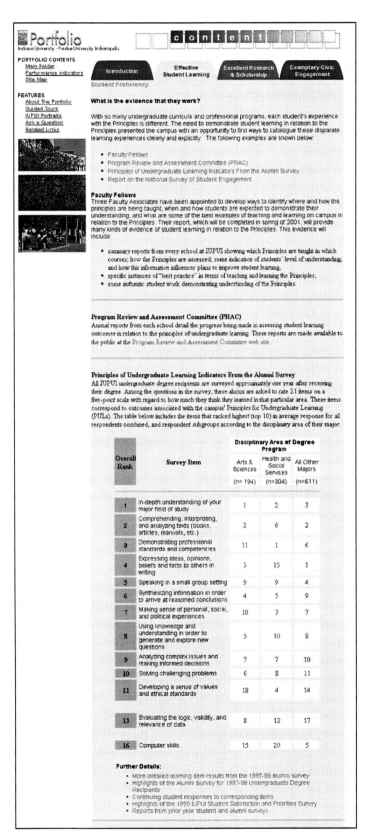

http://www.imir.iupui.edu/iupuifolio/frCont.asp

... explains each principle's requirements ...

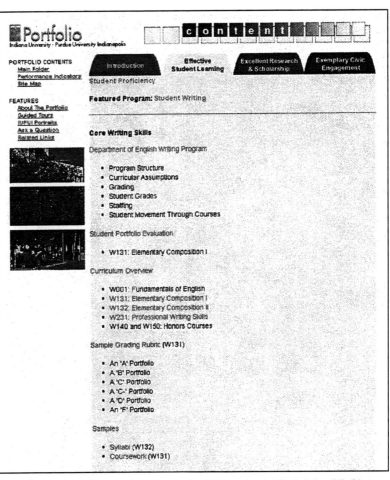

http://www.imir.iupui.edu/iupuifolio/frCont.asp

... and shows examples of achievement of the principles at varying levels

How Poor is Poor?

With the high costs of living, transportation, and medications, some families [Comment1] making too much money to qualify for Medicaid and food programs are barely scraping by. Subsequently, many elderly people who receive Medicare and Social Security [Comment2] are receiving too much money, as defined by the federal poverty line, to get help from public services for certain medical and transportation needs[Comment3]. This essay will focus on a southern California family of three, living in the area known as Silicon Valley, and the struggle [The student is setting the stage for further analytical development of these issues. Goal] living in that area. Jake Ginsky, a writer for the MOJO wire web site and author of *Hi...* class family by federal poverty level standards can have serious financial problems that can be attributed to where they live[Comment4]. This essay will also chronicle the plight of an elderly woman in urban Chicago who also receives too much money (from Social Security) to be eligible for certain medical and transportation costs. *Mama Might Have Been Better Off Dead*, a book written by Laurie Kaye Abraham, tells the story of this elderly lady named Cora Jackson[Comment5]. This evidence presented here will show how the current federal poverty level scale can be extremely misleading and can ultimately cause people to lose medical benefits and financial help with food[Comment6]

In *Mama Might Be Better Off Dead*, Abraham describes the trouble Mrs. Jackson has when trying to acquire a medical card for prescriptions. Mrs. Jackson receives Social Security and Medicare, however, the medical diapers she needs could only have been gotten through the Medicaid program. In order to qualify for Medicaid, Mrs. Jackson needs to "spend down" or pay $394.00 toward medical expenses each month in order to get a green card. Having to spend down a portion of an income is because, according to the poverty line, Mrs. Jackson makes plenty of money with her Social Security to cover her medical expenses. Mrs. Jackson was still struggling to make ends meet[Comment7]. When describing the spend down program, Abraham states, "The program was designed with good intentions, to provide some relief for people with medical costs that

http://www.imir.iupui.edu/iupuifolio/sabol/final.htm

core learning outcomes or goals that every undergraduate student is expected to achieve. Different areas of this part of its portfolio explain, with examples, what the principles are and how they are integrated into curricula and pedagogy across the campus and throughout baccalaureate programs. From these areas of the portfolio, a visitor to the site can link to descriptions of various studies and assessments of students' achievement of the principles, to examples of assessment instruments, to summary results of these assessments, and to discussions of initiatives under way to improve students' learning of the principles.

The portfolio visitor who drills down to Student Writing, part of Principle 1, Core Communication and Quantitative Skills, will find even more detailed information and examples. Under Core Writing Skills, the portfolio includes information on required writing courses, discussion of the assumptions about learning to write that undergird the writing curriculum, and sample course syllabi and assignments. Summary data on grade distribution and course enrollment patterns for the required writing sequence, descriptions of assessment of writing in the courses, grading rubrics with examples of students' writing at each grade level, and a student's essay with hyperlinks to comments by the instructor make up key exhibits and evidence in this section.

The ability of electronic portfolios to present multiple types of information, examples, and measures is one of their great advantages; they can present evidence of effectiveness from a variety of perspectives and capture the diversity and complexity of practices and outcomes. Moreover, different portfolio visitors are likely to be interested in different kinds of information and different degrees of detail. The electronic environment allows visitors to choose the type and amount of information they view (or hear or read); site visitors can, in effect, customize the information to suit their priorities and interests.

Even with the copious amount of information in the IUPUI portfolio, the relationship of each subsection and exhibit to the main themes of the portfolio remains clear. The portfolio's themes, purposes, and intended audiences guide the specific choices of materials and exhibits to include. And throughout the portfolio, the visitor finds hyperlinked narrative and analysis that provide a context for each exhibit and piece of information, explaining what is being presented and why. This framing narrative helps visitors understand what they are looking at and maintains the overall coherence of the portfolio.

A strength of the IUPUI portfolio is its wealth of authentic material. These authentic pieces of student and faculty work make the portfolio richer and more informative than other documentation of institutional accomplishment. The authentic examples bring realism and specificity to the claims made in the portfolio narrative and to the summative institutional data presented. At the heart of the portfolio, these examples are a key reason for its usefulness and effectiveness.

The sidebar opposite on documenting *learning outcomes* offers some suggestions for the kinds of information, evidence, and exhibits that might be included in a portfolio as evidence of institutional work on a learning outcome. The sidebar on this page offers suggestions for materials to document a major *strategic priority;* the example used here is student diversity. No single portfolio is likely to include all the kinds of items listed; rather, the lists are composites of materials found in a number of electronic institutional portfolios.

How should the portfolio be organized in the Web environment to communicate these themes to its audiences?

The portfolio should be organized in a way that makes navigating through it and finding specific information as easy as possible. While this principle may seem obvious, it is difficult to put into practice. The Web environment presents an infinite array of choices for organizing, storing, and presenting information. These choices become even more complex when a portfolio is intended for multiple stakeholders; different groups have varying degrees of familiarity with higher education, while specific concerns about accountability may be quite different from one group to another.

It is tempting, in this situation, simply to pile on the evidence and information in hopes that each visitor to the portfolio will find something of interest in the avalanche of materials. Another temptation is to create many overlapping organizing schemes for the portfolio — by categories of work (teaching, research, service), by organizational units (schools, colleges, departments), by audiences, by strategic planning goals — in hopes that visitors to the site will find some category that draws them into further exploration of the site.

Avoiding these temptations is critical if the portfolio is to communicate clearly to its audiences and if it is to remain a manageable long-term initiative for the institution. In the UUPP, several campuses began with complex, multilayered organizing schemes and simplified them later, in part responding to feedback from internal and external users of the portfolio. Starting with complexity and working toward simplicity may be an effective strategy. Creating a standard structure for the information presented in each major theme is another approach that helps portfolio visitors find specific information relatively quickly and easily.

The following general principles apply to structuring Web-based portfolios:

- *Stay within the selected themes for the portfolio, and keep the portfolio's main purposes and audiences in mind at all times.*
- *Remember that the aim of the portfolio is not to portray or evaluate every program and aspect of the institution but to convey a few clear ideas or pursue a few well defined lines of inquiry. Remember that the portfolio can link to the main campus*

Web site for access to additional information on, for example, admissions procedures, course offerings or requirements in particular programs, student organizations or services, or current events on campus.

- *Keep the organizing structure simple.* When visitors to a Web site cannot find an obvious path from the site's opening page to the information they seek, they leave quickly. According to one summary of several user studies, the average user clicks the "back" button after only two to three seconds if a page does not immediately appear relevant to his or her current goals (Nielsen, 2000). While visitors to an institutional portfolio presumably have more than a casual interest in the site, it is nonetheless essential that the portfolio present clear, simple paths to information if it is to communicate effectively.

  The front page of Portland State University's institutional portfolio presents a photograph of the campus with a quotation from the president that emphasizes the campus's commitment to the Portland community. The next page lists the portfolio's five main themes, selected to illuminate major components of the university's urban mission and context. Alternatively, on the left side of the page, a list of information categories for specific audiences appears; thus, a prospective student can click on "prospective students," an accreditor can click on "higher education boards and agencies," and so on. Each choice on the opening page takes the visitor to a page that introduces a particular theme of the portfolio or introduces the portfolio to a particular audience.

  Visitors to this site thus have a choice between exploring a topic (or theme) or following a path designed to accommodate the interests of the group the visitor represents. Both types of pathways take visitors to some of the same pages and information, but the information has a different context, depending on how the visitor arrived at that area of the site. This scheme is simple, yet it is designed to present clear choices to site visitors that show them how to find the information they are seeking.

- *Give visitors the capability of drilling down to more detailed information.* Site visitors have varying degrees of interest in the portfolio's topics and themes. Some want only very basic information; others may wish to explore a theme in great detail. The site should be designed to give visitors the ability to decide how deeply to delve ("drill down") into a topic to find more detailed information and examples. The initial pages on a topic should be kept fairly simple. For results of a survey or an assessment study, for example, a summary or a set of bulleted highlights might be the first item the site visitor accesses; the list of examples of individual comments or the full report might be linked to this summary page for visitors who drill down to find additional details.

- *Consider a standard structure for each topic addressed.* A set of consistent subcategories for each major portfolio theme not only helps visitors find information easily but also helps those constructing the portfolio to stay focused on exactly what they are trying to communicate. For example, in the IUPUI portfolio, each program or initiative included in the portfolio is presented as a set of responses to four questions (tailored somewhat to fit each topic): What is it? What evidence demonstrates we are doing it? How do we know it is effective? What plans do we have to improve? These questions are purposefully designed to keep the focus on goals, assessment, and improvement as overarching themes of the whole portfolio. (See the IUPUI portfolio example earlier in this chapter.)

- *Get feedback from intended audiences about whether the portfolio is easy to navigate and whether it is communicating clearly.* The importance of keeping the portfolio's intended audiences involved with the process cannot be overstated. At every opportunity to consult with members of these audiences, whether a site visit, focus group, or some other occasion, the user-friendliness and clarity of the portfolio should be discussed. Whenever possible and appropriate, members of audiences for presentations on the portfolio should be encouraged to visit the portfolio beforehand and to comment on it. Some Web portfolios, such as Portland State's, include an area where visitors to the site can make comments.

- *If possible, include a professional Web designer on the portfolio team.* The principles for institutional portfolio design in this section are related to general principles of Web site design, familiar to a professional Web designer. If resources allow, a professional Web designer can contribute invaluably to the effectiveness of an institutional portfolio site. Ideally, designers should be part of the institution's staff and be familiar with general higher education issues and with specific institutional issues. Because many other Web sites are created for promotional or general informational purposes, it may be necessary to orient designers to the issues of accountability and effectiveness.

How will the portfolio be related to the institution's main informational Web site?

In theory, the portfolio serves purposes clearly different from those of the institution's main Web site: The portfolio is used for accountability and improvement, while the campus Web site is used to provide general information on many aspects of the institution. The portfolio is organized around a limited number of distinct themes and focuses related to impact and effectiveness; the campus Web site provides extensive information about activities, programs, and organizational units in the institution. The materials in the institutional portfolio are illustrative; the materials in the campus Web site are as comprehensive as time and resources allow.

In practice, the relationship between the electronic portfolio site and the main campus Web site is likely to be more complex than described above and to evolve over time. The specific relationship and distinctions between the portfolio and the campus site depend on the audiences and purposes for each. Sites will likely link to each other at many points and may exert influence on each other. As Hamilton points out in her essay, parts of the campus site linked to IUPUI's portfolio are being revised and upgraded; it is expected that the portfolio will bring more visitors to those areas of the campus site and that those visitors will expect the campus site to support claims and assertions made in the portfolio.

Although the relationship between the portfolio and campus sites is complicated and not entirely predictable, it is nonetheless helpful to distinguish between the purposes of each. Many visitors to the institutional portfolio will want to know just what they are looking at and see its purpose clearly articulated. Faculty and staff contributing to the portfolio will need to understand (or develop a shared understanding of) how the portfolio context differs from that of the main campus site. It is never too early in the process to articulate the specific purposes of the portfolio as clearly as possible.

What resources will be required to develop and maintain the portfolio?

Development and maintenance of electronic institutional portfolios demand a significant investment of institutional resources. Just how significant that investment is depends on several variables: the institution's ambitions for the portfolio; the size and complexity of the institution; and what is already in place in terms of technological capacity, technical staff skills, and, more broadly, assessment, strategic planning, and other processes that may be represented in the portfolio.

Some issues to consider in determining required resources include available hardware and software, a skilled technical staff, staff time, and committee structure.

Most campuses already have the technical infrastructure needed to mount and maintain a Web site. Requirements include a Web server, Web authoring software, and computer workstations for faculty and staff directly involved in creating and updating the portfolio. Beyond these basic requirements, technical needs depend on how sophisticated the campus wishes the portfolio to be. Streaming video, for example, requires appropriate video equipment and software. Such investment may be worthwhile for a campus that wants its portfolio to include "live" examples of students and faculty at work. A dynamic database that automatically updates institutional data in the portfolio, such as those at Georgia State and IUPUI, requires additional software products. Campuses using their portfolios as tools for planning and decision support have found this software well worth the cost.

The degree of skill needed among the technical staff depends on the campus's technical ambitions for the portfolio. At a minimum, available staff should be conversant with Web authoring, file conversion, server maintenance, and graphic design. For more technically complex portfolios, staff may require expertise in working with multimedia equipment and/or database connections.

Using the experience of the six UUPP universities as a model, institutions beginning portfolios should assign several core staff members to have ongoing responsibility for developing and maintaining the portfolio:

- *A project director,* with one-quarter to one-half time assigned to the institutional portfolio. In most cases, the campus project director is a senior faculty member with some administrative experience or responsibilities. Several campuses have appointed the staff member responsible for assessment (or the faculty member who chairs the assessment committee) as campus project director. This choice makes sense, because portfolios generally focus on learning and assessment and portfolio work may uncover a need for new assessment initiatives. Nonetheless, portfolio development requires a considerable time commitment above and beyond administration of the assessment program; expecting portfolio work to be simply "folded into" ongoing assessment processes is not realistic, at least in the early stages of portfolio work.

- *Institutional research staff (or other staff responsible for gathering, maintaining, and interpreting institutional data).* Campuses with an institutional research office will want an institutional research officer to be involved with the portfolio. This involvement may demand a quarter or a third of the institutional research officer's time, depending on what is included in the portfolio. In addition, another quarter or third of the time of an additional institutional research staff member will be needed for portfolio development and maintenance. Portfolio maintenance, over time, may come to overlap substantially with ongoing institutional research work, decreasing the time commitment necessary for the portfolio itself.

- *Web development and graphic design staff.* At some point in the development of the portfolio, Web developers and/or graphic designers may be needed to create an attractive, unified look for the portfolio and to help structure the site for accessibility and navigability. Involvement of these staff (or outside consultants) is likely to be required on an occasional, rather than an ongoing, basis.

Successful portfolio development is usually accomplished with the help of a small, active working group of faculty and staff that meets fairly regularly — say once a month in the initial stages, less frequently once the portfolio's structure and content are fairly well developed. In addition, for the portfolio to have broad impact on the campus and to represent the work of the campus accurately, other relevant committees should be consulted periodically. The amount of committee time involved depends heavily on the scope of the portfolio and on the size and complexity of the campus.

Again, resources here depend on what is already in place on a campus. For example, if portfolio work reveals that campuswide core learning outcomes for the baccalaureate need to be developed or revisited or that assessment or strategic planning processes are lack-

It is never too early in the process to articulate the specific purposes of the portfolio as clearly as possible.

ing, the institution will need to consider allocating resources to those functions over and above those required for the portfolio.

The extent to which these processes are already established also influences the length of the portfolio start-up period — the period of time for the portfolio to be sufficiently developed so that most work on it is maintenance. A large campus beginning a portfolio in tandem with developing assessment, strategic planning, or institutional research programs may take three to five years to reach the stage of portfolio maintenance. A small campus with well developed processes in the areas to be featured in the portfolio may require only half as long to reach this point.

The UUPP is conducting a functional needs assessment to yield concrete information on the fiscal and human resource implications of portfolio development for large, complex urban campuses. The findings and methodology of that assessment should help other campuses considering portfolios to estimate probable investments and time commitment. It seems safe to say that a regularly updated portfolio probably costs less in the long run than a conventional self-study for regional accreditation. If the portfolio will be used with multiple groups of stakeholders and can substitute for a number of accountability documents that would otherwise need to be produced, its cost-effectiveness will be even greater.

About the Essays in This Section

The essays in this section include advice on developing electronic institutional portfolios and detailed accounts of how several universities went about creating them, exploring the issues in detail from a variety of perspectives. Sharon Hamilton's essay discusses how IUPUI organized its portfolio initiative and conceptualized the portfolio itself. With no models or precedents and only a loose idea of what an electronic institutional portfolio might look like, Hamilton and her colleagues confronted considerable challenges. The IUPUI portfolio is quite ambitious, in breadth, depth of content, and the range of stakeholders it aspires to reach. Hamilton's essay focuses on the initial issues she and her colleagues faced; how they went about designing, implementing, and institutionalizing the portfolio; and the impact of the portfolio on the campus's assessment and improvement efforts.

Like Hamilton, Kathi Ketcheson focuses on the efforts of a campus to create its own model for an electronic institutional portfolio that reflects its specific, urban mission and the ways it ensures effectiveness within that mission. Portland State University's dynamic process for building the portfolio reflects its character as a campus well known for innovation and experimentation. Ketcheson describes steps to establish a process, defines roles of key players, and delineates principles and core elements of the portfolio. She also explains uses of the portfolio and involvement by key audiences in the portfolio's ongoing development. Reflecting the experience of other universities, PSU found that a collaborative approach helped dissolve barriers between administration and faculty and redefined the role of institutional research on the campus.

Victor Borden addresses the role of institutional research and data in institutional portfolios, exploring not only how such data complement other evidence in a portfolio by providing quantitative information about an institution but also how work on a portfolio can enrich and expand the information that institutional researchers offer their institutions. Like Ketcheson, he finds that collaborative campus work on an electronic portfolio has enlarged the scope of issues within the purview of institutional research and helped faculty members and institutional researchers to understand common interests and issues. He also argues for the potential of institutional research to support the scholarship of teaching and learning for the entire institution.

At California State University Sacramento, development of an on-line institutional portfolio for the UUPP led to yet another innovation: creation of a prototype department/program portfolio focused on teaching and learning. Dean Dorn's essay discusses the evolution of the prototype and explores possible uses for a departmental portfolio — to encourage the department's examination of learning outcomes and experiences; to provide a vehicle for departmental self-assessment and reflection, program review, and specialized accreditation; and to use as a valuable adjunct to an electronic institutional portfolio. The model that Dorn and his colleagues developed for the Sociology Department portfolio has already attracted national attention and interest.

Finally, Judie Wexler's essay discusses the uses and usefulness of institutional portfolios for institutional accreditation and describes the work of WASC's Senior College Commission in experimenting with portfolios. Electronic institutional portfolios embody and respond to several key trends in regional accreditation: an increased focus on student learning and educational effectiveness, a recognition that institutions must be evaluated in the context of their specific missions and student bodies, and a commitment to ongoing institutional learning and improvement. As vehicles for both improvement and accountability, portfolios promise to make the accrediting process less burdensome and more genuinely helpful to institutions in the WASC region.

Collectively, these essays make a case for the promise and potential of electronic institutional portfolios to benefit higher education and its stakeholders in a multitude of ways. It is hoped that they also give readers a clear sense of what is involved in developing such portfolios, as well as some concrete ideas about how to begin developing one.

Note

1. The Urban Universities Portfolio Project (UUPP) brings together six leading urban public universities to develop a new medium: an electronic institutional portfolio to demonstrate a university's effectiveness to its stakeholders. The UUPP is

funded by The Pew Charitable Trusts and is cosponsored by the American Association for Higher Education (AAHE) and Indiana University Purdue University Indianapolis (IUPUI). For more information, visit http://www.imir.iupui.edu/portfolio.

References

Barr, R.B., & Tagg, J. (1995, November/December). From teaching to learning: A new paradigm for undergraduate education. *Change 27* (6), 12-25.

Hutchings, P., & Shulman, L.S. (1999, September/October). The scholarship of teaching: New elaborations, new developments, *Change 31* (5), 10-15.

Nielson, J. (2000, January 9). Is navigation useful? *The Alertbox: Current Issues in Web Usability* (http://www.useit.com/alertbox/).

Snake Pit in Cyberspace: The IUPUI Institutional Portfolio

by Sharon J. Hamilton

The institutional portfolio at Indiana University Purdue University Indianapolis (IUPUI) combines product and process to model a form of inquiry that demonstrates institutional self-examination in a public forum. As a product, it provides focused information to multiple stakeholders in the Indianapolis community in particular and higher education in general; as a set of processes, it engenders ongoing opportunities for the campus to define its goals, analyze and evaluate its achievement of those goals, and develop plans to improve its levels of achievement. This chapter focuses primarily on these processes, tracing how conceptualization and development of the portfolio became institutionalized as ongoing processes leading to quality assurance and improvement.

Why Did We Create an Electronic Institutional Portfolio?

A university can be compared to a pit full of snakes: Everything is entwined with everything else, and nothing stays still for a moment. Many segments of the population view universities, like snake pits, with unease and some skepticism. Urban universities in particular, unlike the exotic Ivy League cobras or the mighty land-grant pythons, are the lowly garter snakes of the underground pit, perceived as necessary and modestly useful but with not much potency. They writhe in a morass of missions, visions, and values that aim at providing access to higher education for as many of their respective communities' citizens as possible while also maintaining the highest standards of research and scholarship, and contributing to the economic, social, and physical well-being of their metropolitan communities. Moreover, as urban communities change demographically and economically, the role of urban universities within these communities must change as well. While remaining constant to the core of their mission, they must shed what no longer fits their urban constituencies' needs and continually self-renew, not just in reaction to urban change but also in knowledgeable anticipation of these changes. Urban universities are, by definition, in a state of continual flux.

Sharon Hamilton is Chancellor's Professor of English at Indiana University Purdue University Indianapolis, director of campus writing, and codirector of Indiana University's Faculty Colloquium on Excellence in Teaching. She also serves as IUPUI campus director of the Urban Universities Portfolio Project and is leading a campus initiative on student digital portfolios.

IUPUI is a prime example of an urban university in transition. With the recent establishment of the state's first community college, IUPUI's traditional student demographic is changing, with a profound transformation in the institution's urban mission. Situated in the downtown core of Indianapolis, IUPUI educates more than 27,000 students annually, most of them from the city of Indianapolis and its surrounding counties. It has grown, as Indianapolis has grown, in both size and sophistication. It has more academic units and schools than any other university in the country and educates more Indiana citizens than any other campus in the state. Its graduates grace corporate executive offices, judges' benches, operating theaters, medical and scientific laboratories, local schools and clinics, and countless other workplaces in the city and state. Many of its students, staff, and faculty are bulwarks of the community in terms of stewardship and volunteer activities. The research and scholarship of its faculty garner national and international acclaim. It is considered, nationally, to be among the most innovative and forward-looking of urban metropolitan universities.

Yet many of IUPUI's local stakeholders, including its students, their parents, legislators, and even the Indiana Higher Education Commission, remain unaware of most of these accomplishments. Many in the community still think of IUPUI as a kind of extension campus of Indiana University and Purdue University. Ironically, considering this perception, many of these same people do not realize that IUPUI offers both IU and Purdue degrees. They have little knowledge of the significant role that the campus plays in the life of their community. They do not realize the value and commitment of this institution in the heart of their community.

The fault for this lack of awareness about IUPUI and about many other institutions lies not with community stakeholders but with us in the academy. For too long, we have taken for granted that what we offer and what we do is for the best of the community and our students. In a time of increasing public accountability, universities have remained aloof from widely publicizing their goals, their processes for achieving those goals, and their strategies for improvement in a changing world. Like the lowly garter snake, we slough off the old and self-renew in private. Small wonder that the public is increasingly wary about the functions of higher education and collectively lacking in awareness of the significant role of urban institutions in their communities.

The electronic institutional portfolio has the potential to rectify this situation. The medium itself is widely accessible and its capacity for representation almost limitless. It can be negotiated according to the information needs and interests of each individual viewer, and it can be maintained and updated much more readily than can print publications. On its own, it is an ideal way to inform a diverse array of audiences and local stakeholders about the mission and role of IUPUI in its metropolitan community. But that is only one small part of its potential. Collectively, the institutional portfolios of the six institutions in the Urban Universities Portfolio Project (UUPP)[1] model possible changes for how urban universities are regarded and evaluated across the country.

What Is Involved in Beginning to Create a Portfolio?

Although many questions must be considered in the beginning stages of creating an institutional portfolio, three seem, in retrospect, to have been most important to beginning IUPUI's portfolio: (1) Can the campus infrastructure support an institutional portfolio? (2) Who should be involved in its design, creation, and implementation? (3) What should be the relationship between the campus portfolio and the campus Web site?

Campus infrastructure

While we did not immediately realize and appreciate the relationship between the IUPUI campus infrastructure and the institutional portfolio, its significance became increasingly apparent during the early stages of developing the portfolio. Four facets of campus infrastructure were most important at the start:

An established, respected, and effective office of information management and institutional research. At IUPUI, the associate vice chancellor for information management and institutional research (IMIR) works in partnership with the UUPP campus project director, appointed by the provost, to provide campus-level leadership for the project. An extensive, credible body of institutional data linked to the campus mission and strategic planning processes was vital in conceptualizing the initial framework and processes for the portfolio. Access to what we knew, what we did not know, and what we needed to know about the campus richly informed early decisions about how to proceed and whom to contact. Additionally, IMIR provided initial content, such as the results of alumni and student surveys, to help stakeholders envision the potential of the portfolio and appreciate the value of their participation in its evolution. These results are presented in "Research Briefs" that appear both in summary and in fully elaborated forms in the portfolio, depending on the needs and interests of visitors to the site.

Faculty-approved learning outcomes for all undergraduates. While institutional research, through various surveys, questionnaires, and interpretive distillations of campus-level data, provides indirect measures of student learning, we needed to find ways to provide direct measures of student learning in a meaningful, campuswide manner. Collecting and organizing representative evidence of student learning that transcends individual courses in individual departments and programs present a huge challenge. The five years spent by the IUPUI faculty drawing up, discussing, modifying, and eventually approving six principles of undergraduate learning provided a sound basis for organizing evidence of student learning in the portfolio. (See the end of this essay for a complete list of the principles.) Using the principles as a major part of the conceptual framework for student learning enabled us, for

Access to what we knew, what we did not know, and what we needed to know about the campus richly informed early decisions about how to proceed and whom to contact.

example, to import already extensively developed materials on written communication, one of the foundational skills in the first principle.

In addition to providing an organizational pattern for presenting evidence of student learning, the principles also revealed where we lacked campus-level information about student learning. We quickly realized the need to develop a campus-level strategy to collect and present evidence that students actually learned and grew in their understanding of the principles throughout their academic career at IUPUI. This realization began the interplay between the portfolio as a representation of current campus processes and progress and as a catalyst for improved processes and progress.

Visionary executive leadership. Another important element of the campus infrastructure is the involvement of those in the highest leadership positions on the campus: the provost, the vice chancellor for planning and institutional improvement, and the vice chancellor for external affairs. Our provost, William Plater, is committed at many levels. As a proposer of the Pew-funded UUPP, he is on its national leadership team and is therefore intensely invested in the success of the institutional portfolio at IUPUI. His support in terms of time and resources, such as providing 50% release time as well as full-time secretarial assistance for the campus project director, was invaluable to the portfolio's effective start. Equally important was his willingness to attend as many as possible of the ongoing portfolio-related meetings with faculty, staff, and community members.

The vice chancellor for planning and institutional improvement has also been involved at several levels: Having established procedures and faculty oversight of program review and assessment on campus, she has a vested interest in ensuring and assuring the quality of student learning across the campus. In preparation for the 2002 North Central Association accreditation visit, for example, she is responsible for demonstrating the campus's capacity for public accountability in terms of explicit, measurable indicators of effectiveness and for establishing processes and strategies for measurement and improvement. Her support of the portfolio as a major part of our self-study for accreditation has played a significant role in according it campus-level status.

The vice chancellor for external affairs also played a major role at the outset of the project and, like the others, continues to do so. Her involvement in and knowledge of the Indianapolis community were crucial in identifying local and internal stakeholders to involve in the development of the portfolio. She also helped to create a community-based focus group to assist in the development of strategies to assess the effectiveness of IUPUI's civic engagement and to develop a "guided tour" through the portfolio for community stakeholders.

Campus-level faculty committees. One final aspect of the campus infrastructure that became increasingly significant as the portfolio moved from its earliest stages as a project to becoming an institutionalized feature of the campus was the committee structure for faculty governance, undergraduate education, and program review and assessment. These ongoing committees, while serving initially in primarily a reactive and advisory role, now play a major role in the everyday continuation of the portfolio. For example, the need to demonstrate effective student learning at the campus has initiated a related project: individual electronic student portfolios, showing the development of every IUPUI student in relation to the institution's goals for students' learning, the Principles of Undergraduate Learning (PULs). The Faculty Governance committee has been advising those working on both the institutional portfolio and individual student portfolios about academic policies and procedures that may need to be changed or added to use the students' portfolios for assessment. Similarly, the Council for Undergraduate Learning and the Program Review and Assessment Committee have been engaged to help determine what other policies and procedures need to be developed or changed.

Designers, creators, and implementers

Because the portfolio is intended to reach out to multiple audiences, we tried to involve representatives from diverse publics at the outset. We began with a meeting of 30 people representing IUPUI faculty, staff, and students and Indianapolis community leaders from P-12 education, the Indiana Commission on Higher Education (ICHE), and business and industry. They collaborated to suggest a functional organizing scheme and a list of possible contents for the portfolio. Out of that meeting, we formed two new committees to begin to design the portfolio: first, a core committee comprising the provost and vice chancellors mentioned previously, the campus UUPP director and director of IMIR, and, as they happen to be based on the IUPUI campus, the national UUPP director, her research assistant, and the technology support person for the project; and second, an implementation committee comprising faculty representatives from key campus committees, a student representative, and a representative from ICHE. The core committee played an executive role, advising the campus project director on major decisions and providing the resources, when necessary, to enact those decisions. The implementation committee met monthly to advise the project director on the development of the conceptual frameworks for the portfolio and to react to work accomplished since the previous meeting.

As was the case at Portland State, we learned during that first year that it is crucial to engage faculty and staff, not just in reacting to ongoing developments but also in actually shaping the portfolio. And, like Kathi Ketcheson in Portland, we found it difficult to begin that process. Our method was, during the second year of the portfolio project, to reconstitute the implementation committee as three function-based committees, each responsible for developing the conceptual framework for one of the three major focal areas of the portfolio that had evolved during the first year of the project: student learning, research and scholarship, and civic engagement.

While the work of the teams focusing on research and scholarship and on civic engagement was clearly related to current campus functions of faculty and staff, establishing a team for developing evidence of learning in relation to the PULs presented a special challenge. The PULs were relatively new to the campus community, and no well defined approaches existed to assess students' acquisition of core skills or understanding of key concepts campuswide. We therefore applied for internal funding to establish three renewable faculty associate positions, with a stipend of $5,000 in addition to the base salary, to learn how each IUPUI school went about teaching and evaluating students' understanding of the PULs.

As we began the third and final year of the UUPP-funded grant project, we created two focus groups to be brought together on an ongoing basis: a community group and a student group. The community focus group met first in real time to consider specific questions needing their expertise and experience as members of the community. In the main, they helped determine which features of the portfolio interested the community so that we could develop our external stakeholders' guided tour. During virtual-time meetings every six weeks to two months throughout the year, we refined our guided tour and determined how to evaluate the effectiveness of our campus commitment to civic engagement and the effectiveness of its portrayal in the portfolio. The student focus group met in real time every six weeks to two months. These meetings focused on questions of how to portray student life and learning effectively in the portfolio and how to develop a student-based guided tour through the portfolio.

At IUPUI we advocate broad involvement in the development of the portfolio, with representation, as much as possible, from all intended audiences and stakeholders.

To summarize, at IUPUI we advocate broad involvement in the development of the portfolio, with representation, as much as possible, from all intended audiences and stakeholders. We learned from experience: During the initial phases of the project, we did not adequately communicate to the campus and the community the potential benefits of both the portfolio itself and campus and community participation in it. Working with those who did see the potential, we developed our initial conceptual framework for our portfolio. When we had a basic framework and had begun development for some topics, we began to widen our search for more involvement. When campus and community members made suggestions, we responded flexibly, and in fact changed much of our conceptual framework as additional and diverse viewpoints and perspectives enriched our own evolving understanding of the potential of this project. This interaction among those involved, particularly when actualized through ongoing modifications responsive to a wide range of suggestions, has been an appreciated hallmark of the process of the portfolio at IUPUI.

The relationship between the campus portfolio and the campus Web site

While at first blush the relationship between the portfolio and campus Web site might seem obvious in that the Web site is as comprehensively informative as possible and the portfolio is focused on several major themes, in actuality the relationship is much more complexly and subtly nuanced. In the early months of the project, the principal metaphor delineating the portfolio's form and content was the idea of a narrative: While the campus Web site offered discrete bits of information, the portfolio would tell the story of IUPUI. Faculty, staff, students, and community members were the characters; the activities involved in student learning, research and scholarship, and community engagement were the plot; the urban community was the setting; and the major themes of the portfolio were the organizing themes of the narrative.

While this metaphor of the narrative served in the beginning to distinguish the campus Web site and the portfolio, we soon realized that narrative alone was not sufficient for our purposes. While acknowledging the power of story to provide richly contextualized examples of campus work and achievements, we saw these stories as part of a larger construct, where stories served as one kind of example. We therefore moved to the more compelling metaphor of a persuasive argument to describe the portfolio. The themes of the portfolio thereby became the framework for assertions, claims, and evidence, and the campus Web site became an integrally linked source of much of the evidence to support our claims and assertions.

The power of metaphor derives from the power of association, however, and the possibility that some might associate "persuasion" with "propaganda" and "marketing" demanded that we be very clear in our intentions for the portfolio. Because a persuasive argument presents evidence most appropriate to its claims, we had to ensure that our claims truly reflected processes of institutional self-examination and inquiry, not just statements of achievement. In a sense, the choice of this metaphor of the persuasive argument forced us to confront one of the major issues of the portfolio: How can a public document be both a means of assuring quality to multiple audiences and a means of demonstrating achievement? The next section, on developing the portfolio, shows our response to that issue.

The dynamics of the relationship between the portfolio and the campus Web site changed with this change of metaphor. During the first year, the portfolio linked to campus Web sites but exerted no influence on any features of these sites. During the second year, as the campus Web site became an integral source of evidence to support the claims made in the portfolio, the site began to change in response to the portfolio's needs. For example, on the front page of the campus Web site, there is now a link to the portfolio. Some schools and academic units are beginning to present their research and scholarly activities in a framework that matches the major themes of the portfolio, with the result that links are more seamless.

The nature of the links themselves is also changing. For example, in the section on student learning, the link to the reports of the Program Review and Assessment Committee originally required deeper levels of probing to glean the required information. But these reports are so crucial to providing evidence of student learning that they are now imported as updatable directly into the portfolio. Moreover, because of the heightened visibility of these reports, the work of this committee now includes monitoring the reports to ensure that each school provides evidence of how assessment leads to students' improved learning.

What Is Involved in Development of the Portfolio?

Development of the portfolio was concurrently diachronic and paradigmatic. In other words, we attempted to achieve development in both conceptualization and amplification while concurrently trying to involve as many of our diverse stakeholders as possible. The relationship between the responsibilities of the campus leadership team to move the portfolio project forward and also to garner and incorporate advice from our many stakeholders was complex. We had to find a balance between, on the one hand, pushing forward with our own ideas and then inviting responses and, on the other hand, incorporating direct formative involvement by stakeholders in the actual development of the portfolio in terms of conceptual framework and contents. This section explores this relationship as it occurred in three major aspects of portfolio development: (1) How were the conceptual frameworks determined? (2) How would contents be generated, sorted, and evaluated? (3) How were faculty, staff, students, and community stakeholders involved?

Determining conceptual frameworks

The conceptual framework for the portfolio changed quite significantly over the course of the project.[2] We began with the synthesis of that initial large group meeting of faculty, staff, administrators, students, and community members. We blended their ideas with the mission of the campus, which at that time was articulated through five major goal statements, and came up with six major thematic statements for the portfolio:

1. IUPUI provides a high quality education that is shaped by and relevant to its position in the Indianapolis community.
2. IUPUI is exemplary in measures of research and scholarship.
3. IUPUI promotes diversity and access.
4. IUPUI provides opportunities for lifelong learning.
5. IUPUI uses internal and external collaboration to meet the needs of its urban constituency.
6. IUPUI is accountable in its stewardship of the public trust and economic resources.

To develop each theme statement, the original conceptual framework had four constructs: performance objectives and outcomes, enabling environments, reflective critique, and plans for improvement. Each construct was developed in terms of evidence of effectiveness, hallmark practices, and key indicators.

While this original conceptual framework was integrally tied to our mission and to the ideas of the stakeholders who attended the initial organizational meeting, we soon found it to be cumbersome and, as we were frequently informed, laden with jargon.

Through revisions involving more faculty members, community-related staff, and key campus committees, we finally (we thought) had an ideal conceptual framework for the portfolio.

We had simplified the concept to three major themes: the IUPUI student experience, our urban commitment, and our global commitment. We also had 12 topical areas: an IUPUI education; career and professional preparation; lifelong learning; leadership and service; links with P-12 education; business and education partnerships; arts, humanities, and culture; urban and environmental planning; health, social sciences, and human services; information technologies; science and technology; and breakthroughs and innovations. Each topical area was held accountable to four questions (worded appropriately for each topic but fundamentally engaging with these four areas of inquiry):

- What is it?
- What evidence demonstrates we are doing it?
- How do we know it is effective?
- What plans do we have to improve?

These questions, particularly the last two, are key to enabling the portfolio to lead to internal improvement.

This conceptual framework was elegant in its simplicity compared with its predecessor, and it put the portfolio's urban focus in the foreground while also acknowledging academe's universal function to contribute to the global knowledge base. Concurrently with our efforts, however, a newly formed campus committee was dealing with a major challenge: the establishment of a new state community college in our immediate vicinity. Because this new campus draws heavily on our traditional student demographic, it has significantly influenced the nature of IUPUI's mission, vision, values, and goals. This committee, which were therefore redefining IUPUI's mission, came up with differently worded conceptual constructs. Initially, we thought we could map their constructs onto ours, as their theme of "effective student learning" matched closely with our theme of the IUPUI student experience, their theme of "excellent civic engagement" matched closely with our theme of urban commitment, and their theme of "exemplary research and scholarship" matched closely with our theme of global commitment. We had invested our efforts so thoroughly in the evolution to our portfolio's conceptual framework that we really did not want to change our wording, which, while it could map to the committee's themes, was in our view more broadly engaging.

The initial conceptual framework

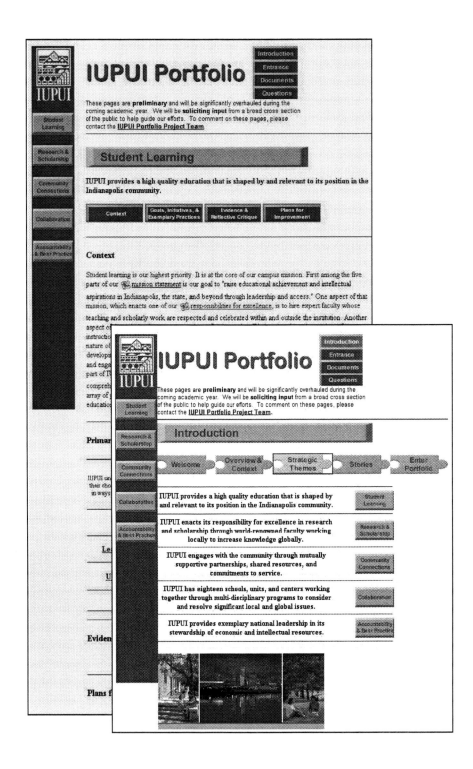

We thus had to decide between adhering to a conceptual framework that finally seemed exactly right and modifying it to match the thinking of a major campus committee defining the future shape of IUPUI. Because the intention of the portfolio project was to become an integral part of campus processes, we decided (appropriately) to modify our conceptual framework yet again by adopting the words and conceptual frameworks of this

The second conceptual framework

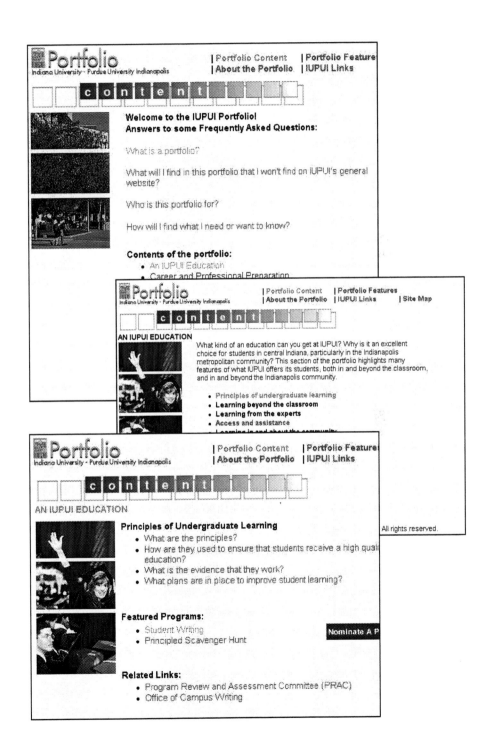

campus-level committee. The consequences of this third reframing were immediately apparent. The members of that committee, representing a wide-ranging hierarchy of influence on campus, began to see the portfolio not as a separate project but as a way to represent the ongoing work of the campus. It was the first major step toward institutionalizing the portfolio.

Generating, sorting, and evaluating contents

If the portfolio is to be an ongoing campus process, then the procedures for generating, sorting, and evaluating content need to be part of the ongoing business of the campus. As mentioned, the Office of Information Management and Institutional Research maintains an updated bank of survey information and other data important to many sections of the portfolio. Importing or linking to that body of information is relatively straightforward. Similarly, every school and academic unit has information on its Web site that we can link to or import as a featured program. For example, in another essay in this section, Dean Dorn offers a prototype for departments to present their achievements as a form of inquiry and self-examination. Determining what should be linked, what should be featured, and how the material should be selected, presented, and evaluated or contextualized is a process that needs to be assigned to appropriate ongoing school and campus committees, student groups, and community groups. While the campus portfolio director must ensure that appropriate assignments are made, it becomes the responsibility of the respective groups to generate, sort, and evaluate the contents.

For representing student learning in the portfolio, we asked two questions: (1) Who should determine what content best demonstrates effective student learning? (2) What ancillary content should be included to show the supports we provide for effective student learning as well as the different kinds of service-learning, experiential learning, and cocurricular learning that occur at IUPUI? The Implementation Committee determined that the Principles of Undergraduate Learning were the best place to begin, as they were part of every undergraduate student's learning experience at IUPUI. We had access to reports about how the PULs were integrated into courses and programs but no hard evidence of where and how they were taught, learned, and assessed, and how that assessment led to curricular and pedagogical changes to improve students' learning. We therefore requested funding for three faculty associates — tenured senior faculty familiar with the PULs and the campus — to develop ways to garner and present this information so that this part of the portfolio can be regularly maintained and kept up to date. During the final year of the UUPP project, we also established a group of students to meet regularly, not only to respond to the student learning part of the portfolio but also to suggest ways to make it informative and appealing to current and future students.

To develop the contents of the excellent civic engagement theme, we began with a small committee of faculty and staff, headed by the vice chancellor for external affairs, to

If the portfolio is to be an ongoing campus process, then the procedures for generating, sorting, and evaluating content need to be part of the ongoing business of the campus.

The third conceptual framework

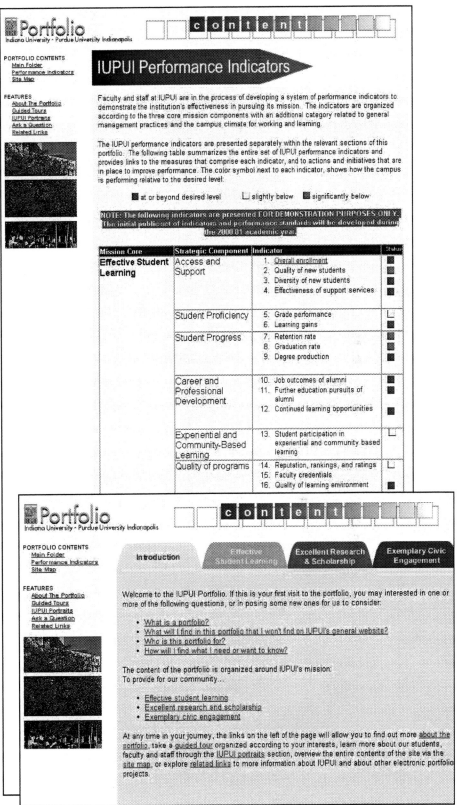

Portfolio
Indiana University - Purdue University Indianapolis

content

PORTFOLIO CONTENTS
Main Folder
Performance Indicators
Site Map

FEATURES
About The Portfolio
Guided Tours
IUPUI Portraits
Ask a Question
Related Links

IUPUI Performance Indicators

Faculty and staff at IUPUI are in the process of developing a system of performance indicators to demonstrate the institution's effectiveness in pursuing its mission. The indicators are organized according to the three core mission components with an additional category related to general management practices and the campus climate for working and learning.

The IUPUI performance indicators are presented separately within the relevant sections of this portfolio. The following table summarizes the entire set of IUPUI performance indicators and provides links to the measures that comprise each indicator, and to actions and initiatives that are in place to improve performance. The color symbol next to each indicator, shows how the campus is performing relative to the desired level:

■ at or beyond desired level   ☐ slightly below   ▓ significantly below

NOTE: The following indicators are presented FOR DEMONSTRATION PURPOSES ONLY. The initial public set of indicators and performance standards will be developed during the 2000-01 academic year.

Mission Core	Strategic Component	Indicator	Status
Effective Student Learning	Access and Support	1. Overall enrollment	▓
		2. Quality of new students	▓
		3. Diversity of new students	▓
		4. Effectiveness of support services	▓
	Student Proficiency	5. Grade performance	☐
		6. Learning gains	▓
	Student Progress	7. Retention rate	▓
		8. Graduation rate	▓
		9. Degree production	▓
	Career and Professional Development	10. Job outcomes of alumni	▓
		11. Further education pursuits of alumni	▓
		12. Continued learning opportunities	▓
	Experiential and Community-Based Learning	13. Student participation in experiential and community based learning	☐
	Quality of programs	14. Reputation, rankings, and ratings	☐
		15. Faculty credentials	
		16. Quality of learning environment	▓

Portfolio
Indiana University - Purdue University Indianapolis

content

PORTFOLIO CONTENTS
Main Folder
Performance Indicators
Site Map

FEATURES
About The Portfolio
Guided Tours
IUPUI Portraits
Ask a Question
Related Links

Introduction | Effective Student Learning | Excellent Research & Scholarship | Exemplary Civic Engagement

Welcome to the IUPUI Portfolio. If this is your first visit to the portfolio, you may interested in one or more of the following questions, or in posing some new ones for us to consider:

- What is a portfolio?
- What will I find in this portfolio that I won't find on IUPUI's general website?
- Who is this portfolio for?
- How will I find what I need or want to know?

The content of the portfolio is organized around IUPUI's mission:
To provide for our community...

- Effective student learning
- Excellent research and scholarship
- Exemplary civic engagement

At any time in your journey, the links on the left of the page will allow you to find out more about the portfolio, take a guided tour organized according to your interests, learn more about our students, faculty and staff through the IUPUI portraits section, overview the entire contents of the site via the site map, or explore related links to more information about IUPUI and about other electronic portfolio projects.

http://www.imir.iupui.edu/iupuifolio

The third conceptual framework, continued

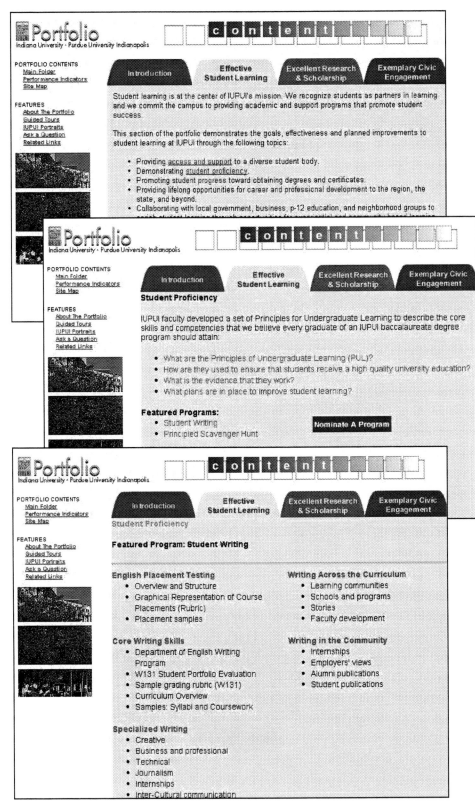

http://www.imir.iupui.edu/iupuifolio

develop a basic format and evaluative procedure for presenting information about community relations. During the final year of the project, we established an ongoing group of community members, with the Chancellor's Board of Advisors at the core, to develop criteria and strategies for involving community members in monitoring and evaluating this part of the portfolio and in suggesting possible items for inclusion.

To develop the framework for the exemplary research and scholarship part of the portfolio, we consulted with the Council of Associate Deans for Research, the vice chancellor for research and scholarship, the dean of the School of Science, and the director of the Undergraduate Research Opportunities Program. The director of the undergraduate program and dean of the School of Science developed a model for presenting and evaluating research and scholarship at IUPUI that was adapted by each school on campus according to its approaches to research and scholarship. The Council of Associate Deans for Research, under the leadership of the vice chancellor for research and scholarship, have undertaken to continue monitoring and evaluating the research and scholarship portion of the portfolio.

The major challenge of institutionalizing the portfolio was not to find ways to present the current status of IUPUI in student learning, research and scholarship, and civic engagement in the portfolio but to establish the underlying processes for reflection and evaluation and the development of strategies for improvement. While faculty members, staff, students, and community members found it relatively easy to identify items for inclusion according to their respective vested interests, they found it rather more difficult to develop strategies for reflection, evaluation, and improvement. Yet these key components differentiate the portfolio from the general campus Web site, and the voices of the intended audiences for the portfolio are essential to its effective development.

Involving faculty, staff, students, and community stakeholders

An electronic institutional portfolio for quality assurance aimed at multiple audiences is without precedent, with no model or blueprint. For that reason, it was difficult to involve as many faculty members, staff, students, and community stakeholders in the formative stages of the process as we would have liked. People wanted to see an example or model of what we were attempting. For the three years of the UUPP project, therefore, we walked a tightrope between involving stakeholders in the formative stages and inviting them to respond to our interpretations of their suggestions. Bearing that generalization in mind, we have discovered six important principles of involvement:

- Involve representatives from each intended audience in both formative and responsive stages.
- Provide meaningful tasks to be achieved at each stage of involvement.
- Inform all those involved at any stage of the process about the progress of the project.

- Inform those whose advice has been used specifically how their advice has been applied to the project.
- Include in the development of the portfolio those in significant positions who might jeopardize the project through lack of understanding, and give them a key role. Provide lots of support and encouragement.
- Use existing committees with campus responsibilities closely allied to the particular aspects of the portfolio that need to be developed, rather than forming new committees.

Now that the IUPUI portfolio is established and its reputation and utility are becoming part of the collective awareness of the campus, it is easier to engage faculty members and staff in its development. In fact, faculty members and staff show ever increasing enthusiasm to have work represented in the portfolio. The same cannot be said yet for students and community members, however, and we continue to work through senior administrative levels to achieve a higher level of involvement by these sectors of our intended audience.

How Does the Portfolio Move From a Funded Project to an Institutionalized Strategy for Assuring Quality to Multiple Publics?

Each year of the UUPP project, we organized a site visit to benefit from an external perspective. The site visit the first year provided a formative critique by the two members of the national project's Institutional Review Board assigned to our campus. For greater involvement and broader perspective, we expanded the composition of the visiting team for the second year's site visit to include two students, two members of the community, and the liaison from our accrediting association.

The comments of this team were instrumental in shaping the final year of the project, particularly the process of institutionalizing the portfolio. The catalyst for this process was a statement by our liaison from North Central, Mary Breslin, who said that in reaching out to our intended audiences we did not need to concern ourselves with what these persons *wanted* to know or what that person or organization might *want* to see. Rather, we should focus on the mission of the campus, on our processes for achieving that mission, and on our plans for improving our level of achievement. In her words, "If it works for IUPUI, it will work for accreditation."

It seems so obvious now, but in our eagerness to please a multitude of diverse audiences, we somehow had lost sight of that fundamental principle. Embedded in Breslin's statement was the method for institutionalizing the portfolio: Make it a part of the work of campus-level committees charged with overseeing the diverse activities and processes related to achieving the mission of the campus. We had already been reporting to these committees for the previous two years and had made them a major part of the site visit. All was in place for this next stage of making the portfolio an integral part of the structure and processes of the campus.

We began by integrating the processes of the portfolio with the processes of the various campus-level committees already described. We also met regularly with members of faculty governance to clarify procedural aspects and other implications of institutionalizing the portfolio. And finally, because the real work of the campus is carried out by departments and programs, we met with every school to discuss how its contributions to student learning, civic engagement, and research and scholarship will be represented in the portfolio on an ongoing basis.

How Has the Portfolio Influenced Campus Strategies for Assuring Quality to Multiple Publics?

For the purposes of the portfolio as a document that can assure quality in the areas of student learning, civic engagement, and research and scholarship, we have been interpreting "quality assurance" as institutionalized processes to assure quality and ensure the development of plans for improvement. The portfolio enacts this interpretation of quality assurance by responding to the following question: *How do visitors to the portfolio site know that IUPUI is identifying areas where improvement is warranted and developing plans for that improvement?*

To answer this question, linking to the Web sites of various schools and programs or campus-level committees is not sufficient. Involving faculty members, staff, and committees in the portrayal of their work in the portfolio is essential to ensure that we are not merely writing a report but are following through with actions to improve and then are demonstrating these processes for improvement in the portfolio. Right now, this realization is in embryonic form, indicating the potential of the portfolio to influence, as well as report, campus processes for improvement; but the realization is not yet demonstrably manifested. Some specific processes have been started, however, to ensure the portfolio provides assurance of quality to diverse audiences.

The earliest campus-level influence of the project was, as previously mentioned, the realization that we needed more information about the PULs. In particular, because PULs are intended to transcend individual courses and to permeate the learning experiences of all undergraduates, we needed evidence to demonstrate where these principles were taught, how we knew they were learned and understood, and how we used evaluation strategies to improve students' understanding of the PULs. As a result, the campus established three faculty associate positions to gather these data for initial presentation in the portfolio and to try to determine how best to represent this body of evidence in the portfolio.

Similarly, the director of campus writing realized that while we had rich data on the placement and first-year writing skills of our students, we had very little data concerning the writing skills of our juniors and seniors. The director subsequently designed and received funding for a pilot program of writing assessment and assistance for juniors and seniors.

Conclusion

In retracing the processes involved in the development of IUPUI's portfolio, I have foregrounded the challenges, the processes of decision making, the flaws and strengths in those processes, and the influence of the portfolio on the campus. My purpose has been to provide suggestions and an institutional context for those who might want to begin to develop an institutional portfolio. I have therefore not spent much time on the actual contents of the portfolio. But while the processes are paramount, the product itself merits attention. It therefore seems fitting for the final word to be the URL for our portfolio: http://www.imir.iupui.edu/iupuifolio.

Notes

1. The Urban Universities Portfolio Project (UUPP) brings together six leading urban public universities to develop a new medium: an electronic institutional portfolio to demonstrate a university's effectiveness to its stakeholders. The UUPP is funded by The Pew Charitable Trusts and is cosponsored by the American Association for Higher Education (AAHE) and Indiana University Purdue University Indianapolis (IUPUI). For more information, visit http://www.imir.iupui.edu/portfolio.

2. The screenshots in this essay reflect the evolution of the IUPUI Institutional Portfolio, and therefore many are not currently active screens. All of this information, however, can be found in the archives section of the current site at http://www.imir.iupui.edu/iupuifolio.

Principles of Undergraduate Learning

1. CORE COMMUNICATION AND QUANTITATIVE SKILLS The foundational areas of writing, reading, speaking, listening, quantitative analysis and use of information technology B the core skills for IUPUI students B are demonstrated, respectively, by the ability to:

    a. express ideas, opinions, beliefs, and facts to others effectively in a variety of written formats (i.e. basic writing composition, general written communication, and professional or research writing);

    b. comprehend, interpret, and analyze written text in reading;

    c. communicate effectively (speak *and* listen) one-on-one and in small and large group settings, as well as identify factors that facilitate and impede communication;

    d. perform quantitative functions and analyses;

    e. use information technology for academic, personal, and professional needs.

    f. These foundational skills are introduced in specific courses and developed and extended throughout the disciplines.

2. CRITICAL THINKING is a sophisticated cognitive process which involves the careful examination of ideas and information from multiple perspectives in order to clarify and improve our understanding and to develop ideas that are unique, useful, and worthy of further elaboration. Critical thinking is demonstrated by

    a. solving challenging problems;

    b. analyzing complex issues and making informed decisions;

    c. synthesizing information to arrive at reasoned conclusions;

    d. evaluating the logic, relevance, and validity of data

    e. using knowledge and understanding to raise and explore new questions.

3. INTELLECTUAL DEPTH, BREADTH, AND ADAPTIVENESS is the ability to examine, organize, and apply disciplinary ways of knowing to specific issues. Intellectual depth is demonstrated by substantial knowledge in one area, usually the major, but, where applicable, in a minor or other concentration of study. Intellectual breadth is demonstrated by the ability to compare and contrast approaches to knowledge in different disciplines and by the ability to define what counts as evidence in each disciplines. Adaptiveness is demonstrated by modifying one=s approach to a problem or question based on the requirements of a particular situation.

4. INTEGRATION AND APPLICATION OF KNOWLEDGE Integration of knowledge is demonstrated when students articulate and apply concepts or constructs from two or more disciplinary areas to personal, academic, professional, or community activities. Application of knowledge occurs when students participate in experiences that enable them to link their knowledge to their own intellectual development, to their professional goals, and to the goals of society.

5. UNDERSTANDING SOCIETY AND CULTURE is the ability to place one=s own cultural traditions in a broader human context. This ability is demonstrated by writing, actions, and speech which indicate knowledge of the range of diversity in traditions, history, and values.

6. VALUES AND ETHICS An undergraduate education fosters the development of a sense of aesthetics, values, and ethical standards. The enactment of values and ethics occurs when students make informed and ethical decisions in their personal, academic, and professional endeavors.

Portland State University's Electronic Institutional Portfolio: Strategy, Planning, and Assessment

by Kathi A. Ketcheson

According to Portland State University's mission statement:

> The University's mission is to enhance the intellectual, social, cultural, and economic
> qualities of urban life by providing access throughout the life span to a quality liberal
> education for undergraduates and to an appropriate array of professional and graduate
> programs especially relevant to the metropolitan area. The University actively promotes
> the development of a network of educational institutions that serves the community, and
> it conducts research and community service to support a high quality educational environ-
> ment and reflect issues important to the metropolitan region.

Culture as the Setting for Innovation

Portland State University (PSU) is recognized as a leader among urban universities in the
United States. As the state's urban public university, PSU is an adaptive, creative, and
entrepreneurial organization open to collaboration with similar institutions. Its organizational culture reflects the trailblazing image that has characterized Oregon's politics and
society, creating an environment in which new ideas are welcomed. Since the early 1990s,
the university has implemented a number of innovations that have created a distinctive
identity for the institution and improved the quality of its programs.

The Urban Universities Portfolio Project (UUPP)[1] has provided an opportunity for PSU to
capitalize on its strengths as an innovator. With its emphasis on assessment, accountability, and reflection, the UUPP and the institutional portfolio concept are compatible with
PSU's priorities in the areas of student learning, research in an urban context, and community engagement. The portfolio is a vehicle for planning through which the university
articulates its vision, focuses its priorities, and emphasizes its strengths to audiences
inside and outside the institution. PSU's faculty-driven approach to the project, character-

Kathi Ketcheson is director and research assistant professor with Portland State University's Office of Institutional
Research and Planning. She also serves as the Portland State campus director of the Urban Universities Portfolio
Project.

ized by openness and collaboration, has resulted in a dynamic and engaging collection of evidence that allows for internal reflection and external commentary.

The Urban Universities Portfolio Project

PSU's experience in the UUPP is an example of how creative thinking about the relationship between faculty and administration can stimulate institutional change. When PSU joined the UUPP in 1998, the provost made two important decisions. He named PSU's institutional research director as UUPP campus project manager and placed responsibility for the project in the institutional research office. Next, he appointed a faculty advisory committee comprising faculty from across the university to work in partnership with the institutional research staff. In doing so, he acknowledged the role faculty play in both teaching and learning excellence and outcomes assessment (Morse & Santiago, 2000, p. 32) and the centrality of institutional research in the information and decision-making structure at the university. By linking the two, the provost ensured the creation of a meaningful product that reflects the goals and values of the institution.

The institutional research role

The new realities facing higher education call for a reconsideration of the role of institutional research in higher education. These realities combine a complex decision-making environment with an increased role for decision makers in making *sense* of information for their constituents (Matier, Sidle & Hurst, 1995, p. 77). Rather than simply collecting and reporting information, institutional research professionals increasingly are called on to conduct research and provide recommendations to their institutions' leaders. They also play an important role in the assessment of student learning outcomes.

Although PSU has maintained a strong institutional research function since the mid-1960s, it did not begin moving toward a new model of institutional research until the close of the 1990s. The portfolio provided a vehicle for advancing this change. In his essay in this section, Victor Borden supports the idea that development of institutional portfolios requires institutional researchers to cultivate closer relationships with a broader range of faculty and staff. At PSU, collaboration with faculty through the UUPP and work on the portfolio permitted institutional research staff to enhance their roles as "information architects, change agents, and consultants of choice" (Matier, Sidle & Hurst, 1995, p. 76). As a result of their participation in the UUPP, institutional researchers at PSU were able to bring the scholarly components of their work to the attention of the campus community and to place themselves within the broader context of the university's academic mission.

Faculty advisory committee

The literature on assessment and accreditation emphasizes the importance of placing faculty at the center of campuswide initiatives related to teaching, learning, and assessment. As Morse and Santiago (2000, p. 33) argue, "Faculty leaders knowledgeable about outcomes assessment can and should take the lead in educating peers about assessment, in setting up institutional structures that facilitate the planning process, and in guiding assessment initiatives toward institutional change." The success of PSU's curricular innovations, such as the University Studies Program and the Center for Science Education, resulted from direct faculty participation in the creation and implementation of these programs. These experiences led to the realization that top-down decision making is a poor fit for projects that require faculty involvement such as development of the institutional portfolio.

In the past, a select group of PSU faculty members were regularly called on to serve on committees, leaving little opportunity for other voices to be heard. For this project, however, the provost appointed people with an eye toward avoiding the "usual suspects." The portfolio committee included creative thinkers actively involved in the improvement of teaching and learning rather than representatives of each university unit. While lacking the perspective of each school or college, the resulting university-wide committee minimized disciplinary differences. Chaired by a senior faculty member (who had served formerly as an academic dean), the committee met quarterly throughout each year of the project.

Defining an active role for faculty

Faculty members often serve as advisers to university initiatives but may have limited opportunities to play an active role in implementation. As Mintzberg (1987, p. 69) states, "Large organizations try to separate the work of minds and hands. In so doing, they often sever the vital feedback link between the two." To bring hands and minds together, the faculty committee was given an active role in designing the portfolio with the institutional research staff. Initially, some administrators believed that faculty members could not be asked to *do* anything but simply should be asked for advice. As a result, the first few committee meetings were frustrating, and little was accomplished. Finally, the project director came up with an idea. If the faculty were asked to do the *thinking* while the institutional research staff did the *work*, perhaps the project could move forward.

Later, one of the most active committee members commented that it was a pleasure for him to be asked to spend two hours creating the design while his partners in the institutional research office brought the ideas to life on the Web. Lively discussions and a free exchange of ideas characterized committee meetings. Some committee members became highly engaged in the project, volunteering time to review drafts of the Web pages, locate consultants in the area of Web site development, and gather content for portfolio pages. By creating an active rather than advisory role for the faculty, the project served as a model for faculty engagement in university-wide initiatives. The committee gained a reputation informally as "the best committee on campus," largely because of its atmosphere of creativity and collaboration.

Forming action teams

To move the project from discussion to action, the committee identified three broad categories of evidence that reflected the university's mission: academic, external, and student issues. Under academic issues, the committee included program assessment, scholarly work on urban issues, faculty issues, and curricular reform. External issues focused on topics that included community connections, university partnerships, K-12 and community college collaboration, national/international higher education, and, overlapping with academic issues, scholarly work on urban issues. Student issues focused on topics including student services, access, and diversity. Four themes were woven through each of the three categories: assessment, diversity, urban mission, and technology.

After the committee divided itself into three action teams, faculty members began outlining specific content that might appear under each broad heading. Building on the university's motto, "Let Knowledge Serve the City," the committee identified programs and activities that could be linked directly to mission, such as community/university partnerships, student outcomes assessment plans, opportunities for lifelong learning through continuing education, and applied research projects. The committee agreed that equal time should be given to activities related to PSU's undergraduate and graduate programs.

Principles of Design

A result of the committee's discussions was the articulation of a philosophical approach and conceptual framework for the portfolio. The philosophical approach is expressed through a list of eight characteristics that have shaped the portfolio and defined its purpose:
- PSU's motto guides the process.
- Faculty are centrally involved in the portfolio's design.
- Content does not comprise a laundry list of activities or serve as a dumping ground for information but forms a strategic document.
- The Web site creates a "place" where many destinations can be reached by various pathways.
- Portfolio Web pages provide a forum for discussion, comments, and feedback, and for conversations about assessment.
- The many voices on campus are represented.
- The portfolio forms the basis for an emergent strategic planning process and for accountability.
- Once completed, the portfolio will appear prominently on the PSU Web site's home page.

This approach in turn led to the development of eight elements that appear throughout the portfolio's content. Examples included in the portfolio would:

- reflect PSU's mission as an urban university,
- demonstrate community engagement,
- contain the elements of assessment and reflection,
- include examples of faculty development,
- focus on student learning,
- highlight diversity,
- be concrete, practical, and visually interesting, and
- focus on interesting and dynamic topics.

Language

Communicating with audiences outside higher education requires language free from jargon. While "service-learning," for example, is a common phrase among colleges and universities, it is less familiar to the public. In PSU's portfolio, narratives and descriptors are clear, concise, and phrased in everyday language as much as possible. Content is displayed using a variety of media. As Susan Kahn notes in the introduction to this section, electronic portfolios make possible the presentation of a wide range of qualitative and quantitative evidence that illustrates the complexity of student learning for a variety of audiences. Some materials are communicated effectively in video and audio, rather than narrative, forms. Pages containing examples of students' experiences in the senior capstone program, for example, demonstrate that listening to conversations with students about learning can be a powerful experience.

Audience

A key feature of PSU's portfolio is its communication to a limited set of audiences, which are defined by the portfolio's overarching message. Advisers from a local Web development firm recommended the selection of three to five audience groups to focus the selection of materials and ensure that the site would be simple and easy to use. Although the range of possible audiences for information about the university is broad, the committee decided on five audience groups, representing a range of interests: prospective students, the university community (faculty, staff, and students), the metropolitan community (local governments, nonprofit agencies, alumni, and the public), the business community, and higher education governing boards and agencies (legislators, the state board of higher education, and accrediting associations).

The overarching message

An electronic portfolio comprises *focused* selections of authentic work. An "overarching message" or unifying theme provides a focus for examples included in the PSU portfolio. Linked to the institution's mission, it provides a rationale for the portfolio's content and for the institution's activities overall. The message communicates what is distinctive or

An electronic portfolio comprises focused selections of authentic work.

special about PSU and flows from its mission as an urban university. It appears in the first two pages and is reiterated in the portfolio themes. Content for each of the portfolio sections is organized around the mission and related activities of the institution, allowing for clear enunciation of the university's message to its constituents.

PSU's portfolio themes structure navigation through the site

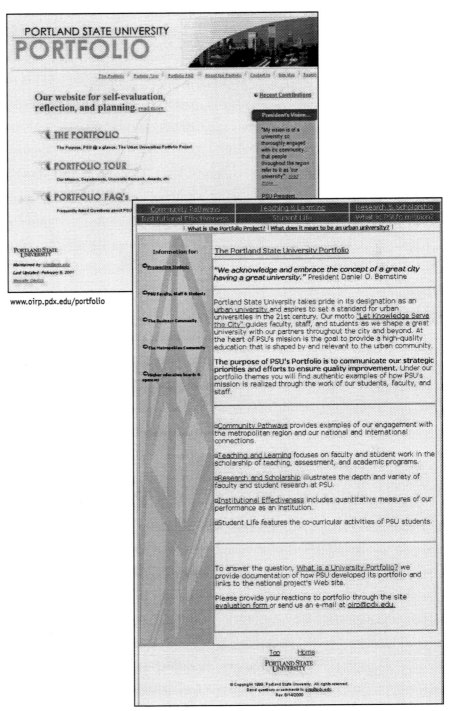

www.oirp.pdx.edu/portfolio

www.oirp.pdx.edu/portfolio/introduction/index.htm

The Portfolio as a Vehicle for Planning and Assessment

Executive leadership

In her essay on IUPUI's experience, Sharon Hamilton points out the importance of strong institutional leadership in bringing campus-level status to the portfolio. A key piece of the administration's planning agenda at PSU is the use of the portfolio as a vehicle for focusing strategic priorities, documenting actions, and engaging internal and external communities in conversations about mission and goals. In promoting it as a planning tool, the campus leadership moved the portfolio from the status of special project to a central place in the university's ongoing activities. Leaders have increased visibility for the project by including it in campuswide events structured around planning themes. They also have been instrumental in broadening the participation of external groups in the design and critique of the project.

Strategy and planning

In the absence of a formal strategic plan, PSU has adopted a planning process based on learning and strategic action. The portfolio provides an effective medium for the university to focus its priorities and learn from its actions. Mintzberg (1987, p. 66) describes an emergent strategy as "a fluid process of learning through which creative strategies evolve," while a deliberate strategy views formulation and implementation as separate activities. At PSU, as in most organizations, planning strategies fall along a continuum between emergent and deliberate, reflecting the real world of decision making and action. Its experiences in curricular reform and institutional change, however, have been characterized by strategic actions based on experimentation and learning rather than deliberate strategic plans. The portfolio gathers these actions together to illustrate the patterns that have emerged from PSU's change efforts and provides for the reflection and assessment that is critical to this form of institutional planning.

The overarching message of PSU's portfolio is linked to its mission and identity as a model of the 21st century urban university. Strategic priorities are articulated through actions documented under the portfolio themes. In contrast to a formal strategic planning document, the portfolio uses multiple media — audio, video, text, graphics — to *illustrate* how planning priorities are being met. The Web allows this information to be contained in one virtual place, accessible to multiple publics in a dynamic environment. It also serves to stimulate conversations about mission, goals, and priorities, both on-line and through campus meetings held throughout the academic year.

Relationship to university assessment efforts

At the end of the 1999-2000 academic year, PSU moved toward a systematic process of assessment and program review. The University Assessment Council appointed a faculty-in-residence to lead program assessment in the schools and colleges. Housed in the Center for Academic Excellence, the faculty-in-residence is responsible for working with academic departments in their efforts to develop assessment plans and collect results. The portfolio serves as a means to communicate the university's progress in program assessment and as a place where faculty and departments can refer to examples that may help them with their own assessment planning.

Ensuring confidentiality

Using authentic examples of students' work, transcripts of interviews, photographs, or other documents and narratives in the portfolio raises issues of confidentiality. Most campuses have institutional review boards that are responsible for overseeing the protection of human subjects in research. At PSU, the responsible committee determined that the portfolio did not constitute "research" but advised that a subject release form, including a statement of informed consent, would protect individuals involved in the project in the event that questions arose over publication of materials. Working together, the institutional research office and office of research and sponsored projects developed a release form that is used whenever information is solicited for the portfolio (see the form reproduced at the end of this essay). The form offers options for participation — documents, interviews, audio or video tapes — and is required for all authentic work contributed to the project. The institutional research office maintains a permanent file of these forms along with an electronic database of participants and their contributions.

The PSU institutional portfolio allows faculty members to see how their work is related to the university's overall priorities and goals.

Involving Audiences

Engaging the campus

The PSU institutional portfolio allows faculty members to see how their work is related to the university's overall priorities and goals. To extend this view to the larger campus community, the PSU team broadened participation in the project to include additional groups of faculty members, staff, and community members. During the 2000-2001 academic year, a public launching of the portfolio was included in the annual fall symposium, organized around the theme of "Great City, Great University." A second forum for publicizing the portfolio was the Faculty Focus before the start of the fall term. Throughout the academic year, campuswide forums serve to stimulate discussion around using the portfolio as a medium for setting strategic priorities and furthering institutional planning. The discussions include a component of critical reflection focused on the portfolio's content. The goal of all these efforts is to engage the campus in efforts to further define the university's identity and set a direction into the 21st century, with the portfolio as a unifying theme.

Involving the community

Portland State University implemented an effective process for including the campus community and external publics in the design and development of the portfolio. An informal focus group comprising eight external and internal participants met with the faculty committee at the end of the project's first year. These individuals represented possible audiences ranging from high school counselors to accrediting board members to business leaders and state or local officials. Following this meeting, the committee convened a second focus group with senior faculty members who were not involved in the project. Both groups provided insight on what targeted audiences would be interested in knowing about PSU and produced a set of ideas that confirmed the principal design elements first articulated by the faculty committee. They suggested that the portfolio should:

- communicate concrete examples of what PSU does for its customers and the community;
- be a practical tool for users;
- facilitate contact between the community and faculty, staff, and students;
- communicate an overarching message, highlighting PSU's connections to the community;
- incorporate a feedback loop for users;
- document current activities, communicate a vision for the future, and provide a method for analyzing progress toward those goals;
- incorporate well defined boundaries for what will and will not be included;
- group audiences under three to five major categories; and
- focus on functional areas within the university and provide a mechanism for sharing information between PSU and its peer institutions.

Throughout the development of the portfolio, the committee continued to solicit feedback from "critical friends" inside and outside the university. These individuals and groups provided expertise and guidance in specific areas and provided suggestions to improve the portfolio's design and content. To gather information directly from Web site users, the project team developed an evaluation form that records responses to scaled items and open-ended comments about the portfolio for later analysis and reporting. An e-mail address for communication with the Web master is included at the bottom of each page.

Involving students

Students' participation is an important element in both design of the portfolio and its viability as a tool for planning and assessment. In the early stages of the project, students' involvement was limited to graduate assistants who were working on the Web site. The need for a student presence in the portfolio was mentioned frequently in focus groups and during presentations to various audiences. During the second year of the project, a reporter for the student newspaper heard about the project from a friend whose capstone project is featured in the portfolio. She published an article promoting the usefulness of the portfolio for students, which led to development of a series of student focus groups during the 2000-2001 academic year. The portfolio theme, entitled "Student Life," is dedicated to the student experience at PSU and is created and directed by student groups engaged in the project.

Accessing Content

PSU's portfolio can be entered through multiple access points, allowing visitors to focus on information of interest to them. One way to access information is through five major themes: community pathways, teaching and learning, research and scholarship, institutional effectiveness, and student life. Under each theme, specific chapters address authentic work, data, and reflection.

However, the main route of entry is through five audience pages, each of which contains strategic questions of interest and links to relevant sites on the PSU home page. On each audience page, the set of strategic questions of interest serves as a means to focus and organize materials and address the needs of various users. Related to the portfolio's overarching message, questions are based on the specific interests of various audiences. For example, a question on the accrediting association's page is "How does PSU ensure the quality of its programs?" Because PSU's mission statement includes quality as a goal, this question is relevant to the portfolio's overall message. A virtual link leads to documentation of assessment plans and student learning. To ensure that the questions posed on each page are the right ones to ask, the faculty committee solicits feedback through interviews and focus groups with individuals representing each audience group.

The Portfolio's Five Themes

Community pathways

The university's motto, "Let Knowledge Serve the City," guided the faculty committee's thinking about how PSU's community connections could be displayed in the portfolio. While knowledge produced at the university serves the city, the city of Portland also provides a natural laboratory for students and a wealth of cultural, political, and practical experiences to enhance classroom learning. The reciprocal nature of this relationship is presented through authentic examples of students' work and commentary from students, faculty, and community partners. International connections also are represented under this theme, highlighting programs and projects demonstrating the global impact of the university's work.

A portfolio "chapter" on the senior capstone, the culminating course in the undergraduate general education curriculum, links student learning to PSU's goals in the area of community engagement. Capstone courses comprise interdisciplinary teams of students involved

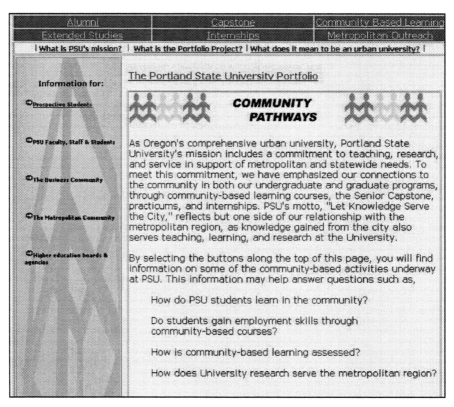

www.oirp.pdx.edu/portfolio/communitypathways

in research, either directly in the community — through agencies and nonprofit organizations — or in the classroom, focusing on issues of concern to the community. Examples
in this chapter include course syllabi, assessment plans, examples of students' work, and
interviews with individual students about their learning experiences. Other portfolio chapters focus on community-based learning, internships, international programs, continuing
education, and community outreach. This last chapter includes narratives introducing virtual links to PSU's Web pages that describe research and degree programs serving the
metropolitan region. Two examples are the Institute for Portland Metropolitan Studies and
the Center for Writing Excellence, which serves Oregon's professional writers' community.

Teaching and learning

This theme includes portfolio chapters on assessment, teaching and learning excellence,
and faculty development. Faculty members engaged in the scholarship of teaching and
links to relevant literature are featured. Self-reflection, related to PSU's success in meeting
its mission and goals, is represented through program assessment results; commentary in
the form of interviews or written narratives from students, faculty, and administrators; and
other evidence of the institution's progress toward its stated aims. Assessment of students'
learning has been identified as a key internal indicator of performance; it is also an
accreditation standard for the Northwest Association of Schools and Colleges. NWASC

requires institutions to produce assessment plans and evidence of learning outcomes as part of the self-study process, and they are included in the portfolio as they are developed.

Research and scholarship

Research productivity is highlighted under research and scholarship. The chapters showcase authentic evidence of faculty members and students engaged in both scholarly and sponsored research. Narrative reports show the increase in research dollars over time and the range of topics covered by sponsored research at PSU.

During development of this theme, an interesting debate arose in the faculty committee. Questions about what constituted "research" versus "scholarship" led to an innovation in the portfolio. While some held a more traditional view, others saw the line between research and scholarship as blurred and indistinct. To address this issue, the committee conceptualized an "issues page" that will be used to connect faculty to other national Web sites focused on faculty issues and provide a place for discussion, either through e-mail postings or on-line in the portfolio site.

Institutional effectiveness

The theme focusing on institutional effectiveness includes a user-friendly version of the statistical portrait, strategic budget priorities, statewide performance indicators, and information related to accreditation. To develop this page, the institutional research staff adopted a broad definition of "data" that includes narratives, graphics, numerical information, and recorded interviews. The thrust of this effort was to make information understandable and accessible to a variety of users while complementing the rows and columns of numbers contained in the existing fact book. Traditional forms of statistical data may be reached through a link to the institutional research Web site.

Student life

The theme of student life allows portfolio users to develop an understanding of the complex nature of the PSU student body and the many ways that PSU's students experience learning — in the classroom, in the community, and through cocurricular activities. The portfolio also provides a way for students to see themselves and their experiences as part of the larger university community and to make connections between the institution's mission and their educational goals. Working with student affairs and student groups, the project team envisions a theme that is student directed but linked to the overarching message of the portfolio.

Future Steps

The processes employed at PSU have been highly successful, ensuring faculty and community involvement and a tangible product. Concerns about the sustainability of the project into the future and issues surrounding the maintenance of the Web site still linger. The portfolio's role as a complement to the self-study process will be further developed as the institution approaches its 10-year accreditation review in 2005. Whatever its future, the portfolio project at PSU has provided a new medium for communication internally and externally and has helped to focus PSU's mission and identity around themes of interest to its multiple publics. The URL for PSU's portfolio site is www.oirp.pdx.edu/portfolio.

Note

1. The Urban Universities Portfolio Project (UUPP) brings together six leading urban public universities to develop a new medium: an electronic institutional portfolio to demonstrate a university's effectiveness to its stakeholders. The UUPP is funded by The Pew Charitable Trusts and is cosponsored by the American Association for Higher Education (AAHE) and Indiana University Purdue University Indianapolis (IUPUI). For more information, visit http://www.imir.iupui.edu/portfolio.

References

Matier, M.W., Sidle, C., & Hurst, P.J. (1995). Institutional researchers' roles in the twenty-first century. In T.R. Sanford (Ed.), *New Directions for Institutional Research* (pp. 75-147). San Francisco: Jossey-Bass.

Mintzberg, H. (1987). Crafting strategy. *Harvard Business Review,* 66-75.

Morse, J.A., & Santiago, G., Jr. (2000). Accreditation and faculty: Working together. *Academe* 86 (1), 30-34.

PSU's release form ensures confidentiality for and informed consent from contributors of authentic work to the portfolio

Portland State University Portfolio Project

Subject Release Form

I agree to be interviewed or provide samples of my work or other relevant materials for the Urban University Portfolio Project and that information I provide may be published on the Web. I understand that, because of my participation in this project, I will have to take time away from my other activities to be interviewed.

The UUPP staff has told me that the purpose of this project is to document programs, classes, and university activities that demonstrate PSU's learning goals, collaboration with the community, and assessment efforts.

I may not receive any direct benefit from taking part in this project, however, the project may help to increase knowledge that will help others in the future.

The UUPP staff has agreed to answer any questions I may have about the project and what I am expected to do. They have promised that all information I provide will be used only for the purposes I indicate below.

I understand that I do not have to participate in this project and may terminate the interview at any time. My willingness or unwillingness to participate will not affect my relationship with Portland State University or the Oregon University System, nor will it affect any evaluations of my work.

Please indicate your permissions with regard to the following:

The UUPP staff...

_____ may _____ may not   videotape my interview and publish it on the Web.

_____ may _____ may not   take my photograph and publish it on the Web.

_____ may _____ may not   audiotape my interview and publish it on the Web.

_____ may _____ may not   quote me in written form on the Web.

_____ may _____ may not   publish samples of my work on the Web.

I have read and understood the above information and agree to be interviewed or provide samples of my work or other relevant materials. I grant permission to use information from the interview in the manner indicated above.

_____   _____

Signature   Date

The Role of Institutional Research and Data in Institutional Portfolios

by Victor M.H. Borden

The essays in this volume describe the potency of using authentic samples of work, such as students' essays, instructors' syllabi, and assessment results, as evidence of personal and now institutional accomplishment. Using an electronic medium provides an efficient platform for storing and organizing for review a relatively large number of examples. As several authors have already pointed out, however, selecting what to include, electronic or otherwise, is one of the key components of portfolio design.

What kinds of evidence are most useful for demonstrating institutional effectiveness? And how much evidence is needed to represent an entire college or university? How can the work of a large and complex institution be represented sufficiently within the bounds of a portfolio? Faculty members and staff from the six institutions that participated in the Urban Universities Portfolio Project (UUPP)[1] have considered these questions and experimented with different forms of evidence. In addition to samples of work from classes, committees, research projects, and other institutional operations, the six universities feature in their portfolios quantitative summaries of the scope and impact of students' and faculty members' work.

Recognizing the important role of quantitative summaries and analyses, the UUPP included from the outset the staff from each campus who had the most experience accessing, analyzing, and summarizing institutional data — institutional researchers.

This essay explores two sets of opposing questions regarding the use of data in electronic institutional portfolios and the relationship between an institution's institutional research capacity and portfolio development:

1. What role do quantitative data play in developing effective institutional portfolios? What does developing an institutional portfolio teach about using quantitative data effectively?

Victor M.H. Borden is associate professor of psychology and associate vice chancellor for information management and institutional research at Indiana University Purdue University Indianapolis. He is a member of the UUPP national leadership team and coordinates the campus IR directors.

2. How do the theory and practice of institutional research inform institutional portfolio development? How does institutional portfolio development inform the theory and practice of institutional research?

Using Data in an Institutional Portfolio

The portfolios described in earlier sections of this volume include samples of work organized to show how students are becoming accomplished critical thinkers, practitioners, and communicators, and how teachers are shaping and supporting these efforts. But even for a small college or for a single academic department, the scope of collective work is too large to evaluate entirely on the basis of individual work samples.

Quantitative data can help summarize the collective work of college students, faculty members, and staff. For example, a university can show its commitment to access for traditionally underserved populations by comparing its ethnic and racial composition with the ethnic and racial composition of its service region. A department can demonstrate the effectiveness of its programs by providing information about how many of its graduates enroll in and complete graduate programs.

Quantitative data can help summarize the collective work of college students, faculty members, and staff.

Experience to date suggests three main approaches to using data to demonstrate effectiveness in institutional portfolios:

- Using *performance indicators* to demonstrate current levels of institutional effectiveness,
- Providing a *statistical portrait* as the context of an institution's work, and
- Showing how the institution uses *management information* to improve continuously.

Performance indicators: using data to reflect progress toward attaining goals

Performance indicators are distinguished from other measures by their direct relevance to institutional goals and objectives (Borden & Bottrill, 1994). Colleges and universities are often characterized by their size (enrollment), control (public or private), program level (undergraduate, professional, doctoral), and disciplinary focus (engineering, arts and sciences, business, and so on). These descriptive characteristics, however, do not relate directly to the institution's primary goals and objectives. Performance indicators focus more directly on core objectives, such as students' learning and achievement, the productivity and quality of research, and the impact of outreach.

Although performance indicators may be the most important type of data in an institutional portfolio, they are extremely difficult to craft. They must reflect the core purposes of the institution in ways that can be displayed in the portfolio to demonstrate effectiveness in meeting mission-critical goals and objectives. They must state objectives in measurable form. These requirements pose significant challenges for capturing the complex purposes and work of educational institutions.

For example, one common objective of undergraduate education is to improve students' abilities to think critically. But efforts by researchers have failed to produce a generally accepted definition of "critical thinking," much less a generally accepted measure for evaluating it (Siegel, 1988). Because we lack consensus on such core educational concepts as critical-thinking ability, colleges and universities are often forced into the position of using the most readily available measures rather than the most directly relevant ones.

The example of critical thinking points to three criteria for selecting performance indicators. Performance indicators must be (1) directly *relevant* to core goals and objectives; (2) based on meaningful, generally accepted, and well defined concepts *(valid)*; and (3) measured in ways that are replicable and consistent *(reliable)*.

Relevance. Relevance is determined by how closely a performance indicator relates to an important goal of the institution. The difficulty in developing relevant indicators usually arises not from determining whether a measure relates to a goal, however, but from deciding how important that goal is to the institution. For example, new students' average entrance test scores (SAT or ACT) may well indicate how attractive an institution is to the most talented students, but this indicator is far less relevant to open-access institutions than to selective institutions. Similarly, the dollar amount of research grants received from the National Science Foundation is most relevant to research universities with a strong focus on the physical and natural sciences but less so to research universities with strengths in health sciences or humanities — and certainly less relevant to universities whose mission focuses on undergraduate education.

Determining the importance of an institutional objective may not seem like a "data" concern. All institutions of higher education, however, face external pressure to track as performance indicators some specific measures, such as retention and graduation rates, without regard to their relevance to institutional objectives. How does an institution reconcile the external pressures to "measure up" in certain ways with the focus on institution-specific mission, goals, and objectives that is central to portfolio development?

On the one hand, the answer to this question entails a close examination of how the institution's mission relates to its constituency's expectations regarding the college experience. On the other hand, portfolio development provides a framework within which one can represent and measure things such as students' progress toward degree attainment in ways more suitable to institution-specific contexts and missions. Urban universities, for example, are challenged to go beyond traditional notions of retention and graduation rates in ways that incorporate elements of institutional context, such as large numbers of transfer students and students who enroll with objectives other than getting a degree.

Validity and reliability. The validity of a performance indicator relates to *what* is being measured and the reliability to *how* it is being measured. Although it is an oversimplification, validity can be thought of as primarily a definitional issue. Measuring some aspect of student learning, such as critical thinking, requires general agreement about its definition. But validity goes beyond definitional clarity in several notable ways. The validity of a concept is also related to whether it is sufficiently distinct from related concepts (e.g., critical thinking as compared with problem-solving ability) and whether it is measurable.

Reliability relates to the accuracy and stability of the method of measurement. For example, some people question whether a paper and pencil exam can really get at critical-thinking ability. Does a student's writing ability supersede critical thinking on such exams? Do situational factors such as lighting, comfortable seating, and mood produce more variation in response than does students' critical-thinking ability?

We have well accepted methods and procedures for establishing the validity and reliability of concepts and measures. Adhering to these methods and procedures is of central importance to the credibility of an institutional portfolio. While the general audience for an institutional portfolio may have little interest in the technical details of validity and reliability, reviewers do need some evidence that the measures were developed using sound methods. One of the advantages of the electronic portfolio is that a developer can make technical details available to the interested reviewer through hyperlinks to further detail. Even if the reviewer is not interested, the availability of the technical details reinforces the credibility of the measures included. For example, information about the employment outcomes of program graduates is made far more credible when accompanied by information about how that information was collected (e.g., survey administration, response rates, and margin of error).

Electronic institutional portfolios also allow performance indicators to be linked to the initiatives and activities that address institutional progress toward the relevant goal. Figure 1 on the next page shows an example from the electronic institutional portfolio of Indiana University Purdue University Indianapolis of the link between a performance indicator and related goal initiatives.

Statistical portrait: data as context for the institution's mission
Data can be used effectively in the institutional portfolio to help paint a statistical portrait of the context for the university's work. This information is crucial for providing the portfolio reviewer with sufficient knowledge about the conditions under which the institu-

Figure 1. Example of a campus performance indicator with links to relevant initiatives

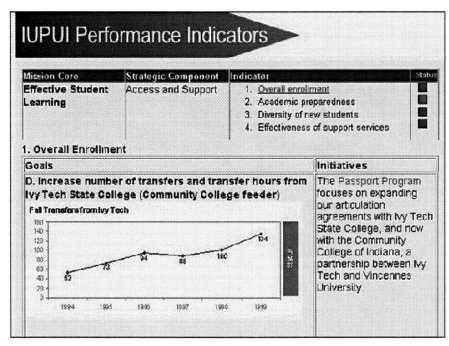

http://www.imir.iupui.edu/iupuifolio
("Performance Indicator" link, accessed August 26, 2000)

tion operates. Knowledge of this context is important for judging not only the effectiveness of the institution but also the appropriateness of its mission.

The universities participating in the UUPP were drawn together, in part, because they face common challenges in demonstrating their impact and value against the prevailing ideas about institutional effectiveness. A large portion of the commonality relates to the types of students who enroll (e.g., significant numbers of older, part-time, and working students) and the common, urban environment within which they work.

A statistical profile of the students attending urban universities provides an excellent example of how this type of data supplies a necessary context for understanding student learning at these universities. Several dimensions of students' diversity characterize urban universities. Ethnic and racial diversity is the most commonly cited dimension, but it is not the only one. Compared with other types of universities, urban universities combine students with a wider range of academic preparation, ages, and cultural backgrounds, including many students who are among the first generation of their family to attend college. Moreover, urban universities often feature larger and diverse professional programs, such as engineering, nursing and other health professions, education, business, and law, compared with traditional universities, which are often dominated academically by the disciplines of the arts, humanities, and sciences.

Expressing these dimensions of diversity requires data. It is one thing to say that students differ and another to show the precise nature of these differences by providing an enrollment profile. Moreover, the conditions of diversity vary widely, even among a group of "similar" institutions. Urban universities on the East and West coasts enroll larger proportions of racial and ethnic minority students, reflecting the greater diversity of the local populace compared with Midwestern urban universities. Midwestern urban universities, however, enroll larger proportions of racial and ethnic minority students than other colleges and universities in their regions. Further, a Midwestern urban university may have a more heterogeneous student population according to other characteristics, such as age, socioeconomic status, and work background.

In some cases, the same data used to paint a statistical portrait may also serve as a performance indicator. For example, if one goal of the institution is to serve a diverse array of learners, then the statistical description of student diversity serves as both portrait and performance indicator. The difference between the two depends on the way in which the data are presented. A table or graph that portrays the racial and ethnic distribution of students is, in and of itself, a portrait. But when those proportions are viewed over time in relation to a goal or target (e.g., consistency with the region's general population distribution), they become a performance indicator.

Figure 2 on the next page provides an example of the use of data as a statistical portrait. Extracted from the University of Massachusetts Boston portfolio, this panel provides an overall summary, with links to further details and additional profile information.

In some cases, the same data used to paint a statistical portrait may also serve as a performance indicator.

Management information: data as evidence of quality assurance processes

While performance indicators focus attention on the institution's core goals and objectives, administrators, faculty members, and staff typically use other types of management information to monitor the success of specific programs and activities that, in turn, are aimed at furthering progress toward core goals and objectives. The portfolio can show that the university has processes in place to gather this information and to use it to make improvements. Data, thus, can also be used in portfolios to show that an institution is constantly seeking to improve its effectiveness.

Whereas performance indicators and statistical portrait data typically consist of aggregate measures for the entire institution, the data of this type appear as more circumscribed examples of quality assurance. For example, measures of turnaround time in processing applications for enrollment demonstrate that the institution seeks to improve its service to students. Similarly, showing how academic managers monitor the availability of classes for students demonstrates that the institution seeks to serve students' needs while managing human and fiscal resources efficiently. This type of evidence is especially critical for

Figure 2. Using data as a
statistical portrait

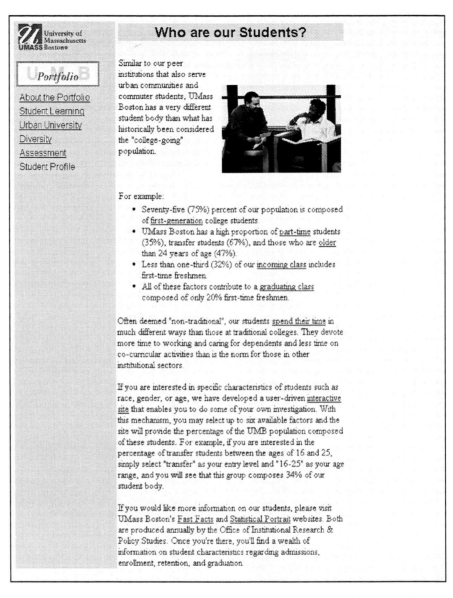

public universities to demonstrate responsible use of public monies. (See Figure 3 on the
following page, extracted from Georgia State University's portfolio.)

Descriptive statistics are the most common form of management information. They
include enrollment trends, student profiles, and reports on faculty workload. Analyses of
process and program effectiveness make up another important category of management
information. These institutional studies may explore, for example, how participating in a
new orientation program affects students' success or whether a new student billing

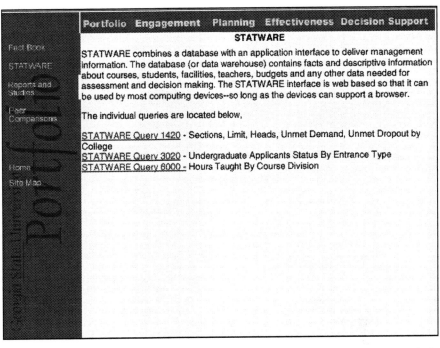

process reduces costs and improves students' satisfaction. Examples of these types of analyses are particularly effective in institutional portfolios, because they have explicit implications for program or process improvement.

In sum, data can be used in an institutional portfolio to show how well an institution is doing in pursuing its goals (performance indicators), to describe the context within which the university derives and implements its mission (statistical portrait), and to demonstrate the effectiveness of the institution's management processes (management information). The next discussion considers the flip side to the issue of using data in electronic institutional portfolios.

How Portfolios Inform the Use of Quantitative Data

Universities are awash with data related to their operations. The federal government, state governments, and commercial publishers consume these data voraciously. These users work conscientiously to develop definitional standards but pay far less attention to contextual relativities.

Yet data derive their meaning from the context in which they are used. For example, a simple chart depicting a downward enrollment trend takes on completely different meanings if it is preceded by a stated enrollment goal or followed by an explanation about new admissions criteria or about a change from a quarter to a semester system. The institutional portfolio provides the kind of context that gives data meaning.

After examining the use of data among seven major research universities, the Knight Higher Education Collaborative (2000) concluded that, individually and collectively, institutions do not make "thoughtful use of data as a gauge of capacity and prospects both within the institution and among higher education institutions as a whole" (p. 2). One of the Knight Collaborative's primary recommendations relates closely to the use of data in institutional portfolios as described here: "Academic leaders should act on the recognition that data take on meaning only as they become parts of a continuing story of an institution's goals and its progress in reaching them" (p. 10).

But some signs of change are on the horizon. For example, the essay in this section by Judie Wexler describes how accrediting agencies, which have been at the forefront of placing context before data, are beginning to experiment with alternative forms of accreditation that require continuous processes of evaluation and improvement in the context of institutional mission and goals. In another instance, The Carnegie Foundation for the Advancement of Teaching is reviewing its classification scheme to accommodate a broader range of mission-related distinctions.

Perhaps most important, portfolio developers are generating measures that recognize the variety of institutional missions.

Institutional portfolios play a pivotal role in this scheme of change. Whether used in a statistical portrait, core performance indicators, or management information, data in institutional portfolios should be related to a context linked directly to institutional goals and progress toward reaching them. Moreover, those who work on developing institutional portfolios learn the importance of interpretive context when presenting data. As more individuals undertake this endeavor, standards for the presentation of data will become increasingly contextual. A measure such as retention will be less likely to be presented in isolation from information about whom the institution serves and the relevance of traditional measures for that student population.

Perhaps most important, portfolio developers are generating measures that recognize the variety of institutional missions. The UUPP universities and a number of other urban institutions have begun a related project toward this very end — the Urban University Statistical Portrait Project (http://www.imir.iupui.edu/urban).

How the Theory and Practice of Institutional Research Inform Portfolio Development

Institutional researchers can play a central role in the development of institutional portfolios because of their knowledge of institutional data, skills in measurement and analysis, and experience in communicating quantitative information. The Association for

Institutional Research Code of Ethics[2] articulates various dimensions of the skills and ethics that institutional researchers should exercise in their work. Specifically, with regard to the execution of reports (Section IIe), certain elements of approach imbue credibility into the processes and products of competent and ethical institutional researchers:

> The institutional researcher shall ensure that all reports of projects are complete; are clearly written in language understandable to decision-makers; fully distinguish among assumptions, speculations, findings, and judgments; employ appropriate statistics and graphics; adequately describe the limitations of the project, of the analytical method, and of the findings; and follow scholarly norms in the attribution of ideas, methods, and expression and in the sources of data.

To be effective, institutional portfolios require the kinds of technical rigor, attention to detail, pragmatic orientation, and stewardship that are central to the theory and practice of institutional research. Although institutional researchers emerge from a broad range of academic backgrounds, they share common values for using empirical evidence for institutional planning, evaluation, and improvement.

The contributions that institutional researchers can make to portfolio development are closely related to the uses of data. If, as suggested earlier, institutional portfolios require data as credible and streamlined forms of evidence, then the theory and practice of institutional research can add great value to the development of institutional portfolios.

How Portfolio Development Informs the Theory and Practice of Institutional Research

Institutional researchers are often asked (or mandated) to provide data with inadequate interpretive contexts. Maintaining lofty ideals about the proper use of data is difficult in working environments that include low levels of empowerment, significant time pressures, and limited resources. Even the most efficient, empowered, and well resourced institutional research operations face pressures to produce data at a rate that does not allow for thoughtful reflection and analysis of context.

Institutional portfolios provide institutional researchers with a contextual anchor for data used to support decisions in such areas as planning, evaluation, and improvement. Portfolio development helps focus institutional efforts more closely on mission-related goals and objectives. If the portfolio is implemented successfully, academic and administrative managers will seek to align their programmatic efforts with institutional goals and therefore make use of common measures. Moreover, the portfolio provides guidance regarding institutional priorities, thereby helping institutional researchers set priorities for allocating scarce resources to projects most critical to the mission.

Electronic institutional portfolios are characterized by a combination of qualitative and quantitative indicators. With notable exceptions, institutional researchers tend to focus more on quantitative forms of evidence. Working with qualitative evidence helps institutional researchers broaden their understanding of evidentiary methods.

Perhaps the greatest contribution that portfolio development makes to the practice of institutional research arises from the collaborative relationships required to implement the portfolio. Some traditional functions of institutional research involve little collaboration with other parts of the institution. For example, responding to external reporting requirements and providing information support to senior administrators consume a significant portion of the resources of many institutional research operations; at the same time, these operations may have little visibility unless problems arise. Developing institutional portfolios, on the other hand, requires institutional researchers to work closely with a broader range of faculty and staff, as Kathi Ketcheson points out in her essay. This collaborative work helps the institutional researcher gain insight into the activities and values of faculty and helps faculty members better understand the purpose and usefulness of institutional research for accountability and institutional improvement.

Hutchings and Shulman (1999) suggest that institutional researchers should take a more active role in supporting the scholarship of teaching and learning. Developing institutional portfolios may well mark the beginning of a transformation of institutional research that takes it beyond decision support for management and planning and toward the scholarship of mission-critical activities in teaching, research, and service.

Notes

1. The Urban Universities Portfolio Project (UUPP) brings together six leading urban public universities to develop a new medium: an electronic institutional portfolio to demonstrate a university's effectiveness to its stakeholders. The UUPP is funded by The Pew Charitable Trusts and is cosponsored by the American Association for Higher Education (AAHE) and Indiana University Purdue University Indianapolis (IUPUI). For more information, visit http://www.imir.iupui.edu/portfolio.

2. The complete text of the association's Code of Ethics is available at http://www.fsu.edu/~air/ethics.htm.

References

Borden, V.M.H., & Bottrill, K.V. (1994). Performance indicators: History, definitions, and methods. In V.M.H. Borden & T.W. Banta (Eds.), *Using Performance Indicators to Guide Strategic Decision Making*. New Directions for Institutional Research, no. 82. San Francisco: Jossey-Bass.

Hutchings, P., & Shulman, L.S. (1999, September/October). The scholarship of teaching: New elaborations, new developments, *Change 31* (5), 10-15.

Knight Higher Education Collaborative. (2000). The data made me do it. *Policy Perspectives 9* (2). Philadelphia: Institute for Research on Higher Education.

Siegel, H. (1988). *Educating Reason: Rationality, Critical Thinking, and Education*. New York: Routledge.

Electronic Department Portfolios: A New Tool for Departmental Learning and Improvement

by Dean S. Dorn

Efforts to improve student learning and assessment have been an important focus of California State University Sacramento (CSUS) for the past 10 years, spurred both by external agencies such as the Western Association of Schools and Colleges and the California State University system and by the campus's own strategic priorities. CSUS has participated in a range of initiatives during this period, including hosting one of the early experimental accreditation visits by WASC (see Judie Wexler's essay in this volume) and participating in the Urban Universities Portfolio Project (UUPP).[1]

The idea for an electronic department portfolio came from several sources. First, involvement in UUPP gave CSUS a conceptual framework for constructing a portfolio for one type of "unit," the whole institution, that was transferable to portfolios for another type of unit, the academic department (or program). Second, the department portfolio idea responded to an interest across the campus in streamlining mandated department program reviews to focus them more explicitly on teaching and learning. If every department put the information and analysis required for the program review process in electronic form and regularly updated this material, the task of preparing the program review every five years would be greatly simplified.

Further, if teaching and student learning were a focus of assessment in the CSUS institutional portfolio, department learning outcomes, in addition to general education learning outcomes, needed to be highlighted. Most students who attend CSUS transfer as juniors, and their main purpose in attending the university is to major in a program or discipline. Departments and programs are thus key units in advancing not only discipline-specific learning outcomes but also university-wide outcomes for the baccalaureate degree.

A search for existing examples of electronic department/program portfolios found none. The then-UUPP campus director and Cecilia Gray, associate vice president for academic affairs, thus decided to develop their own prototype, designed both to meet campus needs and to serve as a model for others. The prototype, a portfolio for the Sociology Department at CSUS, is the focus of this essay. CSUS is developing portfolios for other

Dean S. Dorn is emeritus professor of sociology at California State University Sacramento. He was the original Urban Universities Portfolio Project campus project director for his university. Currently, he is an executive officer of the Pacific Sociological Association.

programs and departments using this prototype, with the idea of linking these portfolios to the main CSUS institutional portfolio.

The portfolio presents a collection of representative work by faculty and students. As with individual student portfolios, the department portfolio is open to assessment and evaluation and aims to demonstrate ongoing development, proficiency, and accountability. Several pages of the CSUS prototype electronic department portfolio are reproduced in this chapter to illustrate the portfolio's basic structure and components.

What Is an Electronic Department Portfolio?

The CSUS electronic department portfolio is a Web-based package of evidence that demonstrates a department's competency, accountability, and efforts to improve. As indicated, it occupies an important place in the institution's assessment efforts, situated between institutional assessment, on the one hand, and individual student and faculty assessment, on the other.

As with individual student portfolios, the department portfolio is open to assessment and evaluation and aims to demonstrate ongoing development, proficiency, and accountability.

The prototype portfolio contains collective evidence about an important group on campus — those who are closest to the process of teaching and learning an academic discipline. It provides an assessment of the context and structure in which students and faculty engage in much of their academic work. As noted, the portfolio can serve as the basis for program evaluation and review.

The prototype department portfolio is intended mainly for audiences of faculty members, faculty and administrative governance bodies, and accreditation associations and commissions charged with evaluating how well CSUS or a program or department in CSUS is achieving the learning outcomes established for students. Although members of the general public, prospective students, parents, and others might find some information in the portfolio useful, they are not its primary audience. As defined here, the prototype department portfolio is not a public relations document that presents only the "good news" about the department or program or that is designed to increase student enrollment. Nor is it the department's general Web page, which presents a variety of information about the department, its faculty, and the major. The portfolio is, however, linked to the department's Web page as well as to the CSUS institutional portfolio.

The CSUS prototype is designed to meet the characteristics of a good assessment program and to support a culture of evidence for assessment. It flows from the department's mission and has a conceptual framework, faculty ownership and responsibility, and institution-wide support. It includes examples of faculty and student work and accomplishments, presents the department's assessment plan and a process for evaluating that plan, uses multiple measures of evaluation, and provides feedback to students and faculty to help them learn to improve through reflection (Cambridge, 1997).

The framework for the prototype includes an introduction and five major themes or categories organized into folders: academic program, teaching and learning, research and creative activities, university and community services, and special accomplishments. The folders are divided into additional subcategories. Because the contents of the prototype cover the most recent three-year period, new content that appears, for example, in 2000 and 2001 replaces content from 1997 and 1998, as the department periodically updates the portfolio.

Introduction to the prototype Sociology department portfolio

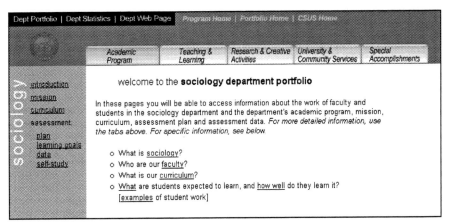

http://www.csus.edu/portfolio/soc_v1/sociology.html

The portfolio's opening page, which represents the first page of the academic folder, links to information about the department's mission, its faculty, its curriculum, its assessment plan, and specific learning expectations for sociology students; to discussion of how students in the department work and learn; and to assessment information on departmental learning outcomes. Additional links lead to more detail about each of these items. Across the top of the front page are links to the department and university home pages, the institutional portfolio, and a statistical portrait of the department (see Victor Borden's chapter in this volume). The page also links to each of the five main folders.

How Can a Department Portfolio Be Used?

Potential uses for a Web-based department portfolio are many. The primary ones, mentioned above, are for assessment, evaluation, and improvement. A portfolio might also be used for specialized accreditation for professional programs and to replace the lengthy and onerous self-study reports that many campuses require for periodic program reviews. CSUS is phasing in the use of department portfolios for program reviews. Once an electronic portfolio is developed, it is easily maintained and updated every year or two. When the time nears for a department's program review, the departmental portfolio already contains the necessary information. Because that information is spread over several years, trend data in the department are readily available. Thus, the program review may consist primarily of questions devoted to reflection on and analysis of the on-line department portfolio.

A Web-based department portfolio might also be useful for institutional accreditation. Although regional commissions do not specifically evaluate departments, they do want to know what the campus is doing to assess and improve student learning. Regional accrediting bodies could easily sample department portfolios on a campus as examples of the institution's commitment to and accomplishments in student learning.

A frequently updated department portfolio site provides an effective way for faculty and others to learn about faculty and student work in the department. By highlighting the

Some other pages of the prototype portfolio

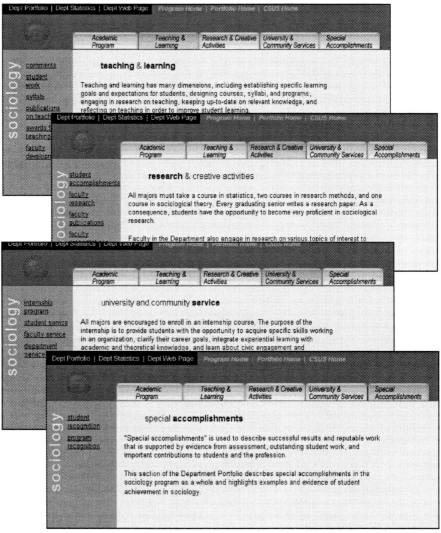

http://www.csus.edu/portfolio/soc_v1/

department's collective achievements and current efforts to improve, the portfolio can contribute to a sense of community among department faculty and students.

Another possible use for department portfolios is in the recruitment process for new part-time or full-time faculty. Potential new hires might visit the portfolio and become familiar with the department's work, assessment efforts, mission, goals, strengths, and weaknesses, giving applicants a quick and honest snapshot of the department. Candidates brought to the campus for an interview might be asked to prepare responses to several questions based on the portfolio — How do you see yourself contributing to helping the department improve, given its assessment? How do you see yourself helping students in the program become successful with the learning outcomes established by the department? Do you see yourself making a contribution to the department community and, if so, in what way?

What Issues Must Be Addressed in Designing and Using an Electronic Department Portfolio?

Departments developing and using a department portfolio must address several major issues, the first of which is the cost of construction and maintenance. The initial labor involved in designing the portfolio to fit the culture of the department and institution can be extensive. This labor includes the Web design, the development of the portfolio's folders and sections, and the work to maintain and update the site. Who will do this work and who will pay for it? Faculty may be reluctant to tackle yet another obligation, especially if the work is added to their normal responsibilities.

One solution here is to ask the college or university Web master to design the framework for the portfolio. If a department is serious about building an electronic portfolio, assigned time may be necessary for the faculty member responsible for the site's content. Ideally, this faculty member should be someone who is involved in activities relevant to the portfolio, such as the chair of the department's assessment committee.

Another issue is the extent to which unfavorable content should be publicly posted. Some faculty members may be concerned that the administration will use such information to punish them or to withdraw resources or that members of the general public may misunderstand data and use it to criticize the department. This issue may well arise even when the portfolio makes clear that its primary purpose is for reflection and improvement. A possible approach to this issue is to get prior cooperation and support from the administration, including protection for the department from members of the public who might use the data to launch an unreasonable attack. Another approach is to protect certain parts of the portfolio by requiring a password for access.

Other faculty may worry about posting examples of students' work — even with each student's permission — because they fear that making such examples publicly accessible will encourage plagiarism. Posting only the title and first two or three pages of a paper, with a notation that more information is available from the department chair or the chair of the department's assessment committee, may help to assuage these fears.

Another issue concerns the links and relationships between a department portfolio and the institution's other electronic portfolios and Web pages. Large and complex institutions have many Web sites. If the college or university has a Web-based institutional portfolio, then direct links to the department portfolio are easy to establish. For example, the institution's learning outcomes and the department's learning outcomes might be linked. Institutional information and data on a department in an institutional portfolio might be linked to the department's own data. A separate button or bar on the institutional portfolio could direct the user to the various department portfolios on the campus. If no institutional portfolio exists, an obvious place to locate the department portfolio is on the department's general Web page or perhaps within an institution's assessment page or academic affairs page.

This CSUS portfolio is a prototype. Readers are invited to visit the prototype, which is meant to represent one possibility among many, at www.csus.edu/soc/portfolio.

The Sociology Department portfolio has prompted serious departmental conversation about learning outcomes and expectations. It has provided department faculty with an opportunity to take a broader perspective on the department and on the important role assessment plays in improvement. It has convinced the administration to develop and support similar portfolios in other departments and to tie the electronic department portfolio to program evaluation. And it has generated wide discussion of electronic department portfolios in the discipline of sociology (Howery, 2000).

Note

1. The Urban Universities Portfolio Project (UUPP) brings together six leading urban public universities to develop a new medium: an electronic institutional portfolio to demonstrate a university's effectiveness to its stakeholders. The UUPP is funded by The Pew Charitable Trusts and is cosponsored by the American Association for Higher Education (AAHE) and Indiana University Purdue University Indianapolis (IUPUI). For more information, visit http://www.imir.iupui.edu/portfolio.

References

Cambridge, B.L. (1997). Learning about assessment. In L.F. Gardiner, C. Anderson, & B.L. Cambridge (Eds.), *Learning Through Assessment* (pp. 1-9). Washington, DC: American Association for Higher Education.

Howery, C. (2000, July/August). *CSU-Sacramento Showcases Its Department Portfolio.* Washington, DC: American Sociological Association.

The Role of Institutional Portfolios in the Revised WASC Accreditation Process

by Judie Gaffin Wexler

Institutional accreditation has traditionally sought to foster educational excellence by ensuring that colleges and universities meet minimum standards of quality and have the resources and capacity needed to pursue their missions responsibly. The vehicles for accomplishing these ends have been the institutional self-study, which provides information on compliance and capacity, and the accreditation visit to the campus by a team of peer reviewers to certify the validity of the self-study's assertions.

The past decade has witnessed rapid changes in the higher education environment and doubts about the adequacy of traditional accreditation procedures to make a real contribution to educational quality. Critics have argued that the self-study is an expensive exercise with little impact on improving the institution and that the focus of accreditation should shift from resources and structures to the key function of educating students effectively.

In 1996, the Accrediting Commission for Senior Colleges and Universities of the Western Association of Schools and Colleges (WASC) began working on a redesign of its accreditation standards and practices to address these criticisms. Work has been based on the premise that all aspects of accreditation, including both standards and practices, must be reexamined if real change is to occur. The revision's three primary goals are to emphasize educational effectiveness and student learning, to promote collaboration between WASC and institutions under review, and to reduce the burden of the accreditation process on institutions.

The revision has proceeded conceptually in retreats and position papers and concretely in experiments jointly designed by WASC and member institutions. The institutional portfolio is one part of the constellation of experiments and changes being implemented. The rationale for the portfolio emerges from the goals for the change process and the resulting new standards and procedures.

Judie Gaffin Wexler is associate executive director of the Senior College Commission of the Western Association of Schools and Colleges. She is working with institutions to develop guidelines for the use of portfolios in the accreditation process.

The Revision Strategy and Results

WASC began its revision efforts with a series of experimental self-studies and site visits. These experiments simultaneously addressed the multiple goals of the revision and explored specific options for change. Each experiment invited the institution to propose themes or issues of internal significance that would frame the accreditation process. At least one theme or issue needed to be related to effective teaching and student learning and to the quality of undergraduate education if the education of undergraduates was a major function for the institution.

All the experiments involved institutions whose accreditation history revealed that basic compliance with minimum standards was not a concern. The institutions thus were free to experiment with alternative ways of presenting data to demonstrate compliance with the broad intent of the standards; they used a variety of approaches to engaging, organizing, and presenting their material.

The experimental work with portfolios began with the large research universities, those institutions that tend to have the most developed data capabilities. This experimental strand focused on an in-depth examination of special topics, accompanied by a data and policy portfolio. These early portfolios were conceived as a way for the institution to present the policies required by accreditation standards and the data that would enable internal and external constituencies to assess effectiveness. Each institution was encouraged to develop its portfolio in a way that was consistent with its own needs and that would enable it to be used for internal purposes as well as for accreditation. This approach resulted in very different types of portfolios, including an increasing number that are Web based.

WASC has now articulated and adopted a new set of standards and a new visit guide and is working on determining elements for institutional presentations. The standards, reduced from nine to four, are phrased in active terms and integrate the key institutional commitments to capacity and educational effectiveness that the Commission has defined as core to the accreditation process:

> Standard 1: Defining Institutional Purposes and Educational Objectives
> Standard 2: Achieving Educational Objectives Through Core Functions
> Standard 3: Developing and Deploying Resources and Organizational Structures to Assure Sustainability
> Standard 4: Creating an Organization Committed to Learning and Improvement.

Each standard emphasizes a key aspect of organizational performance. Taken together, the standards reinforce a concept of institutions as learning organizations committed to distinct missions.

At the same time, the accreditation process has been redefined into three stages: the proposal, the preparatory review, and the review of educational effectiveness. The proposal enables the review to be based on an institution's own context and goals for the accreditation process. The institution specifies themes or issues it would like to address and a format that presents evidence to demonstrate compliance with the standards. The proposal is subject to peer review.

The preparatory review, approximately two years after the proposal is accepted, determines whether an institution fulfills the requirements of the core commitment to institutional capacity. The educational effectiveness review, one year later, considers the institution's core commitment to educational effectiveness. While the process unfolds in three stages over three years, it is one review, not three separate reviews. For this reason, the process requires an integrated and expanded institutional presentation rather than multiple, separate, partially duplicative reports.

The process models the principles of learning-centeredness. Institutions develop goals and outcomes for the accreditation review cycle beyond a demonstration of basic compliance. The three stages of the review allow for multiple points of feedback and enable the entire review to focus on both educational and institutional effectiveness.

The importance of the portfolio evolved to the point that the new accreditation model eliminates the traditional self-study and asks for an institutional portfolio in its place.

The Centrality of Portfolios

Over the course of WASC's experiments, the importance of the portfolio evolved to the point that the new accreditation model eliminates the traditional self-study and asks for an institutional portfolio in its place. The traditional self-study was a large document, written for the Commission by multiple campus committees and edited into one voice. It was generally organized around the standards for accreditation, providing a snapshot of the institution at one point in time. Although self-studies asserted and described the institution's compliance with the standards, little evidence was typically provided to support those assertions. Instead, the visiting team was expected to validate the statements through on-campus interviews and examination of campus documents. The very nature of the self-study encouraged description and limited the potential for making the process learning-oriented.

The institutional portfolio addresses many of the self-study's limitations. Exhibits of data and documents collectively articulate the institution's mission and vision, demonstrate compliance with accreditation standards, and display the scope and quality of educational outcomes. The elements taken together portray the institution in its complexity. Most elements in the portfolio are genuine institutional documents and data rather than presentations created solely for accreditation. That is, the actual primary source material is part of the portfolio, which can be expanded to meet the needs of each stage of the process. Presentations of actual primary materials and activities, instead of description, allow for a dynamic examination of the institution. Through analytic essays that discuss and evaluate exhibits, the portfolio also provides a structure for institutional self-examination, reflection, and analysis.

Portfolios are expected to be selective in their choices of exhibits, providing pertinent information and solid evidence of educational and institutional effectiveness. They do not simply include all available materials related to the accreditation standards and student learning. Moreover, institutional mission and the thematic purposes for which the portfolios are used influence the materials and their arrangement. All portfolios do not look the same.

As the Senior College Commission considered these attributes of institutional portfolios and the goals for accreditation outlined and developed over four years of work in the region, it became convinced that the portfolio was the best vehicle for achieving those goals.

Emphasizing educational effectiveness and student learning

Although standards have long provided for measures of educational effectiveness, planning outcomes, and academic quality, institutions and teams have felt more confident focusing on resources and structures. The evidence for resources and structures is more widely understood, easily presented, and consistent across types of institutions. It can be discussed in a linear form and at the institutional level. Educational effectiveness, planning outcomes, and academic quality are, in contrast, messy to discuss. The evidence varies across institutional type and within institutions. Because the concern is with processes as well as with data, educational and organizational effectiveness are more difficult to describe than are resources and structures.

The portfolio addresses these problems by providing evidence and examples of educational and institutional effectiveness. It displays educational accomplishments for examination by outside evaluators within the context of institutional goals and student profiles. For example, an institution might include material from reviews of general education outcomes or the findings of regularly scheduled academic program review.

Promoting collaboration with institutions

Accreditation attempts to recognize the diversity of institutions but to hold them to a common set of standards. The format of the self-study, with its emphasis on the standards, often eliminated recognition of the institution as a distinct entity with its own issues and priorities. Regardless of an institution's mission, size, or developmental stage, the self-study was organizationally the same. The institutional portfolio, however, documents both the complexity and the individuality of institutions of higher education.

Portfolios include some standard, required elements and other elements selected by the institution, based on its internal priorities and its self-defined themes for the visit. With the opportunity to select themes (to be approved by WASC) and the portfolio elements to be emphasized, accreditation becomes a collaboration among the institution, the visiting team, and the accrediting agency staff. The collaborative stance results in greater institutional ownership of the process and results, but it also requires effective interaction among institution, team, and staff to build trust and mutual understanding of goals.

Reducing the burden of the accreditation process

Institutions of higher education are data- and report-rich. All institutions have multiple forms and sources of data organized for a variety of internal and external audiences. All institutions have reports created by campus committees and departments that reflect on and sometimes lead them to change various aspects of their functioning.

The portfolio includes policies, data, and reports created by the institution as part of its ongoing operations rather than material developed expressly for the accreditation visit, thereby providing a dynamic sense of institutional accountability. By including mainly materials that the institution already has on hand, the flurry of accreditation-directed activity and the burden on the institution are reduced. Further, the accrediting team is able to see directly how actual operations compare with the ideal established by the standards and the institutional mission.

Whereas the self-study was a unitary presentation focused on establishing consistency with standards, the portfolio allows for institutional complexity and distinctiveness by asking the institution to select the documents and data that make its case. Because the institution chooses from existing materials, the presentation reflects its actual operations rather than an attempt to fit practices into a template provided by the standards. Institutional attention is directed toward its own evidence for self-improvement as well as on external standards.

Preparation of the Portfolio

At first glance, it might seem that the office of institutional research working alone could prepare the institutional portfolio. If it is to be useful to the campus as more than simply a vehicle for accreditation, however, the portfolio is best prepared in consultation with various internal constituencies. A number of important questions need to be addressed with these constituencies: Why is the portfolio being prepared? What does the institution hope to learn from it? What kinds of information should be collected? How should the information be analyzed and presented? What areas of the learning process and of the institution should be emphasized?

WASC continues to struggle with the organizing principles for institutional portfolios and with the mix of required, suggested, self-selected, and stipulated elements. Current thinking defines three dimensions or categories of elements: descriptive and contextual information, evaluative materials, and case studies to document students' learning and engagement with educational effectiveness. This delineation supports the new standards and is a departure from the data and policy portfolios created for the experimental self-studies. It continues to be true, however, that no one portfolio model will fit all institutions.

The descriptive and contextual dimension includes exhibits that express the nature of the institution and its student body, such as:

- The institution's mission/vision statement
- Statements of educational objectives for academic programs
- Demographic trend data on faculty, staff, and students
- A list of academic programs
- Trend data on key financial ratios
- Organizational charts.

Currently, WASC is considering asking that such exhibits be included with the proposal submitted by the institution to help WASC understand the context in which the institution is operating. Contextual information adds meaning to the issues and plans delineated in the proposal.

The bulk of the portfolio falls into the evaluative dimension. It includes exhibits that express the institution's status in relation to the standards of accreditation to enable the team to make informed judgments. An accompanying essay indicates why the data elements and exhibits were selected, what they mean to the institution, and how they demonstrate fulfillment of the core commitment to institutional capacity. Because the intent is to focus institutions on the development of their own strategic indicators, the essays are kept brief, with enforced page limits.

Although we distinguish between the preparatory and educational effectiveness stages of the process, the portfolio presentation for the preparatory stage must include exhibits that support all the standards. Because this process is an iterative one, some of those materials are later expanded on for the review of educational effectiveness. For that review, the institution submits an essay that addresses its mechanisms for assessing educational effectiveness, and an in-depth illustration of a relevant topic that has been addressed, the findings, and the application of the findings.

While the experimental visits have focused on in-depth examination of themes or special topics, institutions thus far have tended to choose themes around which they are hoping for institutional improvement, using the accreditation review process as a way to jumpstart campus initiatives. Accordingly, institutions generally report on the early stages of initiatives, before a great deal of concrete assessment data are available. Discussion has thus tended to emphasize the structure of the initiative over its outcomes and efficacy. The shift in the standards, the sequential stages, and the portfolio presentation should change this emphasis. At the same time, we recognize the barriers to change posed by the risk of exposing poor or even mediocre outcomes. Institutions have a right to ask how such outcomes will affect accreditation and be understood by the public.

After decades of using self-studies for accreditation, institutions and reviewers have difficulty moving out of the mind-set that features a self-study and supporting documents in appendices. It is easier to consider doing something different on the Web, however, because the Web makes something different essential. The electronic medium offers three significant advantages in the creation of portfolios: (1) It offers a way to organize and interrelate an enormous amount of information, (2) it mandates an organization different from a print-based presentation, and (3) it makes that information available to the campus community on an ongoing basis. In the electronic format, the same material can be maintained and updated for multiple uses and audiences.

The reasons to use the Web for institutional portfolios are compelling. At the same time, not all institutions have the capacity to create and maintain an electronic portfolio.

The reasons to use the Web for institutional portfolios are compelling. At the same time, not all institutions have the capacity to create and maintain an electronic portfolio, and not all want to commit the resources necessary to place all their materials into electronic format. Moreover, many evaluators have thus far found the Web-based portfolios difficult to use and overwhelming in scope. Evaluators are busy people and customarily read self-studies at odd moments. A Web-based portfolio requires access to the Web, the time to sit in front of the computer, and a certain facility with Web-based documents. Some evaluators have found it difficult to navigate their way through portfolios without instruction from the institution and a map from the team chair or WASC staff. Rather than using the interactive possibilities to follow strands of evidence, some evaluators have requested a printout of the Web pages. We are not yet certain whether evaluators will use the portfolios without printing out large portions of them.

Building Expertise

Our early assessment of the experimental visits suggests that the data portfolios created to show compliance with standards successfully used existing data and materials to reduce the burden of accreditation. The portfolios were produced with less time and effort than were traditional self-studies. Reports on the usefulness of the portfolios as administrative tools beyond regional accreditation are mixed; not all institutions are continuing to maintain the portfolios they created. The majority, however, reported plans to update their portfolios annually as a support for institutional planning and grant development and a resource for public accountability. One institution reported that the portfolio led to dramatic changes in internal accountability procedures. For portfolios to be sustainable, key campus decision makers must perceive them as valuable. Further, the portfolios that have been maintained seem to have had multiple institutional uses. A larger study is under way that should better inform us about the long-term usefulness of the portfolios.

One way in which portfolios can reduce the work of accreditation for individual campuses is through the creation of system-level portfolios. WASC's experiments led the University of California's central office to create a portfolio of shared data, structures, and policies so that each individual campus need not replicate the same material. This initiative has been highly successful in reducing the burden for individual campuses and is being considered by other systems.

While the data from the experimental visits are valuable, we recognize that we are now entering new territory as we move to replace the self-study with portfolios for the entire range of institutions in the region. The portfolios of the future will be more comprehensive than were the data and policy portfolios of the past. Knowing that evaluators have difficulty working with large-scale portfolios, we need to develop techniques to help them move through the material.

Although we recognize that portfolios designed as evaluative tools and those designed for institutional improvement have two goals, we hope that these goals can be combined. Institutional improvement is, we believe, supported by inviting institutions to select and reflect on materials that best mirror their performance in relation to the core commitments to institutional capacity and educational effectiveness. Self-selection of exhibits is also consistent with the WASC commitment to collaboration with institutions. Evaluation would be more difficult, however, if each portfolio were totally unique. Mandated items in the portfolios support evaluative purposes by allowing some comparability across different institutional contexts.

One of the four new WASC standards examines institutions through the lens of their success in "creating an organization committed to learning and improvement." We at WASC also need to look at our own processes and procedures through this lens. As we move into the widespread implementation of institutional portfolios, we need to determine whether they are resulting in greater emphasis on teaching and learning, whether accreditation decisions are more reliable, and whether the original goals of redesigning our accreditation standards and processes are being met. We recognize the danger that once we write something down, it becomes hardened into an absolute, but we know that we can continue to improve the process only by being willing to examine and change it.

In the portfolio, we believe we have found a technique to buttress the development of an accreditation process that is centered on educational effectiveness in context and structure. By supporting institutional accountability, the portfolio helps reduce the dichotomy between internal and external systems, strengthening both.

Learning From Experience

by Susan Kahn

Recent work on electronic institutional portfolios shows that they can be powerful vehicles for fostering internal and external understanding of an institution's mission and work and for bringing together assessment, improvement, and accountability. Because experiments with institutional portfolios are very new, much is to be learned about the most effective ways to organize and implement a portfolio as a sustainable approach to genuine institutional improvement and innovation. The uses of portfolios with external stakeholders are also just beginning to be established; while portfolios may be the wave of the future for regional accreditation, the interest of other external stakeholders in portfolios, and in the ideas about effectiveness and accountability that portfolios embody, has not yet been extensively tested.

This section has included a great deal of advice on developing institutional portfolios, along with detailed accounts of how several universities went about creating such portfolios. Here are a few basic recommendations about developing a portfolio initiative on your campus, distilled from the section's six essays:

- Decide early on the purposes of the portfolio, its intended audiences, and the uses these audiences will make of the portfolio. These decisions should shape and direct the themes and evidence that the portfolio will present.
- Make the portfolio development process inclusive of faculty, administration, and key campus committees if you are seeking real impact and improvement. Involve external stakeholders from the audiences you are interested in reaching, and incorporate their perspectives as early as possible.
- Be extremely selective about the themes, materials, and evidence included in the portfolio. Keep the portfolio linked to major campus priorities and efforts related to assessment, effectiveness, and strategic planning.
- Be sure that the organization of the portfolio is as simple and user-friendly as possible.

Susan Kahn, editor of this section on institutional portfolios, is national director of the Urban Universities Portfolio Project and director of programs and planning in the Office for Professional Development at Indiana University Purdue University Indianapolis. She has written and spoken extensively on electronic institutional portfolios.

A

access *(see also* diversity, permission forms, security)
  digital divide, 10
  viewing of portfolio material, v, 24, 26, 42, 49, 63, 64, 77, 78-79, 91, 98, 102, 118, 122-23, 126, 135, 143, 152, 160, 184, 207-08, 215

accountability *(see also* accreditation, assessment, performance indicators/measures), 94, 135, 136, 137-38, 139, 153, 160, 162, 166, 178, 181, 197, 202, 204, 215, 216, 217
  high-stakes performance, 5, 91, 102
  performance-based funding, 137-38
  quality assurance, 159, 175-76, 197-99, 209

accreditation *(see also* accountability, assessment, institutional effectiveness, summative portfolio), 6, 8, 9, 29, 137-38, 147, 157, 162, 180, 189, 200, 204
  regional accreditation, 6, 29, 60, 67, 136, 137-38, 147, 157, 162, 174, 188-89, 190, 200, 203, 204, 206, 209-16, 217
  self-studies, 6, 8, 137-38, 156, 162, 189, 190, 205, 209, 210-13, 214, 215, 216
  specialized accreditation, 157, 204, 205

advising, 19, 22, 23, 28, 29, 53, 55-56, 58-59, 67

alumni, 2, 161

Alverno College, 6, 22, 23, 24, 30, 83

American Association for Higher Education (AAHE), v, vii, viii, 22, 87, 123, 129, 158, 176, 190, 202, 208

American Association of University Professors, 101

American Historical Association (AHA), 102

American Sociological Association, 208

Annenberg Institute for School Reform, 10, 11

applications *(see* software)

artifacts *(see* exhibits)

assessment *(see also* accountability, accreditation, peer review, portfolio review, program review/improvement, summative portfolio), v, 1-2, 5-7, 11, 16, 17, 20, 37, 43, 45, 50, 51, 52, 54, 60-70, 78, 83, 85, 97, 112, 115, 123, 135, 136, 137-38, 140, 141, 143, 144, 145, 147, 150, 155-56, 163, 166, 170, 173, 176, 178, 179, 180, 182, 184-85, 187, 192, 203, 204, 205, 208, 217
  authentic, 119-20, 123, 138, 150, 192, 212
  self, 2, 5, 6, 8, 17, 19, 22, 29, 45, 49, 50, 51, 61, 62, 83, 115, 143, 157, 159, 170, 188

S

Samford University *(see also* problem-based learning), 76-82, 102
    problem-based learning project, 102
scalability, 38, 87
scholarship *(see also* learning, pedagogy, research, teaching/learning), 92, 94, 99, 117-18, 126, 164, 165, 166, 167, 173, 175, 179, 187, 189
    criteria for, 94-95, 97-98, 118
    of teaching/learning, ii, 94, 101, 104, 117-18, 124, 125, 126-29, 144, 157, 188, 202
security *(see also* access, permission forms), 26, 42, 49, 79, 102, 127, 185, 207-08
Seldin, Peter, 91, 92, 94, 101
selection, 2, 4, 10, 15, 17, 20, 47, 85, 87, 109, 111, 114, 127, 170-73, 182, 192, 212, 217
self-assessment *(see* assessment)
self-studies *(see* accreditation)
service-learning, 3, 18, 170, 182
Sharon (student), 28, 37-42
Shulman, Lee, 94, 98, 99, 144, 202
Siegel, Janice, 96-97
social construction *(see* knowledge)
Social Life of Information, The, vii, viii
social responsibility *(see* civic engagement)
software, 10, 28, 29, 30, 36, 37, 38, 42, 43, 46, 47, 51, 54, 56, 57-58, 64, 71, 77-78, 79, 80, 81-82, 85, 96, 108, 112, 113, 115-16, 121, 154, 198
specialized accreditation *(see* accreditation)
Springfield, Emily, ii, 26, 28, 29, 30, 53-59, 76-82, 86, 87

stakeholders *(see* audience)
Stanford University, 23-25
statistical portrait, 189, 193, 195-99, 205
    Urban University Statistical Portrait Project, 200
Steve (student), 15
Stier, Marc, 96-98, 106-09
storage *(see also* portability), 3, 24-26, 28, 38, 43, 46, 47, 50, 51, 60, 62-65, 77, 83, 99, 102, 103-04, 112, 113-14, 115, 121, 151, 192
strategic planning *(see also* institutional effectiveness), 136, 140-43, 144, 145, 146, 151, 152, 155-56, 178, 181, 184, 185, 201, 215, 217
student evaluations *(see* faculty evaluation)
student learning *(see also* learning, teaching/learning), v, vii, 1-11, 17, 18, 19-20, 24, 29, 32, 37, 38, 39, 45, 49, 50, 51, 52, 73, 74, 92, 96, 100, 101, 102, 117, 122, 123, 124-29, 130, 131, 135, 136, 137, 138, 139, 143-44, 146, 147-50, 161-62, 163, 164, 165, 166, 167-68, 170, 171-72, 175, 178, 182, 187, 188, 193, 195, 196, 203, 206, 209, 210, 212, 214
student learning outcomes/objectives *(see also* learning), 10, 19, 20, 22-23, 24, 29, 32, 46, 53, 58, 59, 60, 61-62, 72, 76, 92, 93, 99, 114, 136, 139, 140, 141, 146, 147, 148-50, 151, 155-56, 157, 161-62, 163, 164, 165, 167, 170, 171-72, 175-76, 177, 179, 181, 189, 194, 196, 203, 204, 208, 211, 212
student ratings *(see* faculty evaluation)

Other AAHE publications about portfolios ...

Making Teaching Community Property: A Menu for Peer Collaboration and Peer Review Describes nine strategies through which faculty can document and "go public" with their teaching, including through a course portfolio. By Pat Hutchings (1996, 128pp)

The Teaching Portfolio: Capturing the Scholarship in Teaching Helped launch the faculty portfolio movement. Provides the *what, why, and how* of what is called a "teaching portfolio" — a faculty member's collection of carefully selected work samples accompanied by reflective commentary. By Russell Edgerton, Pat Hutchings, and Kathleen Quinlan (1991, 72pp)

The Course Portfolio: How Faculty Can Examine Their Teaching to Advance Practice and Improve Student Learning Applies the portfolio concept to document the unfolding of a single course, from conception to results. Also discusses the course portfolio's place in the development of a "scholarship of teaching and learning." Includes nine case studies by faculty in a range of disciplines. Edited by Pat Hutchings, with an introduction by Lee S. Shulman (1998, 132pp)

From Idea to Prototype: The Peer Review of Teaching (A Project Workbook) A three-ring binder of reproducible materials for campuses looking for better ways to document, improve, and evaluate teaching. Provides excerpts from an actual course portfolio, plus exercises, checklists, resource lists, and short articles. Edited by Pat Hutchings (1995, 150pp)

Time Will Tell: Portfolio-Assisted Assessment of General Education Describes implementation and use of student portfolios to assess general-education outcomes at individual and program levels. By Aubrey Forrest et al. (1990, 20pp)

Visit AAHE's online publications catalog at www.aahe.org/catalog.

AAHE
AMERICAN ASSOCIATION
FOR HIGHER EDUCATION

One Dupont Circle, Suite 360
Washington, DC 20036-1110
202/293-6440, fax 202/293-0073